REWARD
STRATEGIES

The Chartered Institute of Personnel and Development is the leading publisher of books and reports for personnel and training professionals, students, and all those concerned with the effective management and development of people at work. For details of all our titles, please contact the Publishing Department:

tel. 020-8263 3387

fax 020-8263 3850

e-mail publish@cipd.co.uk

The catalogue of all CIPD titles can be viewed on the CIPD website:

www.cipd.co.uk/publications

REWARD
STRATEGIES
From intent to impact

Duncan Brown

Chartered Institute of Personnel and Development

First published 2001

Typeset by Fakenham Photosetting Limited, Fakenham
Printed in Great Britain by the Short Run Press, Exeter

British Library Cataloguing-in-Publication Data
A catalogue record for this book is available from the British Library

ISBN 0-85292-905-6

CIPD House, Camp Road, London SW19 4UX
Tel: 020-8971 9000   Fax: 020-8263 3333
E-mail: cipd@cipd.co.uk Website: www.cipd.co.uk
Incorporated by Royal Charter. Registered Charity No. 1079797.

CONTENTS

For Fiona, Tabitha and Genevieve, and Mum and Dad

ACKNOWLEDGEMENTS

Thanks to Towers Perrin colleagues, particularly Sheryl Turping, David Watson, Jamil Husain and Diane Gherson, for their ideas and intelligence, and for their commitment, support, good humour and tolerance. It's a unique place to be, in all senses.

Thanks to all the many organisations and clients who give me access, time and support, inspiration and such wonderful raw material to work on. They make reward management such an interesting, varied and enjoyable field of work.

Thanks to Helen Nagle and Sarah Elder for their invaluable help with the script and the great diagrams.

INTRODUCTION

There is an old joke in consulting about the client who rings up and says he urgently needs to develop a new reward strategy to show to his chief executive. The consultant replies that he will e-mail one over within the hour.

As someone who classifies and codes most of his consulting work under the heading of reward strategy, I must right away declare an increasing ambivalence towards the subject and nomenclature. For many years I argued for a broader, organisation-tailored and purpose- and goal-driven approach to compensation and benefits practices. These, it seemed to me, were often stuck in a technical and administrative backwater, driven by history and spurious ideas as to 'best practice'.

Now, the situation has come full circle, with most organisations proclaiming their reward strategy, which reinforces their business goals and drives regular changes in their pay and benefits practices. Consultants are keen to sell you their universally successful formula for strategic reward success.

Yet as all of us who have developed or been on the receiving end of such changes know, underneath the glossy jargon in the reward strategy policy documentation, the reality is that changing pay and benefits practices is an emotional, sensitive, difficult and time-consuming exercise. In a number of cases, often well-intentioned changes, driven by a desire for better business alignment, have actually demotivated employees and damaged the chances of achieving the firm's strategic goals. Such failures have led some academics to write off the whole idea as fanciful idealism and a waste of time.

But the fault is not with the concept of reward strategy itself, as some critics assert, but with the way in which it is often applied, force-fitted into a 'best practice' and technical 'quick-fix' mindset that, ironically, the whole concept was originally designed to counteract. The answer is not, therefore, to abandon it in order to return to this mentality, or to administrative backwaters, but rather to change the way we think about and operationalise our reward strategies.

'My aim is to help you to develop and operate tailored reward policies'

This is the purpose of this book, so I am afraid if you are looking for the magic off-the-shelf strategy contained in that e-mail, then you are not going to get it from me, and I think that the research evidence is quite clear that you won't get it from anyone else either. My aim is to help you, based on my ideas and experiences in many types of organisation, to develop and operate tailored reward policies that genuinely do support and reinforce your employer's key goals, but that also suit the character and culture of your workforce and genuinely operate as intended in practice.

The book is organised in three parts. The first two look at the 'why' and the 'what' of reward strategies, illustrating why your organisation does need such a strategy and some of the most important components. The chapters are organised as follows:

- *Chapter 1* provides more detail on the history and the current controversy over the value of having a reward strategy; it also outlines the basis for the new concept of reward strategy described in the rest of the book.
- *Chapter 2* addresses the 'top-down' issue of business goal alignment, and provides a methodology – a pathway – for developing pay and benefits practices that really do reinforce the direction and nature of your organisation's goals. This is the entire focus of most of the current reward strategy literature and is a necessary but not sufficient component of an effective reward strategy.
- *Chapter 3* looks at the relationship between reward policies and organisation structures, considering issues such as the appropriate level of hierarchy and centralisation.
- *Chapter 4* considers a number of the most significant and specific strategic and structural trends affecting reward practices today, including globalisation, mergers and acquisitions and e-business.
- *Chapter 5* considers some of the important design questions affecting the detailed content and components of your strategy. There is not the space in this book to cover every aspect of reward practice design in detail, and they are generally well covered in other specialist publications. Nonetheless, the stance you decide

to take on issues such as performance-related rewards and market positioning, and how you integrate and align your practices, are integral aspects of an effective reward strategy.

The third section is for me the critical piece, which addresses the 'how' of reward strategy. It attempts to illustrate how to combine visionary and long-term direction in your reward policies, with practical workability, understanding and effectiveness on the ground.

- *Chapter* 6 argues for a more employee-oriented, bottom-up approach to reward strategy, rooted in the concept of the psychological contract at work. It covers how to tailor the strategy to suit the culture and employee needs in your organisation, and achieve the essential understanding and commitment to it of employees and line managers.
- *Chapter* 7 covers the key processes that are critical to implementing and operating your reward strategy effectively: communications and involvement, performance management and the management of change. It describes common failings in these areas and suggests actions and techniques to overcome them.
- *Chapter* 8 provides a guide to diagnosing the current reward situation and to then designing and implementing an appropriate reward strategy for your own organisation. Practical tools and techniques are illustrated that my colleagues and I use to develop such strategies.
- *Chapter* 9 summarises the key components of effective and ineffective reward strategies and draws some conclusions as to their future requirements and characteristics.

All chapters are informed with actual examples from particular employers, with more detailed case studies at the end. Each chapter starts with a statement of its objectives and key points are summarised at the end.

You won't find the magic solution and supposed 'best' practice, nor will you obtain detailed answers to all of your reward design dilemmas. But hopefully you will end up agreeing with me as to the importance of strategically designed and managed reward policies and understanding how to apply a tried and tested process to best answer the key reward questions facing our rapidly changing organisations and environments.

Chapter 1

Reward strategies – essential or ineffectual?

Chapter objectives

- ✪ dissect the current controversy over the existence and value of reward strategies
- ✪ understand the traditional top-down model of reward strategy
- ✪ review the criticisms of this reward strategy concept
- ✪ profile the characteristics of current reward strategies
- ✪ understand why a strategic approach to reward is essential
- ✪ describe the emergence of a new conceptual framework.

History: from pay administration to strategic reward management

Very few of us with any influence on the pay and reward practices at our employers' would dare to go into work and describe them as 'non-strategic', so all-pervasive have North American notions of strategic human resource management become in this country. In earlier decades pay issues had been strongly influenced by tradition and government policy, and writers and practitioners such as McBeath were critical of the 'large numbers of organisations with no salary policy or plan ... usually associated with high turnover, poor productivity and low morale'. Smith (1982) was of the view that 'technical, political and economic developments have outmoded developments in remuneration', while Gomez-Mejia and Balkin (1987) criticised the narrow-minded technical and administrative approach of compensation and benefits specialists.

Speaking in the late 1980s, Barry Curnow, President of the Institute of Personnel Management (now the Chartered Institute of Personnel and Development), described the discipline as being at the crossroads between a restricted past and a future of great opportunities:

> We can either be compensation technicians, administering existing structures and mechanisms, or we can be compensation strategists, part of the corporate team, supporting the business plan, actively helping our organisations to go where they need to.

The profession's view would be that it is very much this latter course that has been pursued over the past decade. According to the invitation to an Industrial Relations Services conference:

> Pay has undergone a revolution ... increasing competition, globalisation, skill shortages and the new technologies have come together to move pay from a peripheral role to centre stage in influencing and achieving corporate objectives ... pay is an agent of change.

‘ Reward systems become an important means of communicating and reinforcing business goals ’

Ed Lawler (1994) was one of the first experts to champion this concept of reward strategy, describing it as 'an integrated reward approach, linking company strategy, pay systems and employee behaviours' (see Figure 1). Reward systems thus become an important means of communicating and reinforcing the business goals of the organisation, not just because pay represents an important cost for many organisations, but because reward systems can incentivise employees to pursue and achieve these goals, and to develop and apply the essential capabilities and skills sup-

Figure 1
LAWLER'S MODEL OF REWARD STRATEGY

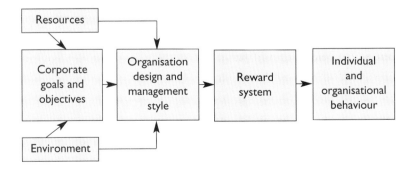

porting them. According to Michael Porter, addressing the IPD's Annual Conference in Harrogate in 1997, 'having the right rewards in place helps people to make the right choices to support your strategy.'

Hurwich (1986) defined reward strategy in delightfully simple terms as 'the incorporation of business issues into decisions on compensation'. However, as well as this derivative 'vertical' link from the business strategy, definitions of reward strategy typically encompass two other important aspects of integration:

- the need for 'horizontal fit' between all of the pay and reward policies with each other and with the other HR policies; this ensures an aligned HR strategy delivering a consistent message to employees about what is needed for the business to succeed, and the HR approach supporting this
- the need for a forward-looking change orientation, so that in rapidly changing environments and organisations reward policies deliver what is required for success in the future, and change to stay aligned with business goals; according to Zingheim and Schuster (2000), two leading exponents of this 'new pay' philosophy, 'companies are using pay to lead change', with 'sweeping and dramatic pay transitions'; the alternative steady-state approach to business and pay management in the new millennium and economy, they argue, will lead to organisational 'road kill'.

Today, therefore, the compensation literature is virtually unanimous in proclaiming that 'reward strategy and policies should be business-driven, responding to the needs of the business' (Armstrong and Murlis 1997), and even that, 'non-strategic reward considerations should be ignored' (Rhodes 1988). And equally grand and expansive claims are made for the effectiveness of these strategies, with a recent report in the USA from one consultancy claiming to 'prove' that 'effective reward strategies boost shareholder value by 9.2 per cent'. A majority of participants in the Towers Perrin (1999b) research referred to below believed that their strategies had been successful in reinforcing business goals and performance.

The characteristics of current reward strategies

So are organisations responding to the exhortations of the compensation writers and gurus? Recent research by Towers Perrin (1999b) amongst 460 organisations in Europe would suggest that they are, or at least they claim to be, strategic in their pay and reward approach. Seventy-eight per cent of these organisations now have an articulated reward strategy, which represents a significant increase over the situation four years earlier, when fewer than half as many did so.

In the context of these strategies, the radical level of change described by Zingheim and Schuster (2000) does appear to be occurring. Ninety-four per cent of these organisations had made significant reward changes in the past three years, and 96 per cent had further changes planned. We describe some of the commonest of these changes in Chapter 5. But according to the study participants, their change agenda is a business-driven one, aiming at better alignment between their business goals and reward systems. Business and broader HR drivers were primary, reinforcing the skills and values required to improve customer service and achieve other key corporate goals through reward practices. The most significant goals driving pay and reward changes among European organisations are (Towers Perrin 1999b):

- improve employees' focus on achieving business goals (81 per cent)
- broaden/improve employees' competencies/skills (68 per cent)
- focus employees on customer needs (54 per cent)
- create competitive advantage through the workforce (51 per cent)
- reinforce corporate values (40 per cent).

Specific reward goals now appear to extend well beyond the traditional recruit, retain, motivate and cost control, in particular linking rewards more closely to the organisation's key success factors and performance. The most common reward strategy goals amongst European organisations (in order of importance) are (Towers Perrin 1999b):

- recruit, motivate and retain high performers
- achieve and maintain market competitiveness
- attract key talent into the organisation
- link pay to the organisation's key success factors
- pay each person based on individual results
- control fixed pay costs
- manage rewards on a total remuneration basis.

A 1998 CIPD survey of performance pay practices similarly concluded that 'organisations are adapting their schemes to improve the fit between

Table 1

THE SHIFTING EMPHASIS IN THE WORK OF COMPENSATION AND BENEFITS STAFF

		Now	Future
Priority	1	Programme design	Developing reward policy and strategy
	2	Developing reward policy and strategy	Providing consulting and process support to line managers
	3	Administration	Programme design
	4	Providing consulting and process support to line managers	Administration

Source: Towers Perrin

rewards and the organisation's business strategy'. These policies can be described as strategic, not only in terms of having clear objectives to support the business goals, but also in that 76 per cent of the organisations with reward strategies in the Towers Perrin (1999b) research involved and consulted with directors and company board members in designing their strategies and the changes they encompass. Moreover, while traditional design work continues to take up the largest part of compensation and benefits specialists' time, reward strategy work seems set to become predominant, as traditional administrative activities are made more efficient, and increasingly, outsourced (see Table 1).

The criticisms of reward strategies

Are these grand strategies anything more than what Professor John Purcell called at a recent conference, 'an illusion in the boardroom'? Critics of the reward strategy concept have become increasingly vocal in the last couple of years and, it would appear, with some justification. The criticisms focus on two areas.

1   In practice, it is very difficult to make changes to pay and reward systems.
2   In reality, therefore, pay and reward schemes are not being primarily influenced by the business strategy.

Based on their research, Cox and Purcell (1998) believe that 'a combination of internal pressures (how would you react if you were told your pay and benefits were being changed?), history and expectations makes the strategic use of reward systems extremely difficult to achieve'. So, 'pay systems may be stronger sources of competitive disadvantage rather than advantage'. According to Marc Thompson (1998a) at Oxford University, in reality 'managing reward is a job of short-term damage limitation, not the strategic lever for change that appears so seductive in the writings of American commentators'.

Two of those commentators, Henderson and Risher (1987), agree, believing that reward strategies exist only in textbooks and that 'pay decisions are mostly short-run, reactive, messy and political'. Pfeffer (1998) even more aggressively attacks the ineffectiveness of performance pay schemes and other 'myths' of pay reinforcing strategy. As Michael Porter observed at the IPD National Conference in 1997, many of these relatively recently developed reward strategies do bear a striking similarity, illustrating that 'HR people often focus on best practice, relying on benchmarking, in the absence of any (genuine) strategic direction'.

Certainly in my work I see plenty of evidence of pay schemes still heavily influenced by tradition and pragmatism, and 'knee-jerk' responses to problems such as skill shortages, which may just be creating even bigger issues for the organisation in the future. Proposals for new incentive schemes have been rejected purely on the basis that they are novel and not in evidence elsewhere in the market. In every other aspect of corporate strategy, the aim is to differentiate yourself from the competition, but often not in respect of rewards.

The Towers Perrin (1999b) research provides evidence to demonstrate that organisations are having problems in implementing their reward strategies, with over two-thirds of them admitting such difficulties, most notably:

● ineffective communications (45 per cent)

- lack of support systems, eg market data (35 per cent)
- poor performance management (28 per cent)
- the system not matching with organisation needs (27 per cent)
- lack of management skills/support (25 per cent).

We consider the nature and causes of these problems in more detail in Chapter 7. But as you can see, they are predominantly concerned with process issues, such as ineffective communication and lack of appropriate line manager skills to implement the schemes as intended.

Moreover, the level of reward change is actually less than was forecast in an equivalent study carried out three years earlier (Towers Perrin 1997), particularly in respect of the most radical 'new pay' initiatives advocated by some US writers. For example, 14 per cent predicted the introduction of team bonus schemes in 1996, when the incidence grew in reality only from 6 to 8 per cent of organisations. Similarly, 29 per cent forecast the introduction of competency-related base pay adjustment, yet only 14 per cent now operate such schemes, up just 3 per cent on three years ago.

Meanwhile, written reward strategies are largely being used within the HR community and not shared with staff, nor even in a majority of cases with line managers, according to our reward study respondents. This must raise questions as to their practical impact.

'There appears to be a sort of strategy-driven determinism at work'

What is even more worrying than Purcell's boardroom illusion is the 'gung-ho' approach to reward changes that some organisations, fuelled by their reading, seem to have taken. There appears to be a sort of strategy-driven determinism at work that, for example, customer service is a key strategic goal so reward schemes must be linked to it. In at least one case I have seen this tried in the absence of any decent measures of customer service actually applying to most employees. In others I have seen it damage all-round service levels, due to the focus incentives induced on a few, narrowly defined service measures.

This approach treats reward strategy as a type of unexplained but automatic black-box process, with 'X' element of business strategy or core values necessarily leading to 'Y' change in reward practice. This not only misses the choices that are always available, but also more importantly ignores the processes of change and operation. A pharmaceutical company wanted to introduce a team bonus scheme, so as to reinforce a core value of the organisation. Teamwork was indeed essential to the success of that research-based company. Yet the internal team structure was highly fluid, with the membership of teams changing regularly during the course of projects, and many staff on multiple and rotating teams. The use of a formal team bonus arrangement would have risked introducing damaging rigidities into this structure, making staff less willing to transfer between teams, for example, as well as huge operating and administrative complexity. So teamwork was reinforced with less direct, non-financial recognition schemes rather than using a team bonus.

Why reward strategies are essential

So, are all of these mushrooming reward strategies evident in organisations just statements of senior managers' and the HR function's views, without any basis in operating reality and suspiciously close to what everyone else in the market is doing? Should we abandon these grand ideas and return to reward practices driven by history and make only tactical and incremental modifications, as infrequently as possible? Is a 'hassle-minimisation' reward strategy the only viable approach worth adopting? During the course of the Towers Perrin (1999b) research, the head of HR in a UK bank told me that 'we deliberately didn't have a reward strategy ... the business might have reacted against the scale of the transformation involved, and the scale of the resources required ... it would have been a nine day wonder'.

A lessening of ambitions and recognition of the time and resource it takes to change reward practices effectively would help in some cases. And yet this organisation had spent three years making significant changes to its HR and reward practices, driven by the transition from being a mutual building society to becoming a quoted PLC, as the case study in Chapter 5 explains. The new business environment necessitated change, and rewards were a powerful tool to reinforce those changes, so as to achieve more demanding customer service and shareholder requirements.

There are three sets of factors that explain why a strategic reward approach is essential in many organisations:

- ❷ decisions over reward systems, even passive ones to continue with the status quo, are big, significant decisions
- ❷ there is a connection between business strategies and particular pay and reward practices
- ❷ human capital is the source of sustained competitive advantage.

The importance of the decision

Pearce and Robinson (1997) describe strategic decisions as those that:

- ❷ require top management involvement
- ❷ entail large amounts of resource
- ❷ have major business consequences
- ❷ are future-oriented
- ❷ impact on the long-term performance of the organisation.

Even the very specific and tactical policy decisions that organisations make seem to fit these criteria pretty well – for example, how to integrate the company car plans in a merging energy company, or how to change the performance measures in an executive incentive plan. As we consider in Chapter 2, reward policies and decisions have the potential to directly frustrate the achievement of business strategies.

The relationship between business strategy and pay and reward practice

As we illustrate more fully in Chapter 2, there is some fairly good research data to indicate that particular business strategies are, over the longer term, associated with particular pay and reward practices. Goold and Campbell (1987), for example, found that performance bonuses were more common and more aggressively used amongst diverse conglomerates with a financial control management style. This, after all, is only common sense. As Towers Perrin (1994) found in a study amongst UK privatised utilities, businesses emphasising a cost leadership strategy are less likely to adopt a high market pay stance, and more likely to relate pay to productivity.

Moreover, while some of the simplistic claims that particular reward practices 'cause' particular improvements in corporate performance are questionable, there is an increasingly impressive body of research evidence to show relationships between business performance and a basket of HR policies and practices, including rewards. Guest and Conway's (1998) research for the CIPD on the psychological contract, the recent Workplace Employee Relations Survey (Culley 1998), Thompson's (1998) research in the aerospace sector and Becker and Huselid's (1996) work in the USA all demonstrate this relationship – see Figure 2 – as well as the interactions with employee satisfaction and commitment. Thompson (1998), for example, found significantly higher levels of value added per employee in companies using a greater number of a defined basket of HR and reward practices, and applying them to a larger proportion of their workforce.

The Towers Perrin (1999b) European research similarly found correlations between business returns to shareholders and certain pay practices, including a greater use of performance pay and more open reward communications. While it is obviously not as simple as pulling reward lever A to achieve business result B, these associations do support Lawler's (1994) contention that even if changing pay systems is difficult, 'they are too important levers for business and cultural change for most organisations to leave alone'.

Figure 2

THE RELATIONSHIP BETWEEN HR AND REWARD PRACTICES AND BUSINESS PERFORMANCE

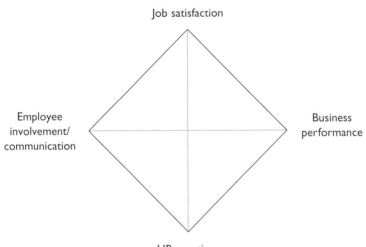

Job satisfaction

Employee involvement/ communication

Business performance

HR practices
(including various reward practices such as pay linked to performance)

Human capital

This is surely the crux of the matter. In our ever-more rapidly changing world and organisations, buffeted by globalisation, social change and intense competitive pressures, all of the business strategy experts – Hamel and Prahalad, Bartlett and Ghoshall, Collins and Porras – tell us that, as the latter pair put it, 'the sources of sustained competitive advantage have shifted from finance, to technology, and now to human capital'.

> **‹ Those people really are your organisation's most important asset ›**

In our new knowledge and service-based economy, in which key skill shortages are increasingly apparent, people costs not only typically represent a much higher proportion of total expenditure, but those people really are your organisation's most important asset. If you do not reward them in the most effective way, ensuring that you recognise and reinforce what will make the business a success, and changing the former as the latter shifts, then you are increasingly likely to be put out of business by someone else who does. And this is true across all sectors – the cost, efficiency, recruitment and retention, and performance pressures are every bit as challenging in the public as in the private sector.

This is the era of 'the talent war', in which 75 per cent of UK organisations report skill shortages and 87 per cent of firms are being held back by a lack of sufficient staff with e-commerce skills, in which US law firms are offering new associates two-year packages worth up to $1 million, where Goldman Sachs has awarded 2 million shares to its junior staff to help retain them, and in which Bain and Accenture (formerly Andersen Consulting) now offer their professionals a stake in their dot.com investment portfolios to help prevent them leaving for new start-up opportunities. As the chairman and chief executive of J.P. Morgan, which operates a similar fund, put it recently, 'If you don't retain and release the energy of great people, then you can say goodbye to those people and to your success.'

The importance of intervention

It may be difficult to effect and manage reward changes but in the new economic scenario, the 'doing nothing', 'leave pay alone', and 'it's too difficult' options are becoming far more dangerous than intervening. That 94 per cent level of change in the Towers Perrin (1999b) European study is not an illusion: these organisations are being forced to intervene. Their less hierarchical, more customer-oriented, more team-based, more talent-hungry, more contribution-focused organisations can no longer tolerate multiple-grade structures, automatic general awards and pay cost-escalation, and inflexible, expensive and misunderstood benefits packages. And they need some kind of strategy to guide that intervention.

Take some examples from my consulting work. There was the insurance company who paid its direct salesforce through commission on product margins – very difficult to change, when commission is an ingrained and long-standing component of the industry's culture which ensures high payments for high performers. But what about customer service? A disastrous year in the 1990s culminated in the company being fined for pensions mis-selling, with the commission scheme identified as an important contributor. The new chief executive subsequently made reform of this pay system one of his top priorities and focused future payments on service and quality.

Or consider the pharmaceutical company who ignored the globalisation of labour markets and refused to break its internal-equity-driven pay arrangements for executives in the UK. A key senior executive was recently lost to a US competitor for a package worth over double his existing one.

Or what about the privatised water company with 98 grades, general above-cost-of-living pay awards, service increments and over 100 separate pay allowances, where the trade unions strongly opposed changes? Explaining its move into broad pay bands and contribution-based rewards in 1998, the company communicated it to staff, 'not as a threat, but a necessity when we have to justify every pound of expenditure to shareholders, customers and regulators'.

Even in a successful, high-growth situation, in this era of hyper-change existing reward practices can quickly become an albatross that damages corporate effectiveness and staff morale. A rapidly growing mobile phone company's entrepreneurial founders, as in most small companies, managed pay on a purely personal basis, and opposed the rigid, job evaluated 'big-company' pay structures that they had experienced earlier in their careers. The trouble is, as the business grows and matures, it becomes very difficult and time-consuming to manage pay on a totally personal basis once you have 3,500 staff, as they were experiencing.

In these and many other cases, reward changes were essential to support a new strategy and respond to new situations. While the changes often were difficult, as one participant in the Towers Perrin (1999b) research told me:

> It's far from perfect, and with hindsight we would have done some things differently. But the difference after all these changes is that now we really do pay people to support the direction the business is going in.

Alastair Ross of the Royal Bank of Scotland similarly explained to me that its reward strategy meant that 'pay is not now driven primarily by internal relativities and status, but by value to the business', while the chief executive of PA Consulting believes that 'a new remuneration structure was central to changing the way PA was managed'.

The need for a new definition and model of reward strategy

Reward policies need to change to support business goals, yet it is very tough to make the changes work, and the speed of change makes lengthy, grand and detailed master plans obsolete before they can be implemented effectively. As the operations director of a privatised utility told me, 'in changing to compete in our new marketplace, pay and reward policies represent the most significant but also the most difficult set of changes we have to make'. So how do we square this circle?

Living strategies

The answer is not to throw the reward strategy baby out with the proverbial bath water, but to alter our concept of what a reward strategy is. The whole discipline of corporate business strategy has changed substantially in recent years to reflect our new environment, a shift brilliantly described by Professor Sumantra Ghoshal (1999) as moving 'from strategy, structure and systems, to purpose, process and people'.

‘Strategy is as much about implementation as planning’

As he and Bartlett illustrate by contrasting the growth of GE with the decline of Westinghouse, fancy strategic plans and corporate structures cannot create sustained success in our fast-moving world where, like ABB, organisations need to be at the same time 'big and small, global and local, decentralised and centralised'. Strategy is as much about implementation as planning, and needs to focus on setting a broad direction and creating the right environment for people to succeed in. The successful business strategy then becomes what Lynda Grattan (2000a) calls 'living strategy', or what Yves Doz at INSEAD referred to as 'a pattern in a stream of decisions' (Doz and Bower, 1992).

Thus HR and compensation professionals, as Grattan (1997) explains, have to recognise that 'the challenges organisations face cannot be addressed by individual techniques and designs' nor dry and detailed plans. Instead, we need to work with 'dynamic, complex integrated systems and processes'. Through a 'focus on trust and aspirations' and creating an appropriate vision, we can genuinely build total HR systems displaying 'vertical linkages with business strategy, horizontal linkages between HR processes and temporal linkages between present and future'.

And in doing so, as Dave Ulrich (1997) elaborates, 'in a world of high amounts of change, agility becomes all important'. It requires 'more flexible, dynamic and responsive HR professionals' who 'cannot assume they will design the perfect programme', but must constantly 'learn and adapt'. HR strategy, according to John Purcell, is therefore 'not simply a question of importing a set of best practices', or just 'adjusting HR practices to get a good fit with the external environment. Instead, the focus has to be on managing change.'

Dynamic, integrated, and achieving business results through a genuine people and process focus over the long term is what all of these thinkers are saying makes a successful HR strategy. This line of thinking means that we need to recognise that effective reward strategies have three components.

1   They have to have clearly planned goals and a well-defined link to the business objectives.
2   There have to be well-designed pay and reward programmes, tailored to the needs of the organisation and its people, and consistent and integrated with each other.

3   Perhaps most important and most neglected, there needs to be effective and supportive HR and reward processes in place.

As Purcell (2000) puts it, 'the emphasis is not so much on high-performing work practices as on HR processes which lead to the successful introduction of changes, uniquely suited to the internal and external circumstances of the organisation – what Boxall has referred to as "the HR advantage".'

Bottom-up strategies

The genuine revolution in reward management over the last decade has been the move beyond a purely technical design focus to encompass a business agenda and strategic perspective. But without extensive employee communications and involvement to create understanding and trust, without effective line and performance management, then the written reward strategy goals that many organisations now have can never be delivered in practice. Their strategies are stillborn.

As the Towers Perrin (1999b) and much contemporary research shows, this is where many of our current business-focused reward strategies are falling down: in the implementation and operating processes. Correspondingly, as Angela Bowey's (1983) research demonstrated nearly 20 years ago, successful pay change initiatives were characterised not just by clear objectives and senior management support, but also by intensive attention to the related processes: of employee communications, teambuilding, performance appraisal and so on.

So the solution is not to abandon our reward strategies and changes, but to adopt a more inclusive, employee and process-focused, evolutionary approach to them. They need to encompass plans, designs and operating processes. We should not of course abandon considerations of business strategy, long-term goals and organisational capabilities and structures (which we consider in Chapters 2, 3 and 4), nor downplay the importance of appropriate design work (described in Chapter 6).

But we need to pay much greater attention to employee needs and values, to culture, and to the realities of organisational life in the

Figure 3
A MORE BALANCED, PRACTICAL REWARD STRATEGY MODEL

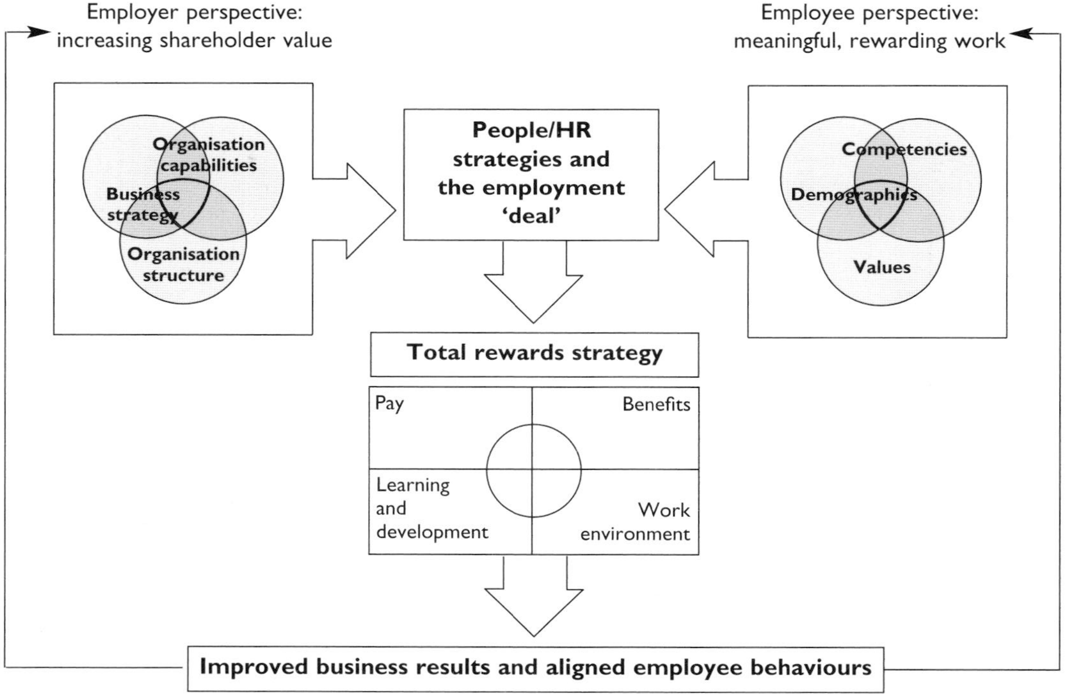

Employer perspective:
increasing shareholder value

Employee perspective:
meaningful, rewarding work

Organisation
capabilities

Business
strategy

Organisation
structure

Competencies

Demographics

Values

People/HR
strategies and
the employment
'deal'

Total rewards strategy

Pay | Benefits

Learning
and
development | Work
environment

Improved business results and aligned employee behaviours

near term when planning and making our reward strategy interventions (described in Chapters 6 and 7). Our model for strategic reward changes needs to become better balanced, multifaceted and more employee- and process-focused – see Figure 3.

As Lawler's (2000a) latest book describes, in the new knowledge-based economy, the traditional direction of strategic rewards (business strategy>reward practices>employee behaviour) almost needs to be turned on its head. 'The new reward challenge', he writes, 'is to attract the right kinds of human capital and to motivate and develop them to perform in ways that increases shareholder value' (reward practices>employee behaviour>business strategy).

And in addressing this challenge, as Zingheim and Schuster (2000) elaborate, we cannot rely on 'bureaucratic and over-designed' pay plans, or market-obsessed 'commodity solutions'. Reward strategies should be 'agile and adaptable, building a focused foundation that can adapt as the organisation changes'. It is a process of 'continual reappraisal and adjustment', tailoring approaches to suit the changing needs of the organisation and its staff.

‘Our effective reward strategy model integrates business, employee and market needs’

So here we have the key components of our new, more effective reward strategy model. To borrow Henry Mintzberg's (1990) business strategy analogy, it involves moving from a tight, forced, 'top-down' greenhouse approach, to a looser 'seed-garden' style, nurturing a mix of broad plans and emergent, 'bottom-up' components. Rather than an exclusive business focus, it integrates business, employee and market needs. As Pfeffer (1998) explains, in the knowledge economy the first strategic question is no longer 'What business are we in?' but 'What do we believe in?'

It takes a total rewards perspective, rather than just focusing on pay and maybe benefits. It encompasses all three aspects of goals, designs and processes, and in doing so involves the HR function in entering into an open partnership with employees and line managers, rather than treating pay issues, as an Irish regional manager described to me recently, 'like the secret service'. And it means abandoning the pursuit of perfection through 'big-bang', 'quick-fix', 'one-hit' changes in favour of a long-term approach of evolution, with regular, adaptive and incremental improvements.

The reward strategy model we now use at Towers Perrin – see Figure 3 – has evolved to recognise the importance of this broader, more balanced and integrated perspective, combining in a sense the humanistic and HRM schools of behavioural and motivation theory with business strategy concepts. The rest of this book looks at how this approach is being applied today, how you can use it in your own organisation, and thereby how you can move your own reward strategies from intent to impact.

Case study

THE NECESSITY OF A REWARD STRATEGY IN A MANUFACTURING PLANT: TOO LITTLE, TOO LATE

Background: the business strategy

This long-established UK plant of a pharmaceutical company employed 600 staff in the production of off-patent products. Its experiences help to demonstrate the dire consequences of failing to change reward and employment practices to match environmental and strategic change.

The business strategy of the operations division stressed productivity improvement so as to raise margins and help fund further research investment to produce new, patented, high-margin products. It moved to a policy of worldwide sourcing, with plants engaged in internal competition to source different country markets, and moving to a structure of fewer, larger and more efficient facilities.

The UK had made some significant changes as part of its efficiency drive, introducing multi-skilling and a team-based organisation on the shop floor, reducing headcount, and boosting productivity by over 30 per cent.

Current reward schemes

Pay arrangements were, however, largely untouched by this transformation. The total package was very competitive by local market standards, but its organisation and delivery were highly complex. There were 19 grades organised into three separate structures, for process, craft and staff workers, each underpinned by different job evaluation schemes. An annual common increase was awarded each January, with service-based increments for the first two groups, and performance-related awards for the staff. It took process operators 14 years to get to the maximum of their scale. There was also a common annual site-wide Christmas bonus scheme covering all employees. Benefits and conditions, such as pension and vacation, were also very competitive for the area.

The new reward strategy

Changes were attempted in 1993, but the proposal to remove increments led to industrial action and was subsequently abandoned. Three years later, however, an in-depth review was undertaken with a brief to improve the cost-effectiveness and simplicity of the current arrangements, while reinforcing personal development and flexible working, and producing stronger relationships between pay and performance on the site.

The review group consulted with managers and staff, looked at external market practice and reviewed data on the current schemes. The consultations revealed some wide divergences in views, but a strong opinion amongst employees that they had not been rewarded for the skill and productivity improvements they had made in recent years. Amongst managers, only the site director saw changes in this area as critical to their survival, and they were surprised at the level of staff support for changes. As one employee put it, 'we know the company have to reduce costs and wages are a major cost'. Market practice revealed contrasting practices in the industry, with approaches ranging from skills and competency pay to equally traditional, incremental structures.

The group reviewed change options in all areas of reward against the agreed goals, and in relation to the effort and disruption required to implement them. Three overall change options were considered, as illustrated in Table 2.

Table 2
THREE BROAD OVERALL APPROACHES TO PAY CHANGES

Aspects of pay and reward	Minimal change approach	Intermediate approach	Radical change approach
Job evaluation	• Tinker with/improve existing systems	• Harmonised grading guidelines to facilitate job slotting	• Single points factor evaluation system
Pay/grading structures	• Reduce number of grades within existing structures	• Common structure with reduced number of grades and broader pay ranges but recognising job family differences	• New single structure of 6–8 grades with broader pay ranges
Pay adjustment	• As intermediate approach	• Revised appraisal and pay adjustment system for staff • Progression based on applied skill steps for process/craft employees	• New common appraisal, relating base pay increases (or bonuses) to: • achievement of objectives • skills application
Performance bonus	• Company bonus scheme with clear measures, targets and payment schedule. Regular communication, interim payment	• Funded according to company performance, modified according to department or possibly smaller teams' performance	• Funded according to company performance, modified according to individual performance

The group was unanimous in supporting changes and broadly rec-ommended the intermediate approach shown, with a number of more radical changes planned for future years. The changes that the directors agreed as part of the new reward strategy included:

- moving to a single, harmonised structure of pay bands, with a common, simple points factor system of job evaluation, and brief generic role profiles replacing detailed specialist job descriptions
- removing pay increments and relating the increases in pay for craft and process workers to defined key skills and behav-iours, and for staff to performance assessed through a new appraisal system
- relating the annual bonus more directly to site performance.

The outline of these changes was communicated to staff, and a joint management and employee group worked out the detail to increase efficiency and flexibility over the next two months. The number of job titles was reduced from more than 150 to 60 roles in order to increase flexibility and efficiency. All of the new roles were evalu-ated into a single five-band structure. The new bonus plan, with service and productivity measures, was modelled and tested.

The group was in the middle of redesigning the new, common appraisal system, which linked personal objectives and compe-tencies to the role profiles, both for pay and development pur-poses, when the whole plant was called to a site meeting. The director announced that the facility was to be closed with the loss of 574 jobs. He thanked all of the employees for their hard work, but said that the restructuring of the pharmaceutical industry and the consequent pressure on prices had forced the decision on the company.

Many factors, of course, contributed to the 30-year-old plant's closure. But the lack of effective reinforcement of the division's goals by its reward arrangements had proved damaging to morale and hampered the required productivity and perform-ance improvements. The speed and enthusiasm with which the changes were greeted and developed so late in the day only served to demonstrate that they were coming too late to affect the fate of the site.

Chapter summary

- Driven primarily by the ideas of strategic human resource management and the criticisms of tradition-bound and narrowly focused pay practices, HR writers and practitioners in the UK have virtually unanimously endorsed the concept of strategic compensation in the last two decades. Pay and reward policies should be driven by business goals and aligned with other HR policies.

- Almost 80 per cent of European organisations now have an articulated reward strategy. In their attempts to achieve a better fit between reward policies and business goals, 94 per cent have made significant changes in the past three years.

- Powerful criticisms of prevailing reward strategy ideas have emerged in the past couple of years. Evidence as to the difficulties in implementing new reward strategies and changes has emerged, leading some critics to state that pay and reward should be relegated to a more tactical and limited role.

- Pay and reward issues are of strategic importance to many organisations and there is evidence for the association between particular business strategies, pay and reward practices, and business success.

- Most significantly, effective reward strategies are even more essential in today's knowledge-driven and human-capital-constrained new economy, in which people really are the key to an organisation's success. Any significant mismatch between the requirements on employees to implement the business's strategic goals, and the behaviours that are rewarded can spell corporate disaster.

- A new concept of reward strategy is required to recognise this rapidly changing world and the implementation problems with the traditional 'top-down' model.

- Key features of the new reward strategy approach include:
  - balancing considerations of business strategy and structure with employee needs and culture, rather than an exclusive focus on the former
  - encompassing the planning, design and operation of reward policies and practices, not just the plans
  - incorporating planned and emergent components, rather than sticking rigidly to plans

- tailoring reward policies and processes to the unique needs of each organisation, rather than borrowing strategies and 'best' practices wholesale from the external market
- moving to a broader consideration of total rewards, rather than a narrow pay and benefits focus
- placing a strong emphasis on reward and related HR processes, such as management training and performance management, and particularly incorporating a high communications and involvement approach, rather than restricting reward strategies to the HR community and a few senior directors
- taking a long-term approach of evolution, incorporating regular, incremental improvements, rather than seeking rapid success through 'big-bang' revolutionary changes.

Chapter 2

The bottom line – aligning rewards with business goals

Chapter objectives

- reinforce the importance of aligning reward practices with business goals and illustrate the dangers of misalignment
- provide a methodology – a pathway – to demonstrate how this alignment can be achieved and give examples of its application
- provide tools to help communicate the relationship between business goals, employee performance and rewards
- highlight the necessary evolution in effective reward management practices to match business and environmental changes.

The problems of misalignment

It was in the early 1970s that US expert Ed Lawler (1971) observed that remarkably few organisations 'examine the potential impact of reward systems on organisational effectiveness and how they relate to the strategic objectives of the organisation'. Yet the whole futility of the academic debate as to the value of reward strategies is demonstrated by the number of real-life examples, 30 years on, of organisations with reward practices that really are getting in the way of the execution of their business strategy. Lawler's comments apply with almost equal force today.

Take a project in a major oil company with a recent record of poor performance. A far-reaching business review had highlighted serious strategic issues: a lack of competitiveness outside of its domestic market; very high production and distribution costs; and a lack of innovation and speed to market. The three-pronged business strategy it adopted, therefore, involved:

- working to become a truly more international organisation
- reducing operating and employment costs
- speeding up response times and new product, market and process innovations.

A brief examination of its reward policies might have suggested just how it got into this situation and the difficulties of emerging from it. A strongly North-American-oriented reward approach ignored local market practices and variations in tax law. It was illustrative of the excessive centralisation in the organisation that was stifling overseas initiatives and growth, and leading to the underutilisation of its international talent.

A universal, upper-quartile pay and benefits stance in the oil market, itself a high-paying sector, contributed to the lack of cost-effectiveness. And the stiflingly detailed, hierarchical, management-by-objectives system for setting personal goals and determining individual pay awards helped to explain the lack of responsiveness and flexibility.

Similarly, a long-established industrial gases company was facing cut-throat international competition, increasingly demanding and sophisticated customers, and a host of technological innovations. The latter potentially opened up new markets for its gases, but were also driving down production costs and prices. Its business strategy aimed at profitable growth through a focus on key market sectors on a global basis, and targeted productivity improvements of at least 4 per cent per annum. The chief executive championed a new set of capabilities and values, which its research had indicated were required in the organisation to deliver these goals. These included teamwork, innovation, customer focus and improved leadership. The traditional culture in the company was typical of an engineering, production and volume-driven organisation, with an autocratic management style and a strong focus on individual results.

But the current reward systems also conflicted with these strategic and cultural requirements. General pay awards and a lack of variable pay meant that there was no relationship between pay and performance for the bulk of employees, and no overall relationship between productivity and pay costs. Meanwhile, a highly detailed job-evaluation-driven pay structure encouraged a 'just do my job' mentality, with no reward or recognition for innovation. Individual management bonuses similarly worked against teamwork and global co-operation, and gave no reward for effective leadership or people management.

These may seem laughably obvious conflicts between rewards and business strategy, hardly requiring expensive consultants to identify them. Yet if we look in our own organisations, most of us will be able to find similar examples of what Steve Kerr (1975), now at GE, once memorably referred to as 'the folly of rewarding for "A", while hoping for "B".'

Evidence of these conflicts continue to litter the UK reward landscape, including:

- a focus in bonus schemes on individual results, when we want co-operation and teamwork
- the lack of any rewards for effective customer service and teamwork
- the lack of any relationship between pay and performance
- the absence of any incentive to people to learn and apply new skills that add value to the business
- actual pay levels and key benefits entitlements still strongly related to length of service
- an inability to reflect external market variations in pay
- complex, significant and often uncontrolled 'add-ons' to base pay
- punishments rather than rewards for risk-taking and innovation.

‘The question is: how do I ensure that rewards reinforce the business strategy’

As in any aspect of life, it is always easy to find fault and to criticise, and no organisation will ever have a perfect reward system. But most of us can improve our current systems. So the key questions to address in this chapter are: how do I solve and avoid these misalignments and ensure that rewards really do reinforce the business strategy, and what do employees have to do to deliver that strategy?

Strategic typologies and life cycle models

Much of the early literature and research on reward strategies concentrated on advocating and demonstrating relationships between particular business strategies and particular reward approaches and practices. Two popular concepts were:

- the use of generic strategic typologies, such as Michael Porter's (1980) classification of cost leadership, focus and differentiation strategies
- the idea of life cycle stages.

Thus Schuler (1988), for example, posited that cost reduction, quality improvement and innovation strategies required different patterns of behaviour by employees in order to execute them effectively. Therefore different sets of HR and reward practices should be employed to develop and recognise these employee characteristics, as illustrated in Table 3. Cost leadership companies, he argued, were more likely to have a hire-and-fire culture, and hierarchical pay structures. The most innovative companies, on the other hand, would operate more flexible, open and market-focused rewards. Carroll (1987) provides a lot more detail on the compensation practices, with the cost leaders characterised by more mechanistic structures and job evaluation, internal equity-based pay, a low to medium market position, and a moderate use of incentives focused on productivity and short-term financial results.

Of course, a company's business strategy will often change as it grows and matures, and Ellig (1987) is one of a number of compen-sation writers who claimed a relationship between the life cycle stage of an organisation and its reward practices. In his view, 'the degree of importance of each compensation element depends on the company's market stage'. A new business is short on cash and keeps pay low, offering instead the hope of future riches from high initial equity shares for employees. As it and its workforce matures, how-ever, pay, perks and benefits become more important to people and so a more comprehensive and balanced reward strategy emerges. A business in decline tends towards high salaries, short-term incentives and benefits, but low long-term incentives.

There is some research support for such associations as these. Gomez-Mejia and Balkin (1987), for example, found relationships between the level of innovation in high technology companies and their reward practices. Towers Perrin (1994) found that utility companies emphasising a cost leadership strategy made greater use of individ-ual performance pay. Those focusing more heavily on enhancing cus-tomer service made greater use of team rewards and were more active in implementing flexible working practices and conditions.

Table 3

SCHULER: MATCHING HR AND REWARD PRACTICES WITH COMPETITIVE STRATEGIES

	Employee characteristics	HR practices
Cost reduction strategy	❷ Predictable, repetitive behaviour ❷ Short-term focus ❷ Relatively independent behaviour ❷ Modest concern for quality ❷ High concern for quantity ❷ High concern for results ❷ Low preference for responsibility ❷ Low flexibility to change ❷ Low tolerance of ambiguity ❷ Narrow skill application ❷ Low job involvement	❷ Low participation ❷ Explicit job criteria ❷ Mostly internal sources ❷ Narrow career paths ❷ Results criteria ❷ Short-term criteria ❷ Mostly individual criteria ❷ Little employment security ❷ Few incentives ❷ Hierarchical pay ❷ Little training ❷ Traditional labour/ management relations
Quality improve-ment strategy	❷ Predictable, repetitive behaviour ❷ Intermediate-term focus ❷ Some co-operative behaviour ❷ High concern for quality ❷ Modest concern for quantity ❷ High concern for process ❷ Preference for responsibility ❷ Modest flexibility to change ❷ Modest tolerance for ambiguity ❷ Modest skill application ❷ High job involvement	❷ High participation ❷ Explicit job criteria ❷ Some external sources ❷ Narrow career paths ❷ Mostly results criteria ❷ Mostly short-term criteria ❷ Some group criteria ❷ Some employment security ❷ Some incentives ❷ Egalitarian pay ❷ Extensive training ❷ Co-operative labour/ management relations
Inno-vation strategy	❷ Creative, innovative behaviour ❷ Long-term focus ❷ Co-operative interdependent behaviour ❷ Modest concern for quality ❷ Modest concern for quantity ❷ Modest concern for process ❷ Preference for responsibility ❷ Flexibility to change ❷ High tolerance of ambiguity ❷ Broad skill application ❷ Modest job involvement	❷ High participation ❷ Implicit job criteria ❷ External sources ❷ Broad career paths ❷ Process and results criteria ❷ Long-term criteria ❷ Some group criteria ❷ Some employment security ❷ Many incentives ❷ Egalitarian pay ❷ Extensive training ❷ Co-operative labour/ management relations

However, generally these writers are strong on prescription but short on the detail, and, in fact, quite often their recommendations contradict each other and what is really happening. Thus, whatever the theory on rewards in start-up businesses, current market data indicates that dot.com companies are paying salary levels, on average, that are 20–30 per cent above their 'old economy' equivalents, as well as awarding generous share grants.

These concepts also miss the dynamism of our new economy, when many organisations have to innovate, be highly cost-efficient and provide high-quality customer service and high-quality products simultaneously. Supposedly mature markets can be transformed by innovative applications of technology – the bagless vacuum cleaner, the 'breathable' raincoat – while new products can become obsolete in months rather than years.

You do have a choice in your reward policies and they are not totally determined by your business and its strategy, nor by the external market, in a totally mechanistic and logical fashion. Schuler's (1988) contention that, 'in selecting a competitive strategy, a firm introduces an imperative for its HRM practices' is just not borne out by my experience, nor by research findings. Ellis and Haftel (1992), for example, found that the success of reward practices bore no relationship to the business strategy of organisations in their research sample, but instead correlated with the intensity and quality of their application.

The Egg Internet bank started off with a reward strategy objective of being as radically different as possible from the reward approach of its blue-blooded owner, the Prudential. The Co-op's Smile equivalent, on the other hand, imported most of its practices directly from its parent. Both can be equally appropriate and successful. In today's environment, as Zingheim and Schuster (2000) explain:

> Reward solutions are becoming less easy to pigeonhole . . . no one solution suits each situation. The reality is a company should do what suits: tailor and mix and match the approach to suit the situation.

This is very much the pattern of extensive, incremental, reward practice changes that Towers Perrin's (1999b) European research demonstrates is occurring, as described in Chapter 5. One of my favourite definitions of reward strategy is by Gomez-Mejia and Welbourne (1987), who call it 'the repertoire of pay choices available to management which under appropriate conditions have a positive impact on organisational performance and the effective use of HR'.

So, while some of these typologies are useful when initially reviewing the reward situation in a company, they do not really help us to address the fundamental reward strategy dilemma, described by one drinks company's HR director as follows:

> We pinned up all our business strategies on sheets on one side of the room, and listed all of our HR and pay policies on the other, and hoped to hell they lined up!

Just how do we select from the bewildering array of reward choices available if these types of classification are ineffective in creating such alignment?

Defining the reward strategy pathway

The solution we have arrived at in Towers Perrin is to build a clear, sequential pathway between the business strategy and the reward practices in order to explain and understand any breakdown or misfits, and then to define and build a robust set of linkages between them.

Essentially, this involves a process of:

1   specifying the key components of the business strategy, such as the major long-term goals, performance objectives and measures of the organisation, its fundamental purpose and mission
2   defining more practically what the organisation has got to be good at, what capabilities it has got to have, in order to execute this strategy
3   defining, through the HR strategy, the cultural and behavioural norms that are desired and required to build the capabilities and execute the strategy – this needs to explain:

 - how the company's investment in its people will be organised and managed
 - the nature of the employment relationship between employer and employees (elaborated in Chapter 6)
 - the core philosophy and tenets of the approach to resourcing, rewarding, communicating and managing in the organisation

4   thereafter considering the reward strategy and its constituent
       goals, programmes and processes, which typically involves two
       stages:

   ● to assess the extent to which the pay and rewards approach
      in the organisation at present reinforces and matches with
      the direction set out by the previous steps
   ● then to make changes and modifications to improve the level
      of alignment.

It is important that this pathway, leading to the reward strategy,
takes into account the stakeholder perspective (eg employee needs
and motivations) and the external context (eg legislation, market
trends and practices).

As Ulrich (1997) points out, the second step is often the critical
missing link in trying to derive HR practices from the business
strategy, which in many cases fails to specify these capabilities.
Having an objective to 'grow shareholder value', for example, is generally not very helpful in determining reward practices for the bulk
of staff, because what is needed is to specify how that is to be
achieved and how employees in general can contribute to it and
achieve it. Defining these capabilities helps the organisation to confirm how it can best be organised, structured and managed to deliver
on the strategy and build and deploy its necessary capabilities. Some
of these capabilities will have implications for the technology and
systems required in the organisation, but from an HR perspective
the most important issue is to identify specifically how our people
contribute to business success and what competencies they need to
apply and actions they need to take to implement the business strategy, through building the required capabilities.

As the pathway model illustrates, this path needs to be followed in
the context of external market demands and requirements, as well as
the needs and motivations of employees and other stakeholders. But
the business needs and requirements have to have a critical role in
driving your reward practices, if they are to be genuinely effective
and value adding.

The case studies throughout this book, and Chapter 8 in particular,
provide more detailed tools that you can use and examples to illus-

trate each stage in the process. The case at the end of this chapter (see page 48) illustrates how the required business capabilities drove the determination of reward practices in an insurance company. When you first confront the pathway on paper, it can seem excessively theoretical, detailed and complex. But fundamentally it is a very straightforward process of alignment, which people should be able to comprehend, identify with and support very rapidly. Some examples are outlined below.

Examples of building the pathway

A UK bank

A new telephone and Internet banking business had a wide choice of possible reward practices to adopt on its greenfield site in the Midlands. But it faced:

- a highly competitive and cut-throat financial services market, leading to a strong emphasis on cost efficiency
- a tight labour market and potential employees who were well aware of the typical 'sweatshop' image of call centres
- investors looking for very rapid growth rates after launch.

An earlier call centre operation operated by the parent company had been plagued by high turnover, low pay and ineffective bonus schemes.

The business strategy of the bank, after a successful and timely market launch, involved an emphasis on customer service (to counter the traditionally poor service image of UK retail banks) and, after building an initial base of deposits, cross-selling across the full product range to grow profitability.

Staff therefore needed to be genuinely committed to building long-term relationships with customers, have good product knowledge and be multiskilled in order to take advantage of the state-of-the-art integrated systems being installed. This in turn led them to define through a series of internal workshops the reward strategy principles.

The reward philosophy was not to throw money at the problems of a competitive labour market, but to use all aspects of reward to create a stimulating and exciting environment to work in. Base pay levels were set at the market median, with future increases related to the development of technical skills and behavioural competencies. Bonus opportunities were introduced for all staff, as well as an extensive programme of recognition awards and fun and celebration days and events to appeal to a workforce with an average age in their low 20s.

A year past launch, the bank had built a capital base of more than 10 times the budgeted level, and surveys showed very high levels of customer satisfaction. Staff too gave very high ratings to their employer in an internal survey, emphasising the benefits of the working environment. Turnover is low by industry standards.

A train company

Okay, you might say, but it is easy in a greenfield situation, without all the headaches of changing people's existing packages. Second then, let us consider the example of a train operating company that inherited all the well-recognised features of the British Rail culture, reinforced by a long-standing set of terms and conditions, with some of the staff allowances dating from the nineteenth century. The pathway here is summarised in Figure 4.

The retail side of the business, covering station and on-train customer-facing staff, had developed a business strategy for the twenty-first century. The core objectives were to make profits and secure the renewal of the franchise through sales growth. Here again, this was totally dependent on high levels of service provided by punctual trains and efficient, knowledgeable, skilled and courteous staff. A major shift in culture and management style would be required, opening up communications and devolving authority to responsible front-line staff.

Perhaps not surprisingly, a day's workshop with a project group identified a clear 'rewarding for "A" and hoping for "B" ' situation. The inherited arrangements were archaic, complex, inflexible and almost certainly discriminatory. As the analysis we carried out shows, far from reinforcing the required standards of service and performance, the opposite behaviours were in many cases being rewarded. Low base pay levels with significant add-on payments encouraged staff to maximise their earnings by receiving additional premium payments for any aspect of work flexibility. The combi-

Figure 4

THE BLOCKAGES ON THE REWARD STRATEGY
PATHWAY IN A TRAIN COMPANY

Business strategy
Good financial returns
Punctual/reliable service
Clean stock
Informed personnel
Secure environment
Increase volume/income by improved customer service
A cost-effective business that is convenient and easy to use

Retail strategy
Functions
Sales experience
Environment
Information
Goals
Provide customer service
Maximise sales
   – integration
   – repeat business
   – coverage/hours
Ensure safety/compliance with regulations
Ensure security
Facilitate cost control

Need to win

Need to play

Structural requirements
Clarity of roles/accountabilities
Effective inter-relationships
   – retail/commercial
Consistent service delivery
Scheduling to match demand
Delegation

People requirements
Informed   } (performance
Knowledgeable } orientation)
Sales-oriented
Customer-oriented
Loyal/committed/trustworthy
Available
Flexible within jobs
Growing in competence
Teamworkers
Actively participating

Pay and remuneration – now
Complex differentiated arrangements
Low basic pay/high overtime rates/supplements
   – uncontrollable
   – not reflecting customer demands
   – administratively complex
System not understood
System inequitable – pay scales are unequal
No job evaluation carried out
Pay is status-based between salaries and hourly-paid
No reinforcement for performance/productivity
System is inflexible – the structure changes, the reward does not
Clerical staff stuck on historically low grades
Location allowances are inflexible
Rates are fixed
Pay is based on 'normal working day'

nation of rigid job demarcations and a lack of objective-setting and appraisal discouraged people from taking on the personal responsibility for addressing passenger needs.

The aims of remuneration in the future that the company identified were as follows:

- to introduce simpler and harmonised schemes
- to pay for personal contribution and performance
- to provide incentives to staff to further the service objectives of the business
- to further work flexibility and the concept of the 24-hour railway
- to improve cost-effectiveness
- to build a company-distinct and branded set of arrangements.

The changes introduced over the next 12 months included the following:

- boosting base pay to more competitive levels, including the consolidation of historical allowances
- addressing sex discrimination issues through the use of a simple, common, evaluation system
- moving all staff to a single review date negotiated as part of a two-year deal, alongside introducing single-table bargaining with all the recognised unions
- adjusting pay levels to reflect increases in job skills and flexibility
- introducing a company-wide performance bonus scheme
- harmonising and simplifying allowances such as shift pay and overtime, and reducing them as a proportion of total pay.

A vehicle importer's dealerships

Finally, here is an example to illustrate the critical importance of rewards to the execution of business strategy. The pathway in this case is summarised in Figure 5. In the highly competitive middle range of the European car market, with wafer-thin margins and huge overcapacity, this car manufacturer adopted a strategy of moving upmarket to sell fewer but more expensive models, with higher profit margins. This was to be achieved with new and attractive models, supported by excellent customer service in the dealerships, so as to improve the company's already high customer repurchase rates. This in turn required higher-skilled staff in the dealerships,

Figure 5

ALIGNING REWARD SYSTEMS WITH BUSINESS STRATEGY

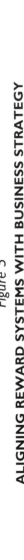

Business strategy

- Move upmarket
- Become service-driven
- Improve higher-than-average customer retention rates
- Increase investment

People/capability requirements

- Higher-skilled sales staff
  - service
  - technical
  - new systems
  'Honest John' not 'Flash Harry'
- Longer time horizons
- Teamwork

Previous reward methods

- Low base pay, high individual commission
- 'I made a packet on one financing deal. She probably won't come back when she finds out'
- 'We say we are a quality marque but we don't pay quality rates'
- 'Teamwork's vital here. Course, you don't get rewarded for that.'

Changes to rewards

- Up to 100% increase in base pay
- Career and competency-based pay structure of 3 pay ranges
- De-geared individual commission
- Individual and team bonus based on 'throughputs'
  - service
  - teamwork
  - mix

working as a team to build long-term relationships with customers, rather than the traditional 'moving metal' approach to selling.

Yet in common with most sales staff in the industry, the pay structure in this company's dealerships consisted of a base pay of around £6,000, with the remainder earned as commission on product margin. In the current market situation, they were earning about £50 in commission for selling a new £15,000 car, which could take up to 15 hours of work. The only way for them to make a decent living was to compete with each other for customers and to go for a fast sale on higher-margin accessories and financing deals.

The quotations in Figure 5 are drawn from my interviews with the salespeople and show that they recognised the fundamental contradiction between meeting customer needs and building relationships, and a pay system that incentivised them to, as one put it, 'screw the customer'.

A whole variety of reforms were made in the dealerships to support the new business strategy, including the introduction of new technology and ordering systems and a new customer care role. Major reform of the pay system was also critical to making the new business strategy an operating reality.

Base pay levels were substantially increased and related to the demonstration of the key competencies required to build long-term relationships with high net-worth customers. All of the staff were put through an assessment centre and a major development programme was introduced to improve skill levels. Dealers were encouraged to introduce pension schemes to provide an element of security in the reward package. The level of individual commission was reduced and a new bonus scheme adopted, rewarding team and individual contribution across all aspects of each dealership's activities. This scheme incorporates customer performance goals, as measured by new customer surveys and statistics on repurchase rates.

‹Often the pathway from strategy to rewards is not so obvious›

The balanced scorecard

This last example was an extreme one, both of change in business strategy and the scale of the corresponding conflict with reward practices. Often the pathway from strategy to rewards is not so obvious and discerning it and communicating it to all employees is much less straightforward. However, as organisations have become much more sophisticated in their performance measurement and management processes in recent years, a number of tools and techniques have been developed to give their strategic goals meaning throughout the organisation. These tools can also be used very effectively to communicate the relationship between strategic goals and employee rewards, either in specific pay plans or by helping employees to understand how the various reward plans integrate and interrelate.

Some of these tools rely on relatively complex financial methodologies, such as economic value added (EVA), which, although they are of great use to managers in understanding what actions really do create value in the long term, are somewhat difficult to explain to employees. They therefore tend only to be used in executive incentive and reward schemes. But one of the best-known and most widely used is the balanced business scorecard, and this is having a direct impact on employee rewards.

Originally developed by Kaplan and Norton (1996), the scorecard essentially provides a framework for organisations to use to define and assess their strategic performance in all of its multifaceted aspects. Thus in their original scorecard they illustrate:

- the financial perspective in terms of traditional measures of profit and returns for shareholders
- the internal business perspective, including measures of operational efficiency such as asset utilisation
- measures of learning and innovation, as an indication of future strategic prospects

❷ the customer perspective in respect of measures of service and market stance.

According to a Business Intelligence Survey, 48 per cent of the organisations attempting to better align compensation practices with their business strategy are now using a balanced scorecard, and 13 per cent are using some type of added value methodology such as EVA. The boards of some very well-known UK companies, such as BA, Boots and BT, have adopted these ideas and use them to guide performance measurement and targeting throughout their organisations.

A number also use the scorecard in their pay and reward systems. According to Kaplan and Norton (1996), 'compensation should be one of several elements linked to the scorecard serving as a reinforcer'. The actual measures and weighting on them obviously varies between organisations and according to the function, level and jobs being considered. But the balanced scorecard provides a common organising framework for defining strategic performance requirements across the organisation.

So, the board in charge of BT's annual bonus is now influenced by selected measures of performance for their employee and customer stakeholders, as well as their shareholders. Sears, the retailing group, has a three-point business strategy for making its business a compelling place to invest by making it a compelling place to shop and a compelling place to work. Its research indicates that a 5 per cent improvement in employee attitudes correlates with a 1.3 per cent increase in customer satisfaction and a 0.5 per cent increase in revenue growth. The long-term incentives of its 200 senior managers are therefore based one-third on investor returns, one-third on customer satisfaction and one-third on employee attitudes.

The breadth of perspectives that the scorecard can encapsulate and communicate has made it particularly useful for public sector organisations, which do not have the clarity of an overriding goal of profits or shareholder returns. But this breadth also means that it can be used effectively to support reward schemes right the way down through the organisation. The scorecard is being used for reward purposes in two senses:

- ✪ to help explain how different aspects of performance are rewarded by various reward schemes
- ✪ to help to select bonus plan measures which both impact on the business's strategic goals and have meaning for staff.

An example of the first type in a UK bank is shown in Figure 6. This example illustrates the pay methods recently introduced for client relationship managers (CRMs), who lead cross-functional teams of staff and are responsible for managing the bank's relationships with its largest clients. The 'hard' financial performance of the client team in achieving income targets through its customer base and measurable customer performance in terms of their perceptions of service levels, and the number of customers in the highest net-worth category affect the annual bonus of the individual CRM.

However, the two other categories of the scorecard are vital to the overall strategic performance of the bank and therefore are regarded not from a pay stance, just as 'nice to have'. The most measurable aspects of performance are not the only ones that need to be rewarded. The internal efficiency of the CRM and his or her team, his or her management style as applied to team members, and the broader contribution the CRM makes to other colleagues in the bank – for example in producing new business leads and referrals – are all used to influence the annual base pay increase, which is totally contribution-based. The bank also argues that through this means it is rewarding immediate past performance in the bonus and the basis for its future success through the base pay vehicle.

Other organisations, such as Bass and Anglian Water, are using their scorecard to ensure that all key strategic goals are reflected in their bonus plans. In the latter case, an all-employee, approved performance-related pay (PRP) plan was replaced by a scorecard-driven bonus, with four components:

- ✪ customer satisfaction, as measured by a customer survey of service satisfaction and perceptions of value for money
- ✪ shareholder returns, as measured by the level of profitability versus target
- ✪ process excellence, as measured by Anglian's position relative to the other water companies in the relevant regulatory league table

Figure 6

**REWARDING DIFFERENT FACETS OF THE BALANCED
SCORECARD WITH BASE PAY AND BONUS**

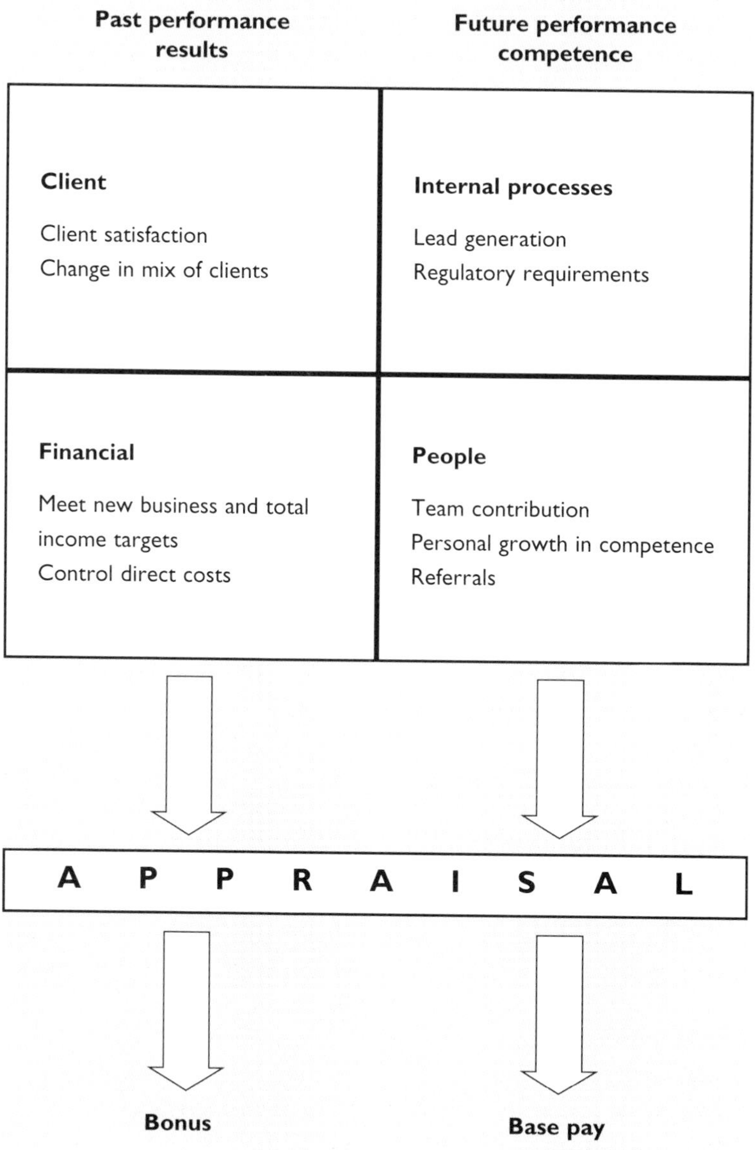

Past performance results	**Future performance competence**
Client Client satisfaction Change in mix of clients	**Internal processes** Lead generation Regulatory requirements
Financial Meet new business and total income targets Control direct costs	**People** Team contribution Personal growth in competence Referrals

A P P R A I S A L

Bonus   **Base pay**

❷ a fourth 'learn and grow' employee-oriented category that reflects employees' perceptions of the appraisal and development processes in the company.

Points are earned for levels of performance above the targeted level in each category, which translate into monetary payments to all employees at the end of the year of up to a maximum of £500. Here is a good example of how a complex and multifaceted set of strategic business goals can be translated into, and reinforced by, a bonus plan that all employees can understand and relate to.

The hourglass

‘Staff need to understand the purpose of reward programmes’

Even without a formal scorecard, consideration of how organisations create value and where most value is added are now often a critical component of business strategies and need to inform your strategic rewards approach. You need to ensure that your incentive plans, for example, are focused on these high value-added areas and measures. Staff also need to understand the purpose of your various reward programmes and how they interrelate.

Another simple tool we have used to do this at Towers Perrin is the hourglass. An example of the approach, from an insurance company, is illustrated in Figure 7, which is drawn from the material used to explain the company's reward strategy to staff.

The value that this company creates for its shareholders, at the top of the hourglass, is produced by the contribution of all of its constituent units and teams. Their contribution is in turn the product of the individual staff in those units. And the contribution that those individual staff members make is a result of them carrying out their tasks and responsibilities and applying their skills and competencies to achieve specific results.

So, this organisation uses different reward schemes to reinforce contribution to their strategic business goals at various points in this

Figure 7

A STRATEGIC APPROACH TO REWARDING CONTRIBUTION IN A UK COMPANY

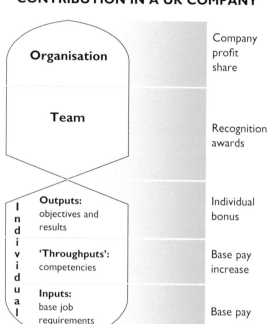

internal value chain. At the base of the hourglass, people's base pay depends on the value of the tasks they carry out and it is increased in relation to the growth in the value of their skills and competencies as they develop. Individually focused bonuses are used as the primary vehicle to incentivise the achievement of individual goals. Team co-operation and achievements are largely supported by development activities and recognised through non-financial means, such as project team awards. Finally, a company profit-sharing and share scheme rewards the combined contribution and co-operation of everyone across the business.

The process of alignment

The examples used in this chapter demonstrate that my view of a reward strategy is not some enormous, complex, 'all-singing, all-dancing', grand master plan that includes all the detail of your reward practices for the next decade. As Glueck (1998) eloquently describes, the rate of change in our organisations and their environments continues to accelerate, and in the future we are going to have to display as reward specialists all of the agility and responsiveness that Ulrich (1997) describes. Fradette and Michaud (2000) advise us in our strategies to 'plan less and react more'.

Reward strategy is more a way of thinking, a process of ensuring that all of your reward practices are regularly subjected to scrutiny in respect of your organisation's goals and what your people need to do to achieve them. Of course, you need to take account of the market, tax considerations, your employees' needs, your managers' capabilities, and all of the other factors described in later chapters, but the simple litmus test for strategic reward management really lies in two questions: do our reward practices support our business direction, and how can I improve that level of support?

It is a way of thinking that can be applied to any reward issue, at any time, no matter how small, specific or detailed, and not just when you are formulating that impressive, written strategy document for the chief executive to approve. This is illustrated with an example from a financial services company which is a market leader in the unit trust market. A number of concerns had been raised with the sales staff incentive plan and so a one-day workshop was organised for a range of interested managers and salespeople. The reward strategy pathway that was constructed on flipcharts is summarised below.

1   *Market:*
- sales opportunities
- increased competition
- cost pressures
- disclosure
- concentration: increasing IFA power.

2   *Business strategy:*
- quality: add value
- profitable growth: sales, less redemptions
- focus/segmentation
- long-term relationships.

3   *Capabilities required:*
- good products
- improved admin

4 *HR approach:*
- best people
- support values
- development
- independent
  (but more managed/responsible).

The business strategy in future emphasised maintaining highly profitable and rapid growth through greater market segmentation and focus, in response to increasing competition in their core market. As well as excellent products and well-qualified sales staff, this also called for improved teamwork between sales staff in each region and greater adaptability to spot and exploit new opportunities, while maintaining long-term relationships. The HR strategy therefore focused on developing such skills in the salesforce, with a much more intensive sales training and development effort, and continuing to resource the top sales staff in the industry.

So how well did the existing reward practices – consisting of a comparatively high and uniform base pay with a low level of commission and extensive recognition awards – support this strategy? Not too well, was the group's conclusion. The package had been in place, with annual increases, since the company had been formed, and reflected its relatively informal and laissez-faire culture. The base pay levels had helped to recruit good people, but there was now a lack of differentiation in the rewards of high-performing individuals and teams in a more mature and longer-serving salesforce.

There was also no incentive to pursue new business opportunities rather than selling through strong existing relationships, nor to focus on a particular market segment which might have high potential but be initially difficult to break into. Nor was there any incentive to sell the products with the highest margins, even though they were more difficult in many cases to sell.

In the afternoon of the workshop alternatives and solutions to these issues were considered. It was decided to move to three pay bands for sales staff, so as to differentiate in base pay according to competence and historic performance, and provide more of a career structure. The competencies required of more clearly defined and segmented sales roles were subsequently defined in workshops with the sales staff.

In addition, although commendably simple, it was decided that the commission plan needed to be changed to reflect the evolution in the market. Different rates for new and existing business and for the different products were introduced, along with a steepening of the payment line over target in order to increase the differential for the highest performers. A series of new team-based cash payments and recognition awards were also introduced.

Plenty of design work followed on from the workshop, but this group were all in agreement that a fairly simple and logical one-day process has led to a series of changes which now mean that reward practices are better placed to continue to reinforce the strategic success of their business.

A moving walkway

‘You can never allow yourself the luxury of resting, having achieved alignment’

As the above example also shows, you are aiming with your reward policies and practices at a continually moving business strategy target. You can design more flexible arrangements to suit a range of shifting situations, but you can never allow yourself the luxury of resting, having achieved a high level of alignment. Because if you do, the business situation will almost certainly have moved on. As Purcell *et al* (2000) elaborate – based on their latest CIPD research in 12 companies into the links between HR practices and business results – 'the search is a constant one ... [with] adjustments and refinements, and sometimes big changes'.

This can be illustrated with the example of the evolution in the reward strategy of a privatised utility in the UK. After privatisation in the early 1990s, the reward strategy was pretty clear. The complex, expensive and divisive nationalised pay structures needed to be replaced by simpler, more cost-effective and performance-related arrangements to help create a common, customer-oriented and 'can-do' culture in the new company.

Considerable progress was made in this direction during that decade, with all but the industrial staff moved into a common pay structure and a new performance management system applied to all staff. Major harmonisation and simplification of allowances and conditions was also undertaken, along with innovations including the adjustment of the annual increase in the base pay budget using a balanced scorecard of corporate performance.

But the market situation by the late 1990s was very different from that at the time of privatisation. A whole host of international competitors were now present, the regulatory regime was much tougher and the impact of customer choice and changing suppliers was far more evident. The company was reorganised into self-standing units to improve the focus on performance and delivery in its various market segments. This put a renewed spotlight on the outstanding reward issues that remained, such as the generally high pay position in the external market, which had been a major factor in the company's decision to sell off its retailing operation. The new business environment also introduced new reward issues, such as a lack of local and divisional pay and benefits flexibility, and highlighted the weak performance–pay relationships at lower levels in the organisation.

The reward strategy has therefore moved on. Competitiveness, cost-effectiveness and pay for performance, as well as business alignment, remain core principles, but supporting the new devolved organisation structure (a topic we consider in more detail in the Chapter 3) is now receiving a stronger emphasis. Pay budgets have been devolved and local pay ranges have been introduced in a number of locations. One unit has withdrawn from the corporate-defined benefit pension plan and set up a money-purchase arrangement for its new staff. A number of units have introduced their own bonus schemes. The process of seeking improved alignment and more powerful reinforcement of business goals goes on.

DERIVING THE REWARD STRATEGY FROM THE CORE CAPABILITIES REQUIRED IN A LARGE FINANCIAL SERVICES ORGANISATION

Background and business strategy

This company employs approximately 10,000 staff across four main business divisions. It had made a series of piecemeal changes to reward schemes in the recent past, but the new HR director felt that it was essential to fundamentally reform the culture in the organisation and saw rewards as a powerful means of reinforcing this.

The business strategy of the company had four main components:

- a focus on specific market segments, with differentiated approaches to match the needs of these different segments
- a focus on profitability
- a focus on efficiency and cost control
- a focus on effective customer relationship management.

Core capabilities and rewards

A series of management workshops and in-depth industry analyses highlighted 14 capabilities that were required in the organisation to deliver this strategy. These included:

- flat, flexible organisation designs
- a strong customer service orientation
- inspiring and open leadership
- appropriate technical expertise
- integrated IT systems.

A project team then assessed the extent to which these capabilities were reinforced by current reward and performance management systems. Despite the differing needs of the four divisions, and some very different personal views on current arrangements expressed by directors, there was strong agreement that these essential capabilities were not being supported effectively, and in some cases the opposite messages were being given. The capabilities provided the link to make the lack of fit between business needs and rewards clear and to establish more effective reinforcement.

The current detailed job evaluation system, for example, worked against structural and job flexibility, with significant delays due to the number of regrading claims. The hierarchical grade structure encouraged technical experts to seek regular promotions and moves into management, rather than continuing to develop their expertise. The uniform, highly competitive and fixed benefits package contributed to a high cost base and took no account of varying staff needs. The flat-rate annual bonus was not related in any systematic way to performance. And creativity and innovation by staff received little encouragement and no rewards.

The new reward strategy
The principles of reward schemes in the future were defined as:

- focusing on delivering a competitive total package, with less emphasis on internal comparisons and relativities
- strengthening links between pay and performance at all levels in the organisation
- relating growth in rewards to things that really add value to the company: higher competence, taking on greater responsibility, increasing contribution
- providing more flexibility to relate rewards to different personal and business needs
- encouraging individuals to play to their strengths, while providing stronger links between individual development and rewards.

The changes that have been made to put these strategic principles into practice include:

- moving from 15 staff grades to five role levels
- focusing the evaluation system on what really matters to the business, simplifying it and making it much more open to staff
- defining technical and, where relevant, managerial competencies for each role, and relating base pay adjustments to growth in these competencies

- introducing different, market-related salary bands for different job families at each job level
- replacing the Christmas bonus with a wide range of individual and team incentives, mostly developed and operated at the local level
- introducing a range of new recognition awards directed at customer service and creative excellence.

The new strategy has been implemented over a two-year period, with different businesses moving at different speeds so as to best address their own particular needs, but also to facilitate learning from the implementation process across the group.

Chapter summary

- Today, despite the greater incidence of written reward strategies, there are still many examples of organisations suffering because their reward practices conflict with what the business strategy requires of their employees. They are rewarding for 'A', while hoping for 'B'.
- Early reward strategy models emphasised the required relationship between particular generic business strategies, such as cost leadership, and particular reward practices. Certain patterns of pay and rewards were also held to be necessary at different stages in a business's life cycle, with a low pay and strong incentive emphasis, for example, in a start-up situation.
- These models generally have little research support, and while they can be useful as an initial thought-starter, they miss the complexity and dynamism of our modern business environment.
- Reward strategy is really a series of choices, and your own choices need to be selected so as to be aligned with what your business requires of your employees. This can be achieved by constructing a reward strategy pathway that:
  - describes as a first step the core components of the business strategy
  - defines the capabilities required in the organisation to deliver on this strategy
  - draws up the HR strategy to build and inculcate these requirements amongst staff

- defines the reward goals, practices and processes necessary to reinforce and recognise these requirements.
- This pathway can be used to assess the level of alignment in current reward practices and then to redesign them so as to improve the 'fit' with business needs.
- The balanced business scorecard – a technique for classifying business performance requirements – and the hourglass are useful tools to help communicate the pathway and to ensure that your reward practices really are adding value to the business. The scorecard is being used both to explain how different aspects of performance are reinforced by different reward schemes, and more directly in helping to define bonus plan measures.
- Effective reward strategies are not detailed plans for determining an organisation's reward practices in a fixed, mechanistic manner from the business strategy. Reward strategy is rather a way of thinking, to continuously appraise, reappraise and adjust your reward practices as your business goals and organisation's environment shift.
- The litmus test of strategic reward management lies in two simple questions:
  - To what extent do our reward practices support our business direction?
  - How can I improve that level of support?

Chapter 3

Relating rewards to the organisation structure

Chapter objectives

- ❷ demonstrate the important features of an organisation's structure that influence the success of its reward policies
- ❷ illustrate how rewards, in turn, reinforce important features of organisation design
- ❷ provide tools and methods to help align your employer's reward and organisation structures.

Rewards and organisation structure

The case study example of the financial services company referred to in Chapter 2 illustrates that how an organisation structures itself to achieve its goals is often as important an influence on the nature of its reward practices as the business strategy and goals themselves. Just as you would expect to see aspects of customer service recognised and rewarded in a business that aimed to be the market leader in terms of service levels, so you might anticipate finding common reward schemes in operation in a highly integrated and centrally managed organisation. Similarly, as some organisations in the public sector have found, the broadbanding of pay structures is difficult to implement if the department or agency stays relatively hierarchical in its structure and management style, and also often in its benefit provisions.

Structural considerations that are liable to influence a reward strategy and its constituent parts include:

- ❷ the overall size and growth rate of the organisation
- ❷ the level of centralisation or – more commonly in these days of lean organisations and empowerment – decentralisation and devolvement
- ❷ the number of layers in the structure and the spans of control of management and supervisory positions
- ❷ the nature of job designs.

Here again, there is a long line of research findings to demonstrate that there are strong associations between organisation and reward structures. A variety of studies have shown that more integrated, centralised and less diversified businesses, with larger head offices, are indeed more likely to have integrated reward strategies, with a common grading structure and benefits plans across the whole organisation. Correspondingly, more decentralised and diverse organisations are more likely to operate with a variety of business unit or divisional reward strategies.

Less obviously, as Kerr (1975) found, more diverse businesses that have pursued a strategy of acquisitive growth and have a looser 'just-deliver-the-results' style of management, make greater use of bonus schemes, with higher payment opportunities and a focus on individual and quantitative, often financial, results.

‹ There are five key aspects of framing and operating your reward strategy ›

But what are some of the practical implications of these relationships? There are five key aspects of structure that you need to consider in framing and operating your reward strategy, which we consider in the following sections:

- the organisation's overall size and growth rate, and their impact on the level of structure and formality in your reward programmes
- the 'vertical' degree of hierarchy in the organisation, which may impact on reward practices such as the number of grades and degree of benefits differentiation
- the level of centralisation in the structure, which will affect the commonality and consistency of reward programmes; here, as in respect of the extent of hierarchy and differentiation in structure and rewards, many organisations are finding that an intermediate approach, harnessing the benefits of control and flexibility, is the best for them
- where responsibilities for reward management – between the different levels and between HR and line managers – lie
- the rate of change in the organisation, and maintaining a sufficiently 'loose' and flexible fit between rewards and structure to allow for this.

Size and formality

The life cycle models that we discussed in Chapter 2 illustrate the fact that as organisations get larger and more mature, and introduce more levels, functions and units into their organisation structure, so they tend to also adopt more structured and formal reward arrangements. As related in the earlier mobile phone company example (see page 12), wholly person-based reward arrangements become impractical above a certain size, beyond which the senior team just cannot know the personal contribution and value of every individual in the company.

Yet there is a danger, as the executives in that company perceived, of importing 'big company' systems of detailed job evaluation and so on which – as in our oil company example cited in the last chapter – really do stifle the speed, flexibility and innovation that is essential to achieving their strategic goals. Ironically, in recent years, many large companies have been attempting to 'free up' their reward systems, devolving more internally, making wider use of share grants and so on, in order to try and replicate some of the entrepreneurial behaviour of their small, rapidly growing competitors.

A key skill of the compensation and benefits professional is not just in the technical design of programmes, but in assessing and delivering the appropriate balance of flexibility and control in reward systems to match with the structure of the organisation. We consider this and the issue of job flexibility in more detail in Chapter 5.

Thus in one government department there had been a wholesale delegation of operating responsibilities and certain budgeted items to small units and teams, with a strong emphasis on creating greater speed and efficiency in decision-making at the local level. Yet if a team, for example, worked particularly hard in achieving its goals despite the loss of staff members, its 'reward' was for the resulting budget surplus to be 'clawed back' at year-end and to receive a new, tighter budget the following year. Now, following the recommendations of the Makinson (2000) Report, this and a number of other large government departments will be introducing gainsharing-type schemes, with employees receiving a share of the gains that their efficiency and high performance produce as bonus payments.

Matching the level of hierarchy and centralisation

Just as there is no universally perfect reward strategy, so there is no one best organisation structure or type of alignment with rewards. Flatter, devolved structures may have been in fashion for the last decade and a half, but a number of retailers, for example, have had considerable market success with a highly focused and centralised organisation.

Similarly, a team in an insurance company concluded that broad-banding and reducing their number of staff grades was not desirable, as much of the work their staff carried out was regulated and required a number of layers of close supervision. In addition, promotion through the grades continued to be a powerful and effective motivator for many of its technically skilled and qualified staff. In reward management, it needs to be very much a case of 'horses for courses', and not simply following the latest trend.

No position on the reward strategy continuum from centralised to decentralised, hierarchical to flat, is therefore right or wrong, but as the government example showed, any significant mismatch between rewards and these structural variables will create problems. They need to be broadly in alignment.

Take another example from the private sector. This utility had a strategy of business-unit-focused growth and had devolved operating responsibilities and reduced the corporate head office accordingly. The fastest-growing business unit was in a market unrelated to the traditional core units. Its strategy was also distinct, focusing on highly technical premium-priced work, as opposed to a stronger volume and price focus in the rest of the organisation. Most of its staff had come from outside and the labour market in this sector was affected by severe skill shortages.

Yet pay and benefits policies in this organisation were still centralised and devised by the corporate HR function, with a common job-evaluated pay structure, single-table trade union bargaining, a defined-benefit service-based pension plan and uniform terms and conditions. The only way this business unit could operate was therefore with a web of unofficial 'fixes', such as the use of 'golden hellos' and secret payments, artificially inflated job evaluation scores and a complex mixture of personal contracts. This created complexity, jealousy and confusion throughout the organisation.

The solution was obvious: to reflect the evolution in the organisation's strategy and structure, and devolve reward practices to the business units so as to re-establish the required alignment. So now this unit has its own pay structure with market-related pay ranges, its own employment contracts and bonus schemes, and its own money-purchase pension plan. The relatively few internal transfers are seconded in for a fixed period on their previous conditions.

Locally designed and operated reward practices, as Purcell and Ahlstrand (1994) found in their research, have generally resulted from the strategic and structural move to hold units accountable for their own performance – a strategy adopted with great success by organisations such as ABB and GE. As a utility business manager said in support of the delegation of pay responsibilities, in the past 'we haven't been involved: pay decisions have been divorced from business realities'.

Just to reinforce the point, however, even heavily delegated and devolved reward arrangements are often far from problem-free. Issues emerging from research in such organisations have included:

- a loss of cost control and a duplication of resources, with pay cost escalation being faster in those local authorities that were the first to pull out of national bargaining, for example
- a lack of local capability to design and operate reward practices
- a loss of accountability for reward issues
- the creation of internal barriers to the career development of staff across the organisation
- internal equality issues such as equal pay for work of equal value.

Thus in an oil company that gave its businesses pay and reward freedoms in the early 1990s, problems soon emerged in moving engineers to the less profitable chemicals business from the upstream exploration division, which had adopted a higher pay stance and set of pay ranges. Similarly, a major retailer abandoned its centralised annual pay review and devolved pay decisions to the store level. But it subsequently found that managers made even less differentiation in pay increases according to local market needs and performance than when they had formerly applied a single, common pay review matrix imposed from the centre. They were unwilling to rob their own lower-performing 'Peters' to pay their higher-performing 'Pauls'.

The reward strategy and structure balance

The majority of organisations are finding that a balanced approach along this centralised/decentralised continuum makes sense, from both a structural and a reward perspective. My clients use different terms for it: flexibility within a framework; co-ordinated decentralisation; controlled autonomy; and so on. But in all cases, what they are trying to do is combine the benefits of local control of reward issues – such as local business and market fit, ownership and speed of decision-making – with the advantages of central co-ordination, in respect of cost-effectiveness and lateral career development.

Research by Towers Perrin (1998) in 50 major UK businesses, as well as demonstrating a relationship between the centralised control of pay and benefits and the level of business centralisation, found a majority of organisations moving from the extremes of a central 'running' structure and a devolved 'targeting' one into an intermediate 'guiding' position. Thus one electronics company operated via heavily independent business units, but gained the benefits of scale through efficiencies and the development of in-depth expertise, by operating with a single research and development function.

An IPD survey (Arkin 1999) similarly found the proverbial pendulum swinging back from the heavy devolvement of power and authority advocated in recent years, helped by the introduction of new technology and HR systems, towards a more balanced, intermediate position. The study found examples of companies, such as BAA, that had experienced operating difficulties and increased costs from high levels of HR decentralisation.

‘Research would suggest that the extent of truly decentralised reward policies has been exaggerated’

In fact, Towers Perrin's (1999b) European rewards research study would suggest that the extent, in practice, of truly decentralised reward policies has anyway been exaggerated. Fifty per cent of the 460 participants described their pay systems as centralised, and 75 per cent operated uniform benefits programmes from the corporate centre. A Warwick University study (Marginson 1993) found that generally pay budgets were the last aspect of rewards to be devolved and that this, in practice, severely constrained any apparent local reward freedoms, as has been evident with pay delegation in much of the Civil Service and National Health Service.

This balance in the structuring of reward strategy is manifest in many different ways. The electronics company referred to earlier largely devolves the design and operation of reward practices to its constituent units. Businesses pay local market rates and design their own incentive plans, for example. But there is a common, company-wide structure of broad pay bands, which allows for the movement of staff between units for the purposes of career development and flexibility in the organisation. There is also central management of benefits schemes – because of the economies of scale involved – and of share schemes.

Similarly in a water company, a meeting of business unit managers supported breaking down their heavily centralised pay and benefits arrangements, which had originated when the UK water industry was a single national organisation. These were becoming increasingly ineffectual in addressing the diverse business and employee needs of customer service staff in the company's call centres, water operators in the field, highly experienced design engineers, security system sales staff and expatriates in the Far East. One size no longer fitted all.

Yet these managers recognised that the effects of a rapid 'abdication' of reward responsibilities, as one put it, could create significant problems. 'We need a clear HR strategy and performance framework before we can effectively develop our own approaches', he explained. Others emphasised the importance of common support mechanisms, for example to provide market data, and also the need to avoid an internal labour market developing in the company.

The intermediate approach it is now introducing has a number of components and levels. Terms and conditions are generally negotiated and managed at the business unit level. However, businesses co-operate to address common issues, such as the introduction of annual hours arrangements to provide greater service flexibility.

A common, flatter pay structure is being retained, but the pay ranges for each band are set locally to match individual market needs. A team has been developing more flexibility in pensions, and choices as to contribution rates are being introduced as an initial step. Bonus schemes are being developed in each business but within a corporate policy framework that supports and encourages their use. The corporate HR function has also been supplying technical expertise to help businesses to design their own schemes.

This evolutionary and intermediate approach allows the businesses to proceed at different speeds to suit their own local needs and competence, increasing the chances that their reward strategy can effectively be delivered and operated in practice.

Making the appropriate balance

But how do you decide what structural balance of reward practices best suits your own organisation? Two of the techniques that we use at Towers Perrin to help assess and define this are:

- an HR and reward structure framework
- a menu of reward design options at various points on the centralisation/de-centralisation axis.

The initial results of an HR and reward structure framework that we developed for a large UK travel group are shown in Figure 8. The organisation had been growing by acquisition and while there was a desire to continue to reflect the different travel brands and operating styles in the different parts of the organisation, there was the recognition of inefficiencies and a duplication of activities. The group's

Figure 8

THE AGREED FRAMEWORK FOR HR AND REWARD POLICIES/SERVICES IN A UK TRAVEL COMPANY

Designed centrally

Delivered centrally

- Management development programmes
- Succession planning
- Generic skills training
- Long-term incentives
- Communication (strategic business decisions, common HR frameworks)
- Senior managers' pay and rewards

- Performance management for corporate groups
- Pay philosophy
- Management bonus decisions etc
- Pay market positioning (big picture)
- Graduate development
- Benefits package design
- Grievance and disciplinary procedures
- Recruitment procedures
- Consultation framework

Delivered locally

- Operational training
- Flexible benefit design and administration

- Operational training
- Base pay and incentives decisions (below corporate group)
- Recruitment
- Performance management (below corporate group)
- Contractual terms and conditions (below corporate group)
- Absence control and monitoring
- Grievance and disciplinary procedures
- Grading

Designed locally

business strategy also emphasised the need for cross-selling between the airline and tour operator businesses, and aimed at improved business integration to boost margins and total revenues.

At an HR staff and line management workshop, we confirmed that each business should retain control of determining pay rates and contractual terms for the bulk of their staff, depending on their local markets and varying levels of profitability. However, it was agreed that there should be a common market stance across the group, with no one paying upper-quartile rates in their market just for the sake of it, for example, and to reduce the chances of internal 'poaching' of staff. In addition, a common pay structure and bonus scheme for managers was agreed to aid business co-ordination and to further management development in the group, which was a key component of the HR strategy.

The decision was also taken to move to single external providers for payroll, pensions and car leasing services. This would allow for flexibility in the various schemes to continue, but create economies of scale in their purchasing and administration.

But the framework also helped to expand the recognition that co-ordination in rewards can be achieved without total central control and uniformity. Thus it was agreed to introduce a common job evaluation system, to guard against some equal pay issues that had emerged, but to operate this scheme in each business, with occasional auditing of its operation.

In terms of performance appraisal, which had a history in the industry of not being carried out effectively, it was agreed that a single team would develop a common approach and support training. However, the system would be operated in each business, and tailored to local needs, to suit the different culture and style of each operation. A different approach, say, would be needed for company representatives in the Mediterranean resorts, compared to the pilots and cabin crews for the charter fleet.

The second technique also helps to balance these reward goals of co-ordination and flexibility, and this is illustrated with an example from a large local authority. It had taken control of pay management out of the national bargaining structure at an early stage, so as to better tailor pay policies to suit its own goals and needs. Various reforms, including performance-related pay, were introduced, but all were applied on a consistent basis across the authority.

Meanwhile, a new chief executive had responded to the external pressures of central government efficiency initiatives and competitive tendering by reorganising into 40 self-standing units. Research found that the employee profiles and business goals of these units varied hugely. Those, for example, open to competitive tendering argued for general reductions in the cost of the reward package and a strong performance emphasis, but the metropolitan-based professional units supported pay increases so as to reduce staff turnover.

An internal workshop initially produced heated debates between these 'decentralisers' who wanted their own local pay freedoms, and those who argued that the council's position as an employer of choice needed to be maintained, with a consistent approach, for example to maternity benefits, across the authority. However, a design team set up subsequently soon came to the conclusion that an intermediate solution, evolving to greater local unit freedom at various speeds, was required. They developed alternatives to move in this direction.

The centralised grading structure in the authority was a constant source of conflict due to its inflexibility, but the team recognised that moving to local unit pay structures, with the skills, data and administration this would require, was a step too far for any unit. Therefore the intermediate solution adopted was to move to a common structure with fewer, broader pay bands, and give the units freedom in positioning their staff within these bands.

Similarly the existing performance pay system had worked well in some operating units, but had been disliked by many professionals and had been difficult to apply to staff organised on a team basis. Again, everybody on the design team recognised the huge task involved if each unit was to develop its own base pay adjustment and bonus schemes.

The balanced solution adopted was to retain a policy of paying for performance, but to develop a menu of different schemes to suit the needs of the different parts of the organisation. Rather than each unit reinventing its own wheel, so to speak, it instead would select the approach from the common menu that best met its own structure and needs: a team bonus, a service- and quality-focused scheme, or whatever.

In terms of benefits, meanwhile, a new cafeteria scheme was developed centrally, ensuring co-ordination and cost savings. But by its very nature this has provided the flexibility to reflect local business and staff needs, and over 70 per cent of the authority's predominantly lower-paid staff made at least one change in their benefits provision in its first year of operation.

Responsibilities in the organisation for reward

This all sounds fine, you might say, trying to combine the benefits of central consistency and co-ordination with the flexibility and empowerment of devolved arrangements. But is there not a danger of a confusion of authority and responsibilities in such a scenario, which many of us who have operated within a matrix organisation structure can probably testify to?

‘The responsibility for designing, operating and maintaining them needs to be crystal clear’

This brings us to the fourth point in respect of the relationship between reward policies and organisation structures: however centralised or decentralised, flexible or controlled, common or varied your reward practices, the responsibility for designing, operating and maintaining them needs to be crystal clear.

Perhaps the worst example I experienced of this was in an initial meeting with a new power company joint venture between an American and a UK utility. The venture had been going for 18 months and had approximately 30 employees. However, while developing my understanding of their initial reward package, my question about life assurance arrangements produced puzzled looks. It emerged that the venture had been operating without any form of life cover for its staff. The US parent assumed the UK had arranged it, and the UK parent and the venture both assumed the other had organised it. An extreme example, possibly, but there are plenty of other examples of devolvement in reward practices leading to the type of abdication that the utility operations manager referred to earlier.

Table 4 outlines a technique that can be used to help ensure that such a situation does not occur. It demonstrates the reward responsibilities that HR staff agreed in the international electronics company referred to earlier. As you can see, the responsibilities vary at different levels in the organisation. The pay and conditions for the top 400 managers are determined, like their personal development, by the corporate HR function. They are treated as a corporate resource and the role of HR staff in each division is purely one of administration.

Correspondingly, local country HR staff in each division have the prime responsibility for setting the terms and conditions for their locally recruited and employed staff. They do, however, need to

Table 4
AGREED RESPONSIBILITIES FOR REWARD MANAGEMENT

Level of HR staff	Types of employee		
	Senior management	*Managers and professionals*	*Staff and manuals*
HR *at corporate HQ*	Design, operation and control of pay	Guidance via principles and advice. Agree to and audit actual systems	Guidance via principles
HR *at divisional HQ*	Administer pay	Design pay systems Operate for HQ employees Advise and audit for country employees	Agree to and audit actual systems
HR *at country operating level*		Operate and administer for local staff	Design systems, operate and administer

adhere to some broad corporate principles, such as equity and legality, and policy changes need to be agreed by divisional HR staff, who also occasionally audit local practice.

Divisional HR staff have the prime responsibility for determining the rewards of middle managers and professionals. Here the corporate principles are more detailed and adherence to them is reviewed more regularly. Nonetheless, there is still considerable freedom in each division to tailor the reward approach to their own particular goals and needs.

My own experience is that it is in a situation of highly devolved responsibilities that this authority structure needs to be agreed most clearly. In one US company, reward responsibilities are heavily devolved, but each year the HR function in each business presents to corporate colleagues a detailed report and plan. This specifies the extent to which the agreed HR and reward goals for that business have been achieved in the preceding year, outstanding issues, and the reward goals, priorities and actions for the next 12 months. This makes clear that with the authority for reward practices comes the responsibility to deliver, just as with the devolvement of business responsibilities.

In addition to well-defined and understood responsibilities within the HR community, the respective roles of line managers and HR staff also need to be clear. The delegation of reward management responsibilities has often also involved the transfer of tasks from the HR function onto the line, again according to the research, with decidedly mixed results. We consider this issue in Chapter 7, but here I would just emphasise again the need for clear and agreed responsibilities and to ensure that line managers have the necessary capabilities and resources to carry out their role as intended.

An example of the responsibilities agreed for the operation of a new pay scheme in a pharmaceuticals company is shown below:

- *line manager*
    - explain overall objectives and workings of pay management in XYZ

- explain basis for grading level and pay level
- provide guidance on personal and career development
- recognise and reward personal and job growth
- make appropriate pay changes in line with organisation pay restructuring

- *HR*
  - distribute and co-ordinate relevant paperwork
  - operate relevant admin procedures
  - review effectiveness of pay systems periodically
  - support communications process
  - authorise pay changes

- *employees*
  - make maximum contribution in their role
  - accept change as essential
  - keep manager informed of significant changes in job content
  - develop their skills.

This clearly sets out the role and contribution of the line managers and HR staff, as well as specifying the expectations of employees. In the financial services company case example referred to at the end of Chapter 5, this is formalised in a brief but specific HR service agreement, which specifies what the line role is and the support that the HR function commits to provide to enable fulfilment of it.

A broad alignment and direction

A general point in terms of the relationships between reward policies and organisation structure is that while you should aim for broad alignment, as with the business strategy, there are no fixed single answers that a particular structure must be associated with a particular set of reward practices. As we have seen, different positions on the decentralised to centralised, hierarchical to flat axes will often be appropriate for different aspects of remuneration, for different employee types, and at different times.

Bill Gates, for example, may never have had his performance rated on a five-point scale through a detailed Microsoft performance and pay review system, but signs of the maturing of the organisation can be seen in the introduction of quite hierarchical multi-graded pay structures in a number of its engineering functions. And in terms of reward practices, even in highly decentralised organisations employee benefits schemes tend to be more centralised because of the complexity and potential economies of scale involved.

In respect of different types of staff, variations in the structural reward balance according to the level in the organisation can be seen in the annual management bonus plans of many UK companies. In an electricity company, for example, a common scheme operates, but the emphasis placed on the different levels of contribution in the company varies by the level of management, as shown in the box below:

Position	Maximum payment	Weighting on different performance measures		
		Corporate	Business	Personal
Director	50%	100%	0%	0%
Senior manager	40%	50%	25%	25%
Manager	30%	25%	25%	50%

Managers at lower levels in the organisation have a less direct influence on shareholder returns at the corporate level, so the incentive focuses more on their own personal and business unit criteria. And in fact, for those in operating units, this skew is even more pronounced than for those in support functions, such as finance, who at a given level are making a broader corporate and less direct business impact.

‘Maintaining an effective reward strategy is akin to painting the Forth road bridge!’

Moreover, just as organisation structures are rarely stable for long in any large organisation, so you need to constantly be adapting your reward arrangements to maintain a broad alignment and to ensure that none of the 'misfits' we saw illustrated earlier in the chapter emerge. Yes, building and maintaining an effective reward strategy really is akin to painting the Forth road bridge!

Evolution in reward strategies to match structural changes

It is not, of course, just in dot.com and fast-growth organisations that the size and structure of the organisation is changing. Ever since the time of the Roman army, large organisations, even as large and bureaucratic as the European Commission, are prone to regular shifts in their designs and structures, and so your reward strategy has to flex to accommodate this, and even hopefully anticipate it. There are unfortunately no right or wrong reward packages that can be plugged into a given structural situation.

The investments division of a large UK plc was set up six years ago to invest in large projects, almost exclusively with the aim of creating work opportunities for the group's other businesses, such as engineering consultancy, although it was required to deliver a given rate of return. At that stage it was staffed largely by accountants, lawyers and engineers from the rest of the group.

But they found that they were good at investing and exceeded the required financial targets. The workforce grew, with much more diverse sources of recruitment, and they engaged in larger and more complex deals, often in conjunction with other companies and finance houses nearer to their London base than corporate headquarters.

And their rewards approach, consistent with that of the rest of the group, then started to seem increasingly misaligned with their needs. After a detailed look at the market, it was agreed that the lack of variable pay and incentives and generous benefits package was indeed damaging to recruitment and retention. While alignment with the group structures was maintained, higher bonus levels and more variation in market rates were introduced, while the business was used as the pilot for the corporate introduction of a car allowance scheme.

Most recently, external capital has been brought into the business and it will be floated off as an independent business next year. They are therefore preparing to put in place a package more reflective of the investments and corporate finance markets than engineering, with a carried-interest long-term incentive, their own defined contribution pension plan and even a reduced holiday entitlement. The more basic requirement for a new payroll supplier is also being sourced at present.

Reward strategy is not all grand schemes and major business issues and restructuring. This strategic way of thinking about rewards – assessing how well they align with the organisation structure and how they need to evolve in line with that structure – can have a major payoff, even in the most detailed and mundane situation.

The second and final example of restructuring is very much at the micro-level. The direct banking call centre of a major UK bank was initially structured along fairly conventional lines. Teams of advisers dealt with basic queries on account balances and statements, and some were paid a higher base pay level to cover more flexible work patterns, in response to variations in customer demand. However, more complex transactions were referred to higher-paid teams of specialist advisers.

The relationship between these various teams was critical to the success of the operation and the initial bonus scheme was introduced to reinforce this essential co-operation. The scheme rewarded everyone on a common basis, according to the achievement of key site-based growth and service goals.

However, the introduction of new technology allowed them to integrate these separate operations so that every adviser could meet the needs of any customer who called. The site was, as a result, reorganised into multifunctional and self-standing teams that covered all aspects of the bank's services. The HR manager correspondingly changed the pay approach to reflect these new dynamics.

Base pay progression was related to a series of skill steps, which meant that staff were rewarded as they acquired the new range of skills that they needed. The bonus was changed to recognise that the individual employee was now even more important to the delivery of all customer requirements and that co-operation between teams was much less critical. The new bonus therefore emphasised individual performance, with a moderate team component, and no site-wide element.

Many years ago, one of the early proponents of business strategy, Alfred Chandler (1962), wrote that 'structure follows strategy'. In this case rewards were following and helping to reinforce and make a reality of the desired structure and thereby to really achieve the bank's strategic goals.

Case study

CREATING REWARD STRATEGY AND STRUCTURAL ALIGNMENT IN A NEW BUSINESS DIVISION OF A MAJOR UTILITY

The business situation

This large established utility recently created a new business division with the aim of providing a unique, customer-focused energy management service to the corporate market. Ambitious growth plans have been put in place for the business.

At the end of its first year of operation it had 20 employees, covering business development, operations, client and fund management functions. The aim is to create a significant business within 10 years. It was deliberately established as a stand-alone division, partly in order to avoid association with the production and engineering culture in the core business and amongst its competitors. It is possible that the business may be floated off independently in the future.

Employees initially came from three sources: from a small acquisition that the company had made some years earlier; from the existing core business; and from the external market. The core business had a typical utility package of a just-competitive base pay, low variable pay and high benefits, while the acquisition had had a generally low pay and reward philosophy.

With the opening up of energy markets in Europe to competition, there is high demand for business development staff, and so recruiting and retaining people with the right package was seen from an early stage as an important business priority. The reward strategy was addressed, for example, at the same time as the division's name and market brand was under development.

Developing the reward strategy

The first step was to survey the external market. The levels and components of remuneration were looked at in three sectors: amongst the energy utilities, amongst blue-chip service companies, and in new start-up businesses. This helped to set the quantum of remuneration for recruitment purposes, but high-lighted the range of practice and choice for the division in terms of how the package was constructed.

An initial 'strawman' reward strategy pathway was drawn up as the basis for debate (see Figure 9). The business strategy empha-sised client service with relatively lengthy customer contracts, but the owners were also looking for a rapid return on their financial investment. Staff would therefore need to be innovative, self-reliant and entrepreneurial, but would also need to look to service customer needs in the long term and focus on financial returns in the short term.

The reward strategy initially focused on three areas:

- the mix of rewards
- the employment deal
- the relationship with reward arrangements in the parent.

First was the issue of the mix of rewards. The new business comparisons pointed to higher variable reward opportunities than was typical for a utility, but with a reasonable focus on the long term to reflect the lengthy contracts at the core of its services.

This latter business feature also supported the adoption of a commitment-based employment deal. Staff needed to stay put and co-operate across functions in order to realise the benefits of long-term contracts and make sure the planned financial returns were delivered, rather than be rewarded with the classic high-risk/high-reward package of the true entrepreneur.

The third key issue was the relationship with reward arrange-ments in the parent. There was a strong feeling that the business needed a distinctive reward package to match its distinctive offering in the market, and the parent had been devolving reward

Figure 9

THE INITIAL REWARD STRATEGY PATHWAY

Business strategy/success criteria

- Long-term growth to £X million in 10 years
- Rapid speed to market: First mover advantage
- Effective contract construction and delivery over full life
- Customer service
- Need to show immediate financial returns
- Possible spin-off/float in future

Culture and HR approach

- Customer-driven
- Commitment-based deal, with employee stakeholding
- Teamwork
- Performance-orientation
- Personal characteristics
  - Innovation
  - Self-motivation
- Entrepreneurial but medium- to long-term focus

Reward package required

- Pay driven by external market and personal contribution
- Emphasis on financial rewards, with a high level of individual flexibility in the package
- Emphasis on variable pay, reflecting a mix of collective performance and individual contribution, rewarding both the short and the long term
- Different structure from other parent businesses, but with some rough read-across

responsibilities to the business unit level for some time. Nonetheless, recruitment shortages pointed to the need to internally transfer some staff and any share-based schemes would need to use the corporate shares as the reward. Uncertainties as to the exact mix of sources for staff recruited in the future, and the fact that some of the parent company's own reward schemes were under review, made it difficult to specify a particular approach.

The new division therefore agreed a set of reward principles to guide its future practices, after consultation with all of the stakeholders involved. These principles included:

- supporting the achievement of business goals and rewarding individual and collective performance, over the short and medium term
- market competitiveness with blue-chip service organisations
- reinforcing the values and culture of the division and giving all employees a stake in its success
- being open and communicating with staff on reward issues
- being flexible to reflect different individual needs and backgrounds, and evolving as the business grows
- recognising that the division is part of a larger group but on an 'opt-in' rather than 'opt-out' basis.

Reward strategy options
The HR staff then developed three alternative packages to put these principles into practice in different future scenarios. These were:

- the integrated option
- the independent option
- the intermediate option.

The *integrated* option assumed that the business stayed close to the core business, provided services to common clients and was forced to transfer in most of its staff. It therefore emphasised alignment with the utility, with 'tweaks' to reflect the different market situation and brand. It was a similar reward package but in a new wrapper, with:

- a loose-grade read-across but greater variation in pay levels and increases

- annual bonus levels 5–10 per cent above the parent, with an element related to group as well as business performance
- application of the group share option scheme, but again with higher opportunities and a wider coverage of staff
- use of the group's flexible benefits plan but offering a lower value of benefits
- emphasis on career development opportunities across the whole group and internationally.

The *independent* option assumed that the business grew rapidly with its own identity and was floated off in the medium term. The majority of staff came from external sources. The emphasis in the reward strategy was therefore to be market- and performance-driven, and to prepare the business for flotation. Policies included:

- paying individual market rates some 10–20 per cent above traditional utilities and, once it had a few hundred employees, establishing its own broadbanded structure
- operating a bonus scheme with payment opportunities up to 50 per cent per annum, based on a mix of business and personal performance
- awarding a proportion of equity in the new business to key employees, with an executive phantom share plan until equity became available, and an all-employee share plan
- providing a bare minimum of benefits, such as life cover, and a group personal pension
- emphasising the excitement and learning of a new business to staff, and with a variety of recognition awards to reinforce the core values and achievement of growth milestones in the business plan.

Finally, the *intermediate* option balanced the reinforcement of a market- and business-performance-driven approach with the benefits of being part of a larger group, for example in terms of administration and development opportunities.

The business and group boards debated the merits of all three options. The integrated option was the fastest and easiest to set up, but represented, it was felt, a missed opportunity to establish and reinforce a new, vibrant business and culture. The independent option provided this excitement and ownership, but there was a feeling it might be too risk-oriented and create conflicts with the parent, particularly if external recruitment continued to be difficult.

The adopted strategy
The directors therefore adopted an evolutionary approach based on the intermediate option. Base pay was initially to be set very flexibly, with a discretionary bonus scheme in the first year, reflecting on the degree of business uncertainty. Interestingly, potential new recruits were happy to accept this when the rationale was explained to them. Transferring in from the parent came on their existing package but with a fixed term for its application, and on the understanding that changes to terms and conditions would be made in the future. New starters were given a cash allowance in lieu of benefits to maintain flexibility.

Since then, the package has evolved, with more formal short- and long-term incentives based predominantly on business performance and a minimum security benefits package has been introduced.

The business has exceeded its initial growth targets and the view amongst both newly recruited and transferred-in staff is that it is an exciting environment in which to work, in which they feel genuinely rewarded and recognised for the success that the business has so far achieved.

Chapter summary

- The structure that an organisation adopts to further the achievement of its strategic goals exerts a major influence on the design and operation of its reward practices. Addressing issues such as how centralised or devolved reward policies should be is a critical component of an effective reward strategy.

- Larger organisations generally adopt more structured, formal remuneration programmes, but there is a need to ensure that this does not stifle the innovation and speed of response that are major contributors to business success in many sectors.

- There is no universally 'right' or 'wrong' position on the axes from centralised to decentralised and hierarchical to egalitarian reward arrangements. Rather, the positioning of reward practices needs to match with that of the other strategic and structural variables. Problems generally result if the strategy and structure change, but reward practices do not. The alignment needs, however, to be a broad and flexible one, with different positions often appropriate for different reward practices and at different times.

● Many organisations are finding in both a structural and a reward sense that a balanced approach, attempting to combine the benefits of local flexibility and empowerment with the efficiency gains of central co-ordination, is the optimum position for them. Examples of this flexibility within a framework include the use of common broadbanded structures with local pay ranges, and flexible benefits programmes with a common menu but which are managed locally.

● This intermediate position also means that different businesses can proceed at different speeds in taking on devolved reward responsibilities.

● It is essential, particularly in very 'loose' organisation structures, to specify where and with whom the responsibilities for different reward policies and for the various employee groups lie. Shared service agreements between HR and line managers are one means of achieving this.

Chapter 4

Addressing specific strategic business situations

Chapter objectives

- illustrate the reward issues commonly evident in situations of major changes in business strategy and structure, including globalisation, mergers and acquisitions, and e-business
- demonstrate the importance of rewards to the successful realisation of these strategic actions
- provide ideas and approaches to help you identify and address these reward issues.

Business strategy specifics and rewards

Globalisation; mergers and acquisitions; e-business: these are some of the most common and all-pervasive aspects of the corporate strategies evident in contemporary organisations. Business strategy as a discipline has become at least as much concerned with managing and implementing these major changes and their impact as it is about traditional business analysis and planning. Yet it is in such specific and often swiftly changing situations that the apparent failings of modern reward strategies we described in Chapter 1 are most apparent. The grand-sounding visions and statements often fall down and fail to provide practical help in addressing the nitty-gritty and often contentious reward issues that emerge and need to be addressed rapidly in such situations, as with:

- how to deal with cross-border differences in salary levels
- whether or not to merge the pay arrangements of a new acquisition with those of the parent company
- how best to provide financial incentives in an e-business division.

All too often, the strategy is forgotten and a series of disconnected and rushed 'solutions' are hastily cooked up, many of which are liable to create severe organisational indigestion and disagreements in the longer term. Yet such issues appear to generally fall between the two disciplinary stools, ignored by both the business strategy texts and the pay and benefits textbooks. So in this chapter we look at these types of highly challenging situation, and demonstrate that a strategic and integrated reward perspective is essential if some of the most common pitfalls are to be avoided.

Global rewards strategies and structures

In Chapter 3 we demonstrated the emergence of a balanced, intermediate position in the organisation and reward structures of many large organisations. We can find evidence for a similar, tailored balance now occurring in the field of international reward.

As financial and product markets have become ever more integrated, and the dominant companies in sectors from consulting through to banking, aerospace and legal services have become ever larger and more international, many of us are being called upon to operate in new geographies and across national boundaries.

Two-thirds of the organisations in the Towers Perrin (1999b) research study of 460 organisations in Europe employed staff in more than one country, and 61 per cent had increased their staffing outside their home country in the previous three years. The worldwide population of expatriates has grown by up to 30 per cent per annum in the late 1990s, and a quarter of the FTSE 100 companies now have a director of North American origin on their board.

So what evidence is there that companies are structuring their reward programmes on a global basis to facilitate these international transfers and support the development of a global mindset in their employees? At an executive level, 64 per cent of these international organisations operate a common long-term incentive plan, and 54 per cent a common worldwide evaluation and grading system. Eighteen per cent have specific plans to move to reward employees on a pan-European basis over the next three years, with over 40 per cent foreseeing greater harmonisation across borders in Europe. Companies such as global pharmaceutical firm Eli Lilly are already showing staff their pay expressed in euros, as well as local currency, on their pay slips.

‹ Barriers to the development of truly global staffing and mindsets persist ›

Yet for the majority of staff at present, pay and benefits practices remain rooted in local national cultures and markets. With continuing major differences evident in the levels and structures of rewards between different countries, and with a trend towards local staffing helping to encourage the growth of host-country as opposed to home-country-based expatriate packages, barriers to the development of truly global staffing and mindsets persist.

There are some key distinguishing characteristics of reward practices evident in our European survey and, of course, there are still major differences in reward levels between say Portugal and Switzerland, even if these can be more easily calibrated in euros. For example, data from the US Bureau of Labor Statistics shows that in 1999 total labour costs in manufacturing were almost five times higher in Germany than Portugal, with base pay levels eight times as high. Compared to the UK, German labour costs were 66 per cent higher, with a base pay differential of 22 per cent.

Common difficulties

Four out of five international organisations reported difficulties in the management of pay and benefits across borders in the Towers Perrin research, with barriers to relocations (41 per cent), variations in employment costs (48 per cent), and relativity and equity disputes between countries (29 per cent) topping the list of problems. Many of the 47 per cent with home-based expatriate pay programmes were critical of their high cost. Yet one UK utility has great concerns about retaining key staff seconded to its North American acquisitions on a home-based package, when the value particularly of long-term incentives in equivalent US companies is so high.

Difficulties such as these, and trying to address what Pucik (1992) calls 'the nightmare of trying to create global equity yet match local conditions', have led some commentators to criticise compensation and benefits professionals for their lack of strategic vision and impact. Lawton (1997) writes of the 'fossilisation, staleness and increasing inadequacy of current paradigms in international reward'.

Emerging solutions

The issue is not as straightforward as simply building massive, integrated and uniform reward systems on a global basis. As we saw in Chapter 3, many large organisations have been decentralising in recent years, in search of greater speed and flexibility. Coca-Cola, for example, recently admitted that it had overcentralised and has instituted moves to give local managers greater freedoms in their own markets. 'Think local, act local' has become the watchword of Chairman and Chief Executive Douglas Daft. Ford abandoned its attempt to create a single global organisation structure and has re-established a powerful and more independent European headquarters.

Even McDonald's varies its menu to a degree to take account of local market tastes. As consumers we want uniformly high levels of service wherever we go, but we still want our personal tastes recognised and our national idiosyncrasies and predilections catered for. And as employees we do not want uniform 'plain vanilla' systems. If I am an American manager then I expect US bonus opportunities, even if they are the highest in the world.

In business strategy and structure, therefore, many international organisations are, like ABB, trying to be at the same time 'global and local, big and small, centralised and decentralised'. And as Stephen Perkins (1997) points out, similarly in their reward practices:

> Organisations are finding it essential to introduce a balance between the standardisation of corporate practice – to communicate a common strategy and provide corporate glue – while at the same time being responsive to the needs for differences in terms of local cultures, values and market practice.

The Towers Perrin (1999b) European study produces a powerful rejoinder to arguments of domestic stasis and lack of global vision in reward policies. A significant level of change is evident in these policies, and 84 per cent of organisations are forecasting further changes as HR managers seek to achieve this balance to better support their business strategy and structure. Planned changes to international reward policies in the next three years, according to the study, include steps to:

- ✪ reduce costs/move away from uniform home-based/balance sheet approaches (44% of respondents)
- ✪ provide greater family assistance to relocating executives (26%)
- ✪ provide improved cultural preparation/training (41%)
- ✪ improve selection, career planning and repatriation (72%)
- ✪ move to reward employees on a pan-European basis (18%)
- ✪ segment staff by region (18%)
- ✪ segment staff by type of move (25%)
- ✪ segment staff by categories of staff (18%).

A key theme in these changes is the move away from simplistic and uniform 'international' approaches, such as the balance sheet method of paying expatriates (which were often simply copied from the market norm), and moving towards more tailored, segmented and flexible reward methods.

The balance in practice

So how are they in practice, and how might you assess and structure the most appropriate balance of practices to best suit your organisation? The following techniques may be useful:

- ✪ Align reward arrangements with the level of globalisation of the organisation.
- ✪ Introduce greater flexibility into the make-up of the compensation packages of mobile employees.

First, you need to align reward arrangements with the level of globalisation of the organisation. The location, scale, structure and nature of international operations will all have an important influence on your reward policies. Paul Hansen (1998) provides a useful model to illustrate how varying degrees of globalisation are associated with different emphases in reward practices – see Table 5. He argues that very few organisations are genuinely global in their operations and culture, and that this, as well as national and cultural barriers, helps to explain the relative lack of truly global reward policies.

Table 5

A MODEL FOR ALIGNING THE HR AND REMUNERATION APPROACH WITH THE LEVEL OF GLOBALISATION

	Level of globalisation			
	Export	**International**	**Multinational**	**Global**
Business focus	Domestic	Domestic, with some developed economies	Multinational	Global
Significance of world business	Minimal	Moderate	Important	Critical
Global strategy	Representation of product/service	Business development and the control/ transfer of technology	Management and expansion of global business efforts	Borderless management and the leverage of international capabilities
Level of global competition	None	Some	Increasing	Significant
Use of human resource	Heavy use of expatriates	Mostly expatriates, some locals	Fewer expatriates, many locals	Cost-effective blend of expatriates and locals
Remuneration emphases	Home country	❷ Still home country ❷ Introducing lower differentials/ more flexibility	❷ Mix of home/host country ❷ Considerable flexibility	❷ Segmented policies ❷ Global cadre ❷ Local focus ❷ Performance-related

Source: Towers Perrin

But their level of internationalisation is increasing, and particularly as greater economic integration becomes evident in Europe we are seeing more regional reward structures being introduced. Forty-five per cent of European multinationals plan to introduce regional pay structures for their mobile staff. A pharmaceutical company, for example, has just introduced a common Euro-net pay structure of three broad bands for its managers throughout Europe. Unilever has moved its entire staff into five, commonly defined work levels, although the actual pay ranges at each level vary by business and by country, a perfect illustration of the global/local balance.

Second, organisations are introducing greater flexibility and choice into the make-up of the compensation package for mobile employees and abandoning 'one-size-fits-all' international HR approaches, which usually do not. We consider this from the employee's perspective, and the greater level of choice in how their package is constructed, even where it is paid, in Chapter 5.

But from the employer's point of view, we are seeing a much greater diversity of resourcing strategies, combining locals and expatriate staff, and short-term secondments combined with the traditional expatriate 'stint'. This flexibility is also evident in the increasing segmentation of reward policies to suit different business needs and employee groups. Changes in this direction have occurred and are forecast by one-third of companies in the Towers Perrin (1999b) study.

‛ Fit with the business, structure and HR strategy is the key driver ›

Thus the home-country, gold-card approach may continue to be used for mid-career expatriates with top management potential in the core business. But a destination-pricing, host-country package may be used for unencumbered young professionals in particular divisions, who want and need to build their international experience for future progress inside or outside the company. Fit with the business, structure and HR strategy is now the key driver of international reward practices, rather than using a common policy that often does not meet the needs of anyone.

This segmented approach is exactly the one being adopted by an international bank following a significant merger. Improved global capital flows was one objective of the merger, but the bank is sensitive to local market needs and is now structured into fairly autonomous operating divisions. Efficiency was another goal and this helped to hasten the demise of a uniform, home-country approach for expatriates that had been applied in both organisations. An elite cadre of staff will, however, now be placed on a global package, largely reflecting US norms, to ensure the development of a pool of managers for senior positions in the future.

The gas company we discussed in Chapter 2 now has a strategy of leveraging its expertise in industrial sectors on a global basis, with many customers seeking worldwide sourcing agreements. Its key HR requirement is therefore to increase its population of internationally mobile staff. It has a worldwide structure of grades to help facilitate international moves, and to increase the diversity of its expatriate population it has moved to a policy of the best of home- or host-country packages for its mobile employees.

These two different examples help to demonstrate that there are no universally 'right' or 'wrong' international reward strategies. Rather, we need to structure our policies to deliver the core themes and components that the business strategy requires, reflecting practices in the markets in which we operate and flexing in response to the changing structure of the organisation. 'Global' and 'local' policies do not start or stop at particular points, but need to permeate our reward policies to the extent that our sector and business strategy, and our employees and their cultures, require.

Mergers and acquisitions

There can be few more dramatic shifts in an organisation's structure than those occasioned by a major acquisition or merger. We are seeing record numbers of intra-industry, cross-sector and cross-border consolidations at the moment in our globalising economy. The value of mergers and acquisitions worldwide increased by 24 per cent in 1999 to $3,029 billion. In the UK in 1998, merger activity by overseas companies rose to £31.5 billion, over three times the 1996 figure.

Mergers also typically demonstrate the critical importance of reward issues to organisational well-being. Reward policies need to reflect the business and structural impact of the organisational changes involved, yet they in turn are often critical to the realisation of the business goals of the parties involved.

Potential high-profile mergers recently, in pharmaceuticals and energy, have foundered, amongst other things, on a failure to reconcile differences in executive remuneration arrangements between the two engaged organisations. More critically, research continues to demonstrate a success rate of less than 50 per cent in the subsequent realisation of the goals of the acquirer, and HR issues are generally predominant in explaining these problems.

A failure to assess the cultural compatibility of the two parties in advance and to look at anything to do with pay and reward systems beyond perhaps a quick overview of total payroll costs as part of the 'due diligence' exercise can contribute to the new organisation being stillborn. As Judy Brown (2000) explains, 'people managers must make their case more forcefully, give strategic input, and consult more' in such situations.

Key employees on either side of the merger or acquisition may leave as a result of the disruption it creates. Then, the inability to create a new culture and sense of purpose, and to break through the immediate concerns and conflicts, often sinks the new organisation, whatever its supposedly enhanced market power. Reward policies have a crucial role to play in building and reinforcing the desired and united culture, and moving from what Cartwright and Cooper (2000) call a situation of '"them" and "us" to "we"'. They may also be critical to realising the efficiency goals of the acquirer. And who is to say that the incentive structures of the corporate bankers and deal-makers are not, in their own way, contributing to the merger boom?

The subject of reward issues in mergers and acquisitions is worthy of a book in its own right and there certainly is not the space here to provide detailed guidance on how to handle the wealth of reward issues emerging in these situations. However, Zingheim and Schuster (2000) make a useful categorisation of the pre- and post-merger situations from a reward standpoint, and between the immediate and the longer-term issues involved.

As they say, the change can act to 'unfreeze' past organisational practices and so to enable rewards in the future 'to communicate new directions and futures in a positive and unifying fashion'. But there are also the immediate tasks of encouraging people who have a part to play in the new organisation to commit to it, while dealing with any issues of duplication and downsizing in a fair and humane way and taking account of all relevant legislation. As Zingheim and Schuster (2000) express it, get it right and rewards can exert a major influence in 'uniting and focusing' people in the new organisation. Get it wrong and you have a major contributor to demotivation, staff turnover and business integration failure.

Planning and preparing

We have all heard the horror stories about HR staff reading about an acquisition by their employer in the press. My own experience is that the earlier HR and compensation staff are involved in the process and the earlier the key employment and reward issues raised and debated, then not only the better the reward policies and outcomes that emerge in the new organisation, but also the more successful the whole acquisition and integration process subsequently is.

Due diligence is essentially a checking process, ultimately leading to a 'go' or 'stop' decision. It typically focuses heavily on the cost aspects of reward and HR in the target company: how efficient are they, can we achieve headcount savings, what are the pension liabilities, what is the opportunity to reduce fixed pay costs and introduce more variability, what are the costs of any 'poison pills' or 'golden parachutes' being triggered, can we integrate and automate payroll operations? These are all important questions to address, and the more the business rationale for the acquisition focuses on efficiencies and cost savings, as in a merger of two similar organisations in the same market, for example, then the more critical they become.

But in an increasing number of situations, as already discussed, the success of business strategies of acquisition depend on harnessing and uniting the talents of key staff in the two organisations, and this means that the HR and rewards assessment needs to be more wide-ranging and more detailed. Perhaps the two key questions to address are:

- ❷ What is the level of 'fit' between the two organisations' cultures and their HR and reward systems?
- ❷ What approach therefore looks the best one for managing and integrating rewards in the post-merger scenario?

Addressing these questions requires a lot more information and thinking than a few ballpark cost numbers. One organisation, for example, characterised the base pay approach of the target company as consistent with its own because both 'paid for performance'. Yet the acquirer had moved to high levels of variable pay in recent years, whereas the target company had performance-related base pay increments, which virtually all staff received. The two approaches were very different and so integrating them would have represented a major effort. Cross-border mergers often make the challenges of information gathering and assessment, and any subsequent integration of activities, even more challenging.

Initially formulating the retention strategy is also key at an early stage. Is our strategy one of retaining key talent, major downsizing or wholesale staff retention? What share options and awards will be triggered by the takeover? Who are we going to want to retain, and how are we going to identify them and then lock them into the new organisation?

Of course, the level of the 'friendliness' of the discussions between the two parties will affect the ease of acquiring answers to these questions, and you will never get all of the information that you want. But it is important to get some initial hypotheses established as to what the key reward issues will be for the new organisation, and how you are going to handle them, as well as a plan to set out who will be responsible and over what timescale the issues will be addressed.

Figure 10 illustrates part of the initial plan that a financial organisation made to handle HR and reward issues as its discussions with a potential partner progressed. It changed thereafter on virtually a weekly basis but still played a vital part in focusing all the staff involved on the key tasks and deliverables.

Figure 10

PLANNING SHORT-TERM ISSUES IN AN ACQUISITION SITUATION

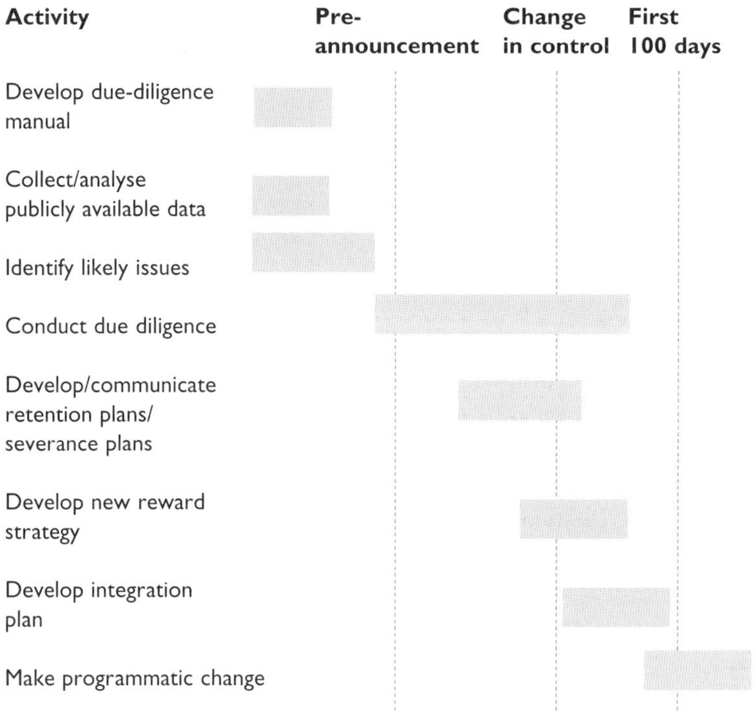
Activity
Pre-announcement
Change in control
First 100 days
Develop due-diligence manual
Collect/analyse publicly available data
Identify likely issues
Conduct due diligence
Develop/communicate retention plans/ severance plans
Develop new reward strategy
Develop integration plan
Make programmatic change

Identifying and prioritising the key issues is vital, given the high level of information and activity overload apparent in the increasingly frenetic weeks running up to the announcement and consummation of a merger or acquisition. At Towers Perrin, working as part of an in-house HR merger team, we have often used a simple matrix to help do this. We brainstorm potential issues (eg short-term retention, pension plan differences) and then rank them in terms both of criticality and ease of implementation. It is amazing how accurate this simple process often is in predicting the key reward issues that subsequently emerge as the takeover proceeds, and the ways in which they should be addressed in order to deliver on the primary business goals of creating synergies, cost savings or whatever.

Designing rewards in the new organisation

> ‘The two most important issues are reward communication and integrating reward arrangements ’

Once the merger or acquisition is agreed and proceeds, then typically a whole raft of transition teams are formed to work on the integration, and here again, reward issues need to be given due priority and attention. A whole host of immediate design tasks generally emerge and need to be rapidly addressed: the packages for the senior team, new incentive and share schemes, redundancy packages, and so on. Generally the priority, probably rightly, with reward practices is given to addressing the issues of senior management reward and retention.

But perhaps the two most important issues that need to be kept in mind, and an appropriate strategic direction set and maintained for them, are those of:

- reward communications
- the nature, level and speed of the approach to integrating reward arrangements in the two organisations.

As Cartwright and Cooper (2000) describe, people's normal reaction to a change of ownership is to seek answers to three questions: What's happening? Do I have a job/future here? Will I lose out? Once people know that they do have a future role, then attention swings very quickly to reward issues. The whole process of communications on rewards is considered in more depth in Chapter 7, but the key points in respect of mergers and acquisitions are as follows:

- Heavily involve and communicate with managers and staff from both the acquirer and the acquired organisation in the process, and from as early a stage as possible. Of course there are sensitive and controversial issues involved, as well as some legal constraints, but there is no doubt that openness and honesty in these situations pays off. Involve people on transition and design teams, regularly update them, survey their views

and opinions, and address any 'hot' issues or spots that
emerge.

- Do not get caught up in the complexity and detail of reward programmes and any changes to them. Focus on making the business rationale and logic for them clear.
- Segment your population of employees carefully in terms of how
the merger/acquisition affects them, and then tailor your core
messages accordingly. Get to the bottom of any commitments or
'promises' made, unofficially or officially, during the transition
period.
- Do not be afraid to keep on repeating the key messages, nor to
say 'I don't know, yet.'

In terms of the strategy for integration, there are a number of generic approaches:

- Implement the reward programmes of the dominant company,
which is most commonly apparent after a hostile takeover. This
approach has the advantages of extending a working formula, but
makes it tough to develop the 'we' mentality amongst the
acquired company's employees. Interestingly, in the current climate of using acquisitions to build new competencies in the
organisation, there have been a number of successful examples of
the reverse in recent months, with an oil company applying the
broadbanded approach of its smaller acquisition to the whole
organisation, and a bank that applied the very flexible base pay
increase scheme from a small specialist subsidiary to the whole
organisation.
- Blend the practices of the two organisations, which is most likely
to happen in a merger of equals. This is often adopted as a 'quick
win' approach to reward in the new organisation, but the real
danger is that it rapidly degenerates into an 'equalisation up'
process, whereby the highest level of provision between the two
organisations is selected as the one for the future. The obvious
danger is of increasing employment costs with no obvious business return, as well as failing to address problems with the existing approaches.
- Do nothing and leave the distinct approaches of the two organisations intact. This is a surprisingly common approach, encouraged by inertia and by the complexity of the Transfer of
Undertakings (Protection of Employment) Regulations 1981. If

the level of integration of the new organisation is low and the level of independence high, it can make a lot of sense. It is also commonly used in cross-border acquisitions, when often only a handful of senior staff address international issues and operate outside their local markets. When it is adopted simply as the easiest option, it can just be storing up problems for the future. Zingheim and Schuster (2000) suggest that a change of structure and ownership presents a window of opportunity to really get a better fit between business needs and rewards, which can thereby be missed.

● Design a totally new rewards approach. This is the least common strategy, usually due to the time constraints imposed, and yet when achieved, it can have a massive influence in promulgating and cementing the values of a new organisation. Generally in the current climate, both parties will have been considering and making reward changes recently, and on occasions this creative power can be harmonised to make a fresh start, do away with legacy issues and genuinely create a rewards package that reinforces your business goals and cultural requirements. Some of my most interesting and value-adding work as a consultant has been in organisations with the courage to contemplate this approach.

The timing issue as to when any reward change or integration is made obviously is important, yet merger and acquisition situations often have the most ludicrous time deadlines. However, it is best not to be rushed into overhasty reactions on the one hand, nor paralysed by the workload and do nothing on the other. Set out and agree a clear strategic direction in terms of how rewards will support the business in the future, what the objectives are and the level and nature of any integration required to achieve them. Then set out a realistic timetable to develop and deliver the approach. Be cognisant of essential and possible 'quick wins' and the need to demonstrate progress, but allow sufficient time to develop and implement any major structural reward changes, which usually involves phasing over a number of months.

Examples of success and failure

Two UK banks that merged had very different histories and cultures. On paper, their reward approaches seemed surprisingly similar, both having 16 grades and a merit pay scheme, for example. However, as its director of reward – who led the development of the new reward strategy – explained, differences in the application of these practices meant that the simplest approach of slotting the two together would have created a large number of anomalies and staff on protected salaries.

More fundamentally, his design team soon concluded that neither approach suited the future environment of 'low inflation, tremendous competitive cost pressures and the promise of delivering major savings from the merger to shareholders'. Operating managers they spoke to saw existing grade structures as a major inhibitor to the necessary restructuring and job changes in the bank.

The new strategy took 12 months to create. The team rapidly developed the strategic framework – see Figure 11 – and then worked on the constituent programmes. Their work was completed with the move of all staff into a new harmonised structure of eight broad bands, providing the necessary flexibility to reward growth in contribution and different market values. New flexible benefits programmes and share schemes completed the first phase of the changes, with new bonus schemes, performance management systems and flexible working coming in over the following 12 months.

Responsibilities for reward management have been heavily devolved to 'enable us to manage rewards in different ways to suit different parts of the business, but with an underlying, consistent philosophy'. The training of line managers and HR staff in the new approach gave the opportunity to mix people up from different backgrounds and really develop a shared understanding and commitment to it.

The three points the director of reward stressed, reflecting on his experience, were:

- focus on two or three key themes in your reward strategy
- allow enough time, whatever the immediate pressures
- get across the concept of reward schemes having a natural life span, which necessitates regular change.

Silicon Valley-based Cisco Systems has successfully grown to be a $100 billion corporation in 12 years by applying such a values-driven approach to the more than 40 acquisitions it has made in the last six years.

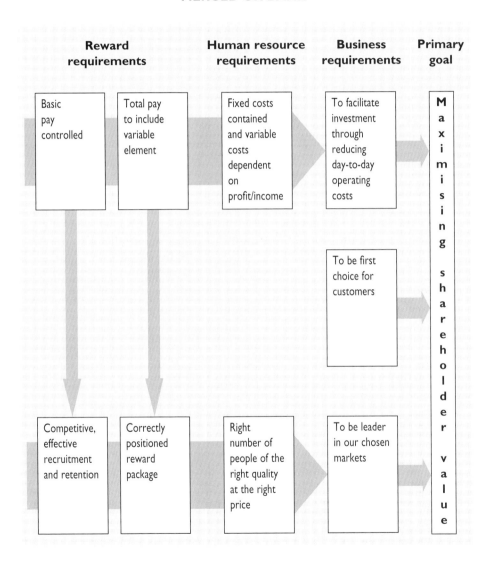

Figure 11

**ALIGNING REWARDS TO BUSINESS STRATEGY IN A
MERGED UK BANK**

Two North American banks had a much less positive experience. The acquired company had a very strong commercial portfolio of mid-sized businesses, which was a major reason for its attraction to other parties. Businesses were serviced by cross-functional teams in each region. The acquiring bank meanwhile had a much more individualistic culture and a functional organisation structure.

The reward approach adopted after the acquisition was to impose the acquirer's reward practices. The heavily team-focused incentives in the smaller entity were replaced with the aggressive and individual bonuses of the parent company, and later, the regional team structure was also eliminated. The new designs were developed almost exclusively by HR staff in the acquirer.

The results have not been good. The bank has lost market share, particularly in the middle market, and the board faces criticism for failing to deliver the promised gains of the merger to shareholders. It now is itself described in the financial press as a potential target, and one can only hope that anyone acquiring it adopts a more thought-through and high-involvement approach to the HR and reward issues that arise.

Reward strategies for e-business

There are contradictory opinions being expressed at the moment on the long-term impact of e-business, and the phenomenon of the dot.com companies, with their contrasting paper-millionaire founders, such as Martha Lane-Fox, and bankruptcies and liquidations, like boo.com. My own view is that beneath the hype and the ups and downs of the stock market from week to week, a fundamental structural change in the economy is under way that is forcing all organisations to radically question how they do business and how they can survive in the future.

'Annual bonus cycles often make no sense at all in this environment'

From a reward standpoint, my work with these types of company is some of the most interesting and challenging that I undertake. It really has led me to question all of the assumptions about motivation and 'good' pay and reward systems that I have built up over the years. Annual bonus cycles, for example, often make no sense at all in this environment, in which major events, such as each stage of venture capital findings, are often key.

How do you address the type of dilemma that Dixons faced with its Freeserve business? The corporate share price was heavily affected by Freeserve's success, but the only way to retain key executives in it was to float the business off so that they could have access to the size of equity-based rewards that they would have been able to obtain in a wholly independent venture. Meanwhile for other staff, as Stephanie Oerton (2000) explains, the traditional pay and benefits structures of the parent were 'inappropriate for attracting and keeping people in this fast-moving environment'. Thirteen pay grades were replaced by four bands, quarterly bonuses and a dress-down policy in Freeserve.

To some extent, the challenges and reward approaches for e-businesses in the new economy are not dissimilar to those facing any entrepreneurial, high-growth, start-up company, and many of the principles of the life cycle models of reward we examined in Chapter 2 can be applied. Cash is often short and intrinsic motivation and a risk-taking ethos strong amongst the founders of these companies, so a low-cash/high-equity ownership approach to rewards for the top team is often appropriate.

Just as these independent companies often do not have a business plan (outside the one presented to their financiers) and are instead directed by an idea, a vision in the founder's head that everyone shares, so there is generally no formal reward strategy or professional HR presence in place at the outset. The business situation and organisational logic make the reward strategy totally emergent. All they generally require is advice on dealing with the equity arrangements.

But there are three issues that often do need thinking through and addressing in these companies and divisions at an early stage, and a failure to do so often spells serious trouble later on. These are:

- ❷ the nature of the employment and rewards 'deal' in these businesses
- ❷ the relationship between the rewards in the subsidiary division and the rest of the parent company
- ❷ changes in the reward arrangements as the business grows and evolves.

As Meg Carter (2000) describes, 'it is ironic that dot-com start-ups, which thrive on enterprise and creative talent, rarely structure their business with HR concerns in mind', contributing to a Silicon Valley-type situation of 'minimal HR investment and high staff turnover'. At a recent Towers Perrin seminar, 75 per cent of the participants had not as yet established an e-reward strategy for their e-business.

The workforce deal

We examine the broad issue of the increasing bargaining power of employees and the importance therefore of defining a clear employment 'deal' and total rewards proposition in Chapter 6. However, it is in the often extreme environment of these small, growing, technology-based companies that the criticality of this issue is perhaps most apparent. For outside of the small group of founders, the workers attracted to these companies are no longer the type of naive 'geeks' described so well in Tracy Kidder's (1995) book about the foundation of DEC. They accepted a deal based on 'hard work, thankless hours for not a lot of pay' because 'it's at the cutting-edge, the job for the best ... for the pride, the intellectual challenge'.

As Bronson (1999) describes in his modern-day depiction of Silicon Valley, 'the world is a lot different now'. Today's technically sophisticated young professionals with the 'click' mentality are still just as interested in intellectual challenge and interesting and skills-developing work, but they are 'no longer nerds in the backroom. They live interesting lives', 'they want ownership *and* they want money', and 'loyalty is not part of the equation anymore: people stay because they are waiting for options to vest, and a chance to put their own idea into practice'. They are much more self-reliant and confident, and are fully aware of their value in an economy where a headhunter will pay $80 for an engineer's phone number. They work to live rather than live to work, and are suspicious of investing in relationships with employers, be that a large, established corporation or a growing dot.com.

This means that you need to define and 'sell' your company's reward proposition to these employees if you are going to recruit and hopefully retain them for any period of time. As Ann Lucas, Head of HR at Razorfish, explains, 'creating the right culture is vital in attracting and retaining people', and they have grown to 14,000 staff. Razorfish adopts a very broad approach to rewards, emphasising the benefits of the environment and development it provides to staff. Everyone has an individual training plan and a personal development champion.

Another good example of this is a fast-growing venture, based on an Internet service, that has been established in the UK by two telecom companies. It now has over 200 staff. Its first and recently installed HR director calls it the HR and reward 'brand' rather than an HR strategy, emphasising that they need an emergent and adaptable approach in such a rapidly changing marketplace. Nonetheless, there is now a clear framework of reward policies and responsibilities in place.

From a pay and benefits standpoint, this includes:

- high pay for the best people in the industry, adopting an upper-quartile market positioning (currently in the UK, surveys suggest that many entrepreneurial start-ups are actually having to pay more than well-established employers in the prevailing labour market conditions)
- share ownership for all
- high levels of differentiation based on performance
- highly flexible and relatively low-cost benefits.

But strong emphasis is placed on the broader aspects of a rewarding experience at the company, with:

- challenging and cutting-edge work
- a personal development fund and regular career coaching
- a fun, fast-paced, open and genuinely non-hierarchical environment
- a compelling future proposition of being the first to succeed within a new market but with the backing of two powerful parents.

On paper, this can look contrived and trite, but potential recruits have reacted very positively to the openness, clarity, honesty and appeal of this branding. In addition, although it is a loose framework, line managers have signed up to all of its components and to their role in making it a working reality. So there is now none of the 'special' deals done by particular managers with individual employees, which often characterise these types of fast-growth companies and which can create so much disharmony when they emerge later on. In addition, managers are held to account if the regular 'pulse' surveys of staff reveal a lack of attention to the development of their people.

Structuring the relationship to the parent

Many commentators believe that the future (and the place to invest) is not in the dot.coms, but in the dot.corps, the larger organisations with e-business interests who have the size and muscle to succeed long-term in this roller coaster environment.

In this last example, the role of the parent companies in the e-business venture was very much a back-seat one of investors, with the odd borrowing of, say, an equal opportunities policy to avoid 'reinventing the wheel'. But how such relationships are structured varies substantially, and some of the most interesting and challenging reward issues are evident not in wholly independent start-ups, but when the e-businesses are subsidiaries of larger organisations.

Do we let them have their own share and long-term incentive plan, and if so, do we use corporate or phantom subsidiary shares, or real stakes in the venture? Should we provide very large share incentives, even though the risks are typically lower than a wholly independent start-up, and the investment banking-derived incentive strategy is often not appropriate? Should they just pay the rates they have to in their market, or should there be a read-across with the rest of the organisation? Should their incentives be aligned with the rest of the organisation, or reflect higher rates of risk with higher variable pay? And even in pensions, while the corporate plan may not suit their workforce profile, do they want to go through the hassle of setting up and running their own scheme?

‘ Match the structural relationship between the parent and its e-business with your rewards approach ’

Here again, many of the principles and approaches we considered in respect of decentralised organisations can be applied, although the issues may be more extreme. Companies, for example, have had independent reward arrangements in their research and development divisions and IT departments for many years. The key is to match the nature of the structural relationship between the parent and its e-business with your rewards approach.

Based on our research and experience at Towers Perrin, we have developed a framework that represents some typical relationships between structural and HR and reward variables in e-business organ-isations. Some companies have set up e-business divisions purely for internal purposes, such as establishing and operating online pur-chasing and distribution systems. Not surprisingly, the reward arrangements in these divisions are highly consistent with the rest of the organisation, with only minor concessions to the different staff profiles.

On the other hand, the corporate strategy in some companies is to grow the venture rapidly and then partially or wholly spin it out, and many of the staff may be recruited externally. In these cases much more independent and market-facing reward arrangements are more likely to be employed, sometimes with a view to establishing the type of reward policies that will apply after the business is indepen-dently floated.

The situation for many of these businesses is that they are somewhere in-between these two extremes, as in the energy company case study at the end of Chapter 3. Carter speaks of the benefits of a balanced approach, with 'the large traditional corporates learning how to replicate the appeal of the dot.com environment to attract and retain staff', and the dot.coms 'developing HR and reward strategies that value and develop staff, without compromising their buccaneering cultures'. The new HR director of an Internet company who could find no records anywhere of past share grants or annual bonus targets in the company would certainly echo this latter point.

It is in such situations that there is usually a wide choice of approaches and practices, and the HR professional's skill is in select-ing the most appropriate for that stage in the business's evolution, and usually anticipating the next stage, but possibly with legacies from its former stage. Each venture is different and its uniqueness needs to be reflected in your rewards approach.

Evolving reward strategies in e-business

The relationship of these companies to their parents often changes, and it is in the fast-moving world of e-business that this requirement for flexibility and adaptability in the reward strategy is most evident.

Sabeer, the founder of Hotmail (which Microsoft bought out making him a multi-millionaire), has a leadership style described as 'not micro-management, but setting the right direction, getting everyone focused, telling the same story, harmonising' (Bronson, 1999). Reward strategies in this environment often also need to be a loose framework with a clear direction that can shift as the company's strategy and structure change.

There are some situations in which it is better not to finalise the fine detail of reward arrangements, such as how bonus payments would be determined, until it is apparent how the business is actually going to develop. If HR is clear and open in telling employees why this is being done, they will most probably accept it.

But what is critical is that the reward strategy does move on, for it is in this environment that the danger of it becoming obsolescent and an albatross around the neck of the changing company's business goals is possibly most evident. A philosophy of work interest, excitement, low pay and high stock grants can work superbly for a new start-up. But what happens two or three years later, when you have made history but face a maturing and increasingly competitive market, reflected in a plateaued stock price; with a larger and geographically stretched organisation; and with parts of the workforce in jobs that mean they need to work to exist, buy food and pay the mortgage, rather than have a fun, fulfilling and meaningful lifestyle?

The answer is: you have to change the reward strategy – and the dot.com company in the case study below experienced severe recruitment and motivation problems because it recognised this too late.

In fact, often the people who lead the high-growth phase in these businesses, the 'architects', are not those who will manage the larger and more established organisation that it hopefully grows into. A different set of reward arrangements may well be appropriate for them compared to the 'residents' of the business even though both groups will often be in the organisation for a period concurrently. Segmentation of your reward strategy, for different periods and for different groups of employees, is therefore also often important in these situations.

Case study

THE NEED FOR STRATEGIC REWARD CHANGES IN A MATURING DOT.COM COMPANY

Background: rapid growth and evolution

The drain of talent to the exciting opportunities created by dot.com companies has created major headaches for established firms in a range of sectors. Yet the dot.coms themselves are experiencing a variety of retention and motivation issues, and in this case, the failure to address these problems by reward changes had a major negative impact on the business.

The company concerned is one of the best-known Internet companies, which has rapidly established a worldwide presence and reputation for the online retailing of its merchandise. Set up in the mid-1990s, it now has over 7,000 employees, and has been rapidly expanding its range of stock, as well as its own distribution and customer service functions, in the last two years.

The reward approach and its problems

Here was an unwritten but crystal-clear reward strategy, stemming directly from the experiences and views of the charismatic founders: come here to work hard, in an unfettered and exciting environment, providing a wholly new service. Pay levels were set very low – at around the tenth percentile position in the market – with a minimal benefits package. But very high share grants (over 200 per cent of the market average) were made to all staff in a classic risk/reward situation. In the early days, it worked brilliantly in attracting and motivating the creative North American entrepreneurs who powered the early success of the business.

But in a large and maturing organisation, with a growing proportion of lower-paid staff and with a plateaued share price, it became increasingly problematic. Recruiting staff on such a high-risk package became very difficult, and the use of signing-on bonuses multiplied. Amongst existing employees there were a range of problems. Star performers from the early days had millions in share options, and their departure would represent a huge loss of leadership and intellectual capital to the business. Other, sometimes less high-performing staff with longer service often could not afford to leave. Newer staff with underwater options had very little to tie them to the business and represented an easy target for the headhunters and increasingly aggressive imitators and competitors. Staff turnover increased rapidly and the internal climate took a noticeable turn for the worse.

The new reward strategy

Recognising these problems, the HR staff in the company reviewed the situation in detail and came up with a more formalised reward strategy that took account of the organisation and its markets. Presenting it to the board, they emphasised that this total rewards transition strategy was critical to the business's survival and future. This approach is summarised below. It incorporates four aspects of reward.

1 *Individual growth:*
   - performance and talent management
   - development through growth opportunities – talent portfolio management.

2 *Total pay:*
   - base pay
   - variable pay, including stock options
   - benefits
   - recognition and celebration.

3 *Compelling future:*
   - company growth, success, image and reputation
   - ownership and goal alignment.

4 *Workplace:*
- lots of teams with 'smart' colleagues
- challenging work and 'just-do-it' style
- two-way communications, fun and fast.

In respect of financial rewards the strategy included the following:

- adopting a structure of eight job levels for reward allocation and career development purposes, covering all 200 roles in the company
- varying pay ranges on these levels by function and country, but providing a framework for moving in stages to more market-aligned salaries; non-professional staff are now paid at the market median, professional staff in the second quartile, with a lower positioning retained for executives
- setting base pay increases in relation to individual ongoing value to the business, assessed in terms of personal competence and performance
- ensuring that signing-on bonuses are more consistently applied for professional staff, but primarily used only for executives
- setting share grants at a nominal level for more junior staff but at a level remaining significant for professionals and executives; future grants are, however, related to an assessment of the individual's criticality to the business and long-term potential
- keeping benefits provisions comparatively low, but to reflect the more diverse and ageing workforce, a range of family benefits such as medical insurance were introduced.

A more systematic and organised approach to development and 'talent management' was also proposed and introduced. The new performance management process is kept deliberately brief and administered through the intranet, but it ensures that the development needs of all employees are considered and performance issues identified and addressed. A simple competency framework supports the process, with a strong emphasis on teamwork and supporting the company's culture. An open system of job vacancy posting has also been introduced.

The board's initial response to these proposals was somewhat hostile, regarding them as overstructured and in conflict with the entrepreneurial ethos of the company. However, they came to recognise that many of these changes, such as having to pay market rates for distribution staff, were already being forced on them. In addition, the attention to the other non-financial aspects of reward and motivation in the framework was strongly supported.

The company's environment and culture was recognised as being a powerful motivation for staff and so these have been incorporated into the rewards framework. The informal, open and 'fun' aspects continue, but the company's values have been codified, and more deliberate recognition of their display introduced. Hard work is still a core feature, but performance expectations and measures are now being more clearly defined and specified.

Finally, the company has put a lot of effort into redefining its future. This has maintained the original philosophy of continuing to give every employee a stake in that future, and with more systematic celebration and communication of what the company has achieved so far. But there has also been deliberate recognition of the need to move on in order to continue to succeed in the future. New and more specific business goals have been defined, following discussions with all staff, with ambitious targets in terms of customer service, growth and innovation. These goals are now being cascaded down through the organisation.

The majority of these changes are now up and running in the company, and the recruitment and retention situation has already improved, particularly in Europe. The market remains a highly volatile and competitive one, but it now has a rewards structure in place that better facilitates the move into the next phase of this still young company's evolution.

Chapter summary

❷ Reward strategies have to be able to provide specific guidance in addressing the reward issues that emerge in commonly occurring situations of major business change. Correspondingly, the success of these business changes can be jeopardised if the reward issues are not addressed in an effective and strategic fashion.

❷ The increasingly international nature of the business world is affecting both organisation structures and reward strategies. Many organisations report problems with their predominantly local reward practices, such as barriers to international mobility and the high cost of expatriate programmes.

● In response, reward professionals are developing more tailored and segmented programmes, attempting to combine the benefits of global integration and local flexibility. Examples include different expatriate reward packages for different staff groups and operating some programmes, such as share schemes, globally, while leaving others, such as general staff pay, rooted in local markets.

● Mergers and acquisitions represent a dramatic shift in an organisation's size, structure and character with major implications for reward.

● Research suggests that many mergers and takeovers fail due to the lack of attention given to HR and reward issues. Reward policies are often critical in building a new sense of 'we' in the combined organisation, as well as in realising the efficiency gains promised to shareholders.

● In the pre-merger phase, reward considerations need to be raised at an early stage. The level of compatibility between practices in the two organisations needs to be thoroughly researched, the potential reward issues from integration raised, and an initial plan for addressing them constructed.

● Post-merger, two critical reward issues concern communications and the approach adopted to integration.

● Communications need to be as open and frequent as possible, with managers and staff involved in addressing reward issues, and a strong business logic regularly reinforced for the emerging solutions. Set out a clear direction as to how rewards will support the business direction in the future and the level and nature of change and integration required to achieve this.

● In respect of integration, the alternatives include:
  ● imposing the reward systems of the acquiring organisation, which may get in the way of creating a sense of shared purpose in the new organisation
  ● integrating the arrangements from the previous organisations, which risks producing increases in reward costs
  ● leaving the pre-existing, different arrangements in place, which may also create internal barriers and inequities

- ❷ developing wholly new reward arrangements, which may take time, but can be very effective in promulgating and supporting a new organisation culture.
- ❷ The challenge that e-business represents to many large, established companies is mirrored in the implications for reward programmes. While they challenge many traditional reward structures and shibboleths, there are also some significant strategic reward issues evident in the fast-growth dot.com companies themselves.
- ❷ For the dot.coms, the initial reward approach is normally emergent, often with a low-cash/high-equity emphasis.
- ❷ Thereafter, it is critical to define a clear reward strategy and brand in terms that can attract and retain the sort of technology-literate staff who are driving the e-business revolution. This often needs to encompass non-financial as well as monetary components.
- ❷ In large organisations the relationship between the reward policies in the e-business and the rest of the company is often a vital issue. These policies need to be consistent with the business and structural relationships, generally being much more distinct, for example, if the intention is to float the business off.
- ❷ In e-business, as indeed in many modern environments, it is critical that reward strategies evolve and change to match with changes in the organisation's structure, involving a continual process of reappraisal and modification.

Chapter 5

Reward methods and designs

Chapter objectives

- illustrate the most widespread trends in reward programme design, occasioned by moves to better reinforce strategic business goals
- describe some of the most significant reward issues and design choices facing UK organisations
- provide ideas and tools to help structure an integrated and strategic approach to reward programme design.

A pathway through the detail

'Ah yes,' said the stores director who we were trying to arm-twist agreement out of to our newly constructed reward strategy principles, 'but the devil is in the detail.' Her obfuscation, presumably to support continuation of her own personal approach to reward management in the stores, highlights the dilemma in adopting a strategic approach to reward management for many HR and compensation professionals.

On the one hand, we want to avoid getting bogged down in the nitty-gritty details of reward practices, which can cloud the direction and core messages – of business alignment, cultural support and so on – that our reward strategy is meant to convey. As in the stores case, this often just serves to support a continuance of the status quo and a focus on tactical and maintenance issues. Hurwich (1986) even plotted on a graph a strategic reward approach at one end of a continuum, with a technical design focus at the opposite end.

‘Without adequate answers your reward strategy is liable to fall down at the first hurdle’

On the other hand, we do have to populate our reward strategy with something – with designs and programmes that structure and organise how pay and reward in our organisation is managed. The breadth and range of programmes and alternatives seems virtually endless: Which do I address first? What alternatives do I have? How should I redesign it? How would we make it work? These and a hundred and one other questions soon emerge. And without adequate answers, your reward strategy is liable to fall down at the first hurdle.

The solution to this dilemma is not to retreat into high-flown reward theories and principles. But we also need to recognise that our reward strategy cannot be a fully finished, detailed blueprint of what every reward practice in our organisation is going to look like for the next 10 years. Rather, an effective reward strategy sets out a direction and provides clear guidance, a pathway, to address the major reward issues that emerge in your organisation, by developing and redesigning reward practices in ways that support what your business and employees require to succeed.

In this chapter there is not the space to provide detailed descriptions of all of the options, possibilities and scheme designs in every area of reward management. These are generally well covered already in a number of pay and benefits textbooks.

A real danger of the traditional reward focus on scheme designs is the encouragement of HR fads and fashions, as organisations follow supposed 'best' and predominant practice and pursue individual technical solutions unrelated to their real business needs or their other HR and reward practices. I have a real fear of the headlong, roller-coaster rush into individual performance-related pay, for example, being repeated with team pay. Initial enthusiasm leads to widespread adoption irrespective of the need or situation, with impossibly high intentions and expectations, which is then followed rapidly by perceived failure, disillusionment and disappointment. As Thompson (1998a) says, 'the hard lessons from the UK experiment with [individual] performance pay may encourage a more reflective and strategic approach to pay in the future.'

It is important to design schemes that suit the unique needs of your own organisation and its staff and ignore the generic prescriptions of supposed experts, which as Fitz-Enz (1997) puts it, 'are neither universal nor generally applicable'.

Nonetheless, there are common reward patterns and themes evident as UK organisations respond to the business and environmental challenges that they face. Towers Perrin's (1999b) European reward study found high levels of change occurring and forecast in virtually all areas of pay and reward (eg 70 per cent changing bonuses, 48 per cent pay structures and 41 per cent pay reviews). Some of the most commonly listed objectives and themes mentioned by the participants in this study as underpinning their design changes included:

- introducing more flexibility and variability into rewards programmes, rather than continuing with control-oriented, highly structured systems; 'we've got to loosen up' was how one participant expressed it
- moving from internally focused to more market-driven rewards
- reflecting a more flexible, person-based rather than a wholly job-based rewards approach
- placing a greater emphasis on variable pay, rather than continuing with what one HR director referred to as 'our base pay obsession'
- adopting a broader concept of relating rewards to contribution in their organisation, rather than maintaining a narrow focus on paying only for individual results
- using a much wider variety of reward tools, rather than a narrow pay and benefits focus
- involving line managers and staff more in reward issues, rather than the HR function controlling reward schemes.

The aim of this chapter is to highlight some of these important themes and issues, which many UK organisations are currently facing, and the choices in scheme designs that they present, the opportunities and the dilemmas. Hopefully it will also provide you with some tools and ideas to help you make these choices, now and in the future, in an integrated, strategic fashion.

Reward objectives

Any reward scheme succeeds to the extent that it achieves the objectives set out for it. In one setting – say a long-established utility facing intense competition and requiring new ideas and creativity to succeed – a scheme that encourages higher employee turnover might be deemed highly successful. The same scheme in an IT company with a high rate of attrition and facing key skills shortages would be disastrous.

The first step in negotiating a strategic pathway through the reward design jungle is therefore to arm yourself with a clear set of objectives. This may seem a blindingly obvious point, yet it is one that many organisations ignore.

Thompson (1992), for example, found that the reason for the failure of the majority of the performance pay schemes that he studied lay not in their design but in the absence of any clear and agreed objectives for these schemes. In much of the public sector, for example, they were introduced as a means of obtaining greater flexibility to pay market rates, and so it is scarcely surprising that they have often not effectively rewarded personal performance. Similarly, when my colleague Mike Langley (1987) researched the impact of sales incentive plans, he found only one company that had any clear objectives against which to review the success of their schemes.

A clear and agreed set of objectives, therefore, provides you with a touchstone against which you can assess the effectiveness of your existing reward schemes and the viability of alternative designs. Hopefully these objectives will relate back up the pathway to the business goals and structures in your organisation, in the manner defined in previous chapters, but simply having some is an enormous help in addressing specific design issues.

Format and examples

The form and detail that these objectives take obviously varies enormously between organisations. In some cases they are relatively brief and generic. At a small financial services company, the objectives of all of their pay and reward schemes are to:

- recruit and retain staff
- motivate them highly
- support the achievement of business goals
- be controllable and easy to administer.

Similarly, in a technology company, the aims of sales reward schemes are to:

- drive the achievement of business goals
- support what the customer requires
- motivate the sales staff and meet their needs
- match with the sales roles and what staff are expected to and can do
- provide competitive remuneration to recruit and retain
- be manageable, controllable and affordable
- form an integrated part of the sales management process.

Other organisations have more far-reaching and detailed goals. The list below summarises the general reward principles that apply in a large water utility and against which all corporate and business unit schemes are periodically audited.

- *Strategy-driven:* pay and reward policies should be aligned with corporate and local business strategies, reinforcing the achievement of business goals.
- *Performance-based:* clear relationships should operate between contribution, performance and reward, related to results achieved and how those results are achieved.
- *Value-based:* pay and reward policies should be aligned with corporate values, reinforcing the actions and behaviours necessary to realise our vision.
- *Common framework:* pay and reward policies should operate within a common strategic framework, facilitating cross-business mobility, realising economies of scale and sharing best practice.
- *Business and market-driven:* pay and reward policies should reflect local business needs and circumstances, such as the cost structure, ability to pay, employee profile and market competitiveness.
- *Flexible:* policies must be responsive to changes in the businesses and external environment.
- *Recognition:* the full range of financial rewards should be used to recognise the success of our employees. Success will be openly celebrated and an ownership mentality encouraged.
- *Fair:* pay and reward policies should be fair, equitable, defensible and legally compliant.
- *Open:* reward information should be openly communicated with employees. They will be consulted as early as possible when changes are being considered.

Similarly, a major reward change programme in a large mutual insurer has been co-ordinated around the following objectives agreed by the board:

- to achieve greater flexibility, in order to:
  - reflect different market rates
  - support job changes and restructuring
  - support career development and mobility
  - evolve over time
- to be more externally market-driven, in order to recruit and retain staff of the appropriate calibre and recognise the increasing and varied market pressures in different functions
- to reward individual contribution and the 'right' things
- to facilitate career development and advancement throughout the organisation and reward potential
- to remove the current overemphasis on grade and status.

Many of the core themes mentioned earlier are evident here and they have led to a range of design changes, including a move to distinct, job-family-based pay structures and increasing levels of variable pay.

'The reward strategy may be just a common set of objectives and success criteria'

The content and detail of these objectives need to be tailored to your particular situation. But the vital point, and the foundation of a strategic approach to rewards, is to have them, agree them and use them. Particularly in a highly diverse and devolved organisation, the reward strategy may be just this: a common set of objectives and success criteria that everyone has bought into, even though the scheme designs might vary, often substantially, in each unit according to particular local needs.

Horizontal alignment and total rewards

There is undoubtedly a temptation – given the range of reward programmes in many organisations and the increasingly complexity of employment law and tax regimes – to adopt a narrow focus on single programmes and to make specific, one-off changes and improvements. This should be resisted, and instead a broad, total rewards approach should be adopted, which is why the term reward, rather than pay and benefits, strategy is emphasised throughout this book.

This is not to say that you cannot address specific issues as they arise, nor that you need to change everything all at once. However, moving within the framework of an integrated approach will be much more effective for your organisation in the longer term than single 'one-hit' interventions. There are three main reasons for this:

- the need to align reward schemes with each other and with other HR programmes
- the fact that monetary rewards are not the only motivators at work
- the need to apply interdisciplinary solutions to complex issues.

Aligning reward and HR programmes

First, as Ian Kessler pointed out at a recent IRS conference, a great deal of attention has been paid in recent years to the 'vertical' alignment of reward programmes with business goals. Yet far too little account has been taken of the need for horizontal alignment between all of the various reward and HR programmes. Without such alignment and integration, there are a number of risks, including:

- Mixed and confusing messages, which weaken the overall power of your reward strategy – as in the use of performance bonuses alongside service-related base pay progression – are sent to employees. Only a third of directors in a Towers Perrin (1994) survey felt that their HR practices were well integrated and delivered a consistent message to employees.
- There is not adequate support for individual pay practices from other HR policies. For example, however well designed your individual bonus scheme, it will fail if there is not an effective performance measurement and management system in place, or if participants do not have the skills and competence to actually achieve the targets that are set. Similarly, the CIPD's latest research on broadbanding highlights that such changes in your grading structure may fail if insufficient attention is paid to how pay is subsequently adjusted within the broader pay ranges.

A good example of a well-integrated reward strategy and set of changes is provided by the mutual insurer referred to on page 112.

The goals of more flexible pay arrangements were addressed by the design of distinct job-family-based pay and development structures. But the design team also thought through how this would impact on the other aspects of pay management. Their changes addressed the need for supporting actions in other HR areas such as performance management and communications. Specific owners for the job families were identified, for example, to take formal responsibility for creating effective pay management and development processes within each family.

A US telecom provider similarly took a total rewards perspective in response to the requirements of an increasingly international business operating in seven countries. Its business strategy focused on corporate customers who wanted global deals and uniformly high levels of service. Current problems were found, in part, to relate to inconsistent reward programmes delivering inconsistent messages in their different locations. A variety of changes followed, including improved international career planning and a global bonus programme focused on customer service.

The total rewards bundle

The second reason you need to take a total rewards perspective is that, as we all know from our personal experience, money is not the only, or often the main, motivator at work. If you list why you took the job you are doing now and why you stay doing it, the major reasons are often to do with the more intangible rewards: for the challenge, the job interest, the exciting environment, having bright colleagues and so on. We all know this and research on employee motivation consistently reinforces the point. Yet even in these resource-constrained times, when the spotlight is on total employee costs more intensely than ever, these non-financial items are often ignored and are therefore hugely underleveraged in many organisations.

‹Money is not the only, or often the main, motivator at work›

Thirdly, as O'Neal (1998) points out, in our increasingly fast-changing and heterogeneous world, in which national and sector boundaries are breaking down, complex problems are now demanding interdisciplinary solutions in everything from medicine to the social services, and also therefore in HR management.

At Towers Perrin, we use a simple matrix (shown in Figure 12) to help consider the total rewards strategy in an organisation. The financial rewards in the upper two quadrants represent transactional rewards that are essential to recruit and retain staff. But as Bloom and Milkovich (1995) observe, these rewards alone cannot extract the behaviours that distinguish outstanding from ordinary performance and that create the mindset required for your staff to voluntarily commit to fully contribute to the competitive success of your organisation. They can also, generally, be easily copied by competitors.

Figure 12
A WAY OF THINKING ABOUT TOTAL REWARDS

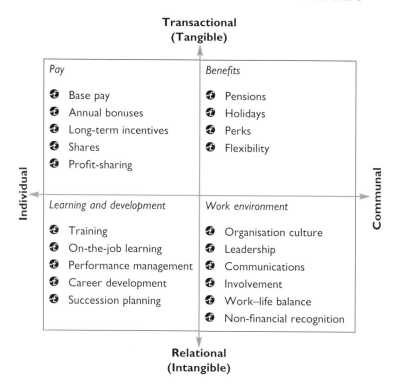

**Transactional
(Tangible)**

Pay
- Base pay
- Annual bonuses
- Long-term incentives
- Shares
- Profit-sharing

Benefits
- Pensions
- Holidays
- Perks
- Flexibility

Individual ← → Communal

Learning and development
- Training
- On-the-job learning
- Performance management
- Career development
- Succession planning

Work environment
- Organisation culture
- Leadership
- Communications
- Involvement
- Work–life balance
- Non-financial recognition

**Relational
(Intangible)**

Relational rewards, on the other hand, result from the lower quadrants in the framework of learning and development and the work environment, and these enhance the value of the upper quadrants. Together they create what we saw referred to in some of our case examples as a reward and cultural 'brand', which is much more difficult for competitors to copy. How many of us have turned down a job offer with a higher salary because we did not fancy other aspects of the company: the politics, the arrogance, the lack of development and so on?

A variety of research studies support this, showing that a broad and flexible employment relationship secures employee commitment to common goals, values and long-term success. Bloom (1995), for example, demonstrates that a broad 'bundle' of valued rewards must be offered in exchange for a 'cluster' of employee contributions to the business. As the HR director at clothing company Land's End puts it, its rewards policies need to 'be concerned with the entire workplace'.

Using this framework of total rewards is also a useful way of considering and making significant overall choices within your reward strategy. From the business angle, where do you need to place your emphasis and how best can you invest the available funds? How would the investments in a new online development centre or a global share plan compare in terms of costs and returns?

We recently carried out a study for a large UK retailer that highlighted that their traditional competitors invested a comparatively large amount in benefits (30 per cent of their total rewards expenditure), which was not always appreciated by their employees. By contrast, a wider sample of blue-chip companies they had been benchmarking in respect of business performance invested less in benefits (22 per cent) but a larger amount in employee development (25 per cent compared to 18 per cent in the retailers). The company therefore altered the balance and mix of their reward investments.

From the employees' perspective, what choices can you offer them to maximise the perceived value of their rewards package at an equivalent cost to their employer, or even just to recognise that people like making a choice? The rewards director in a bank told me a story of how one married call centre employee with children took 90 per cent of her salary in retail vouchers under their flexible benefits scheme. She thereby benefited from a volume discount they had negotiated with large retailers (£10 vouchers for £9) and the savings on National Insurance. As he explained, competitors would need to offer her a substantially greater pay package to entice her away. According to Towers Perrin's (1999b) latest research, 60 per cent of UK employers now offer staff choices between different rewards, and 55 per cent of European companies plan to introduce flexible benefits in the next three years.

The move to total rewards

There is now plenty of other evidence to demonstrate that this message is getting through to organisations, and that a total rewards approach is being adopted, beyond simply the move to rechristen compensation and benefits specialists as reward managers. The 460 participants in the Towers Perrin (1999b) European research predicted a lower emphasis on the goals of performance-related pay and pay cost control in the future. But they foresaw greater attention to the goals of managing rewards on a total remuneration basis and offering employees more choice in the make-up of their rewards package, in order to support their HR objective of becoming an employer of choice.

Lower levels of change than in recent years were forecast in the survey in respect of virtually all areas of pay management, with attention switching to the other three quadrants. Seventy-five per cent of companies forecast changes in their benefits plans, with almost half having increased their benefits spend in the last three years. So much for the predicted trend towards 'clean cash'!

In terms of what one of my accountancy friends calls the 'below the line' rewards, illustrated in Figure 12, 72 per cent of organisations had similarly increased their training and development spend over the same period, with a median provision of between three and five days' training per employee and a particular focus in the UK on the development of high-potential employees. Career planning continues to be a major focus of attention in companies such as Unilever and Phillips and research suggests that training and development opportunities are a key factor in the retention of the techno-literate, job-hopping 'Generation X' staff.

This was very much the case in the IT department of a recently merged insurance company, where attitude studies demonstrated that cash bonuses were not the main factor in preventing their highly prized systems and web specialists being lured to higher-paying consultancies. These staff did want competitive pay and financial recognition for their individual contribution. But what really kept them and motivated them was the challenge and development offered by the large IT projects in the company, as well as the open and laissez-faire environment in which they worked.

Many employees, with their increasingly frenetic lifestyles, are looking for greater flexibility in their roles and the organisation of their working lives. For instance, this book was written on a sabbatical break from consulting. Seventy per cent of companies, and 90 per cent in the public sector, already operate schemes to help their employees balance their work and home lives, a key feature of policies in the lower right-hand quadrant of our framework. These include things such as offering flexible working hours (70 per cent of employers), homeworking (which 46 per cent plan to introduce) and job-sharing (operated by 31 per cent).

Just ask anyone who works in a call centre how important the physical environment and operating style in their company are. An intense work environment is the primary cause of staff turnover in these centres according to recent IDS research (2000). As we saw in the Chapter 4 discussion on globalisation, companies are increasingly turning their attention away from selecting the latest purchasing power parity formula for their expatriates' financial package and focusing instead on the environmental and career issues that correlate more strongly with the continuing high failure rates in expatriate placements. Seventy-two per cent of international companies are making improvements to their selection, career planning and repatriation policies, while 41 per cent are introducing improved cultural preparation and spouse support programmes.

Recognition schemes

In many companies at the moment non-financial recognition schemes are being dusted down and modified to increase their impact in support of the goals of the business and its reward strategy. The schemes are particularly prevalent in knowledge and technology-based sectors, as well as sales and service functions. There can be few better illustrations of the need to tailor reward schemes to your own circumstances than the common failure of the ubiquitous 'employee of the month' scheme!

Happily, much greater diversity and creativity is evident in this field at present and with some impressive business returns. Common trends in their usage, to achieve this greater business impact, include:

- putting a greater focus on recognising key strategic business goals and values, such as teamwork and customer service, which in some cases can be difficult to formally reinforce with pay
- adopting a more inclusive philosophy of recognising as many 'winners' as possible, rather than concentrating on a narrow élite of exceptional performers; in many sectors it is the contribution of all employees, not just a few superstars, who will really ramp up the organisation to world-class performance standards
- using a wider range of rewards – letters of thanks, gifts, points, vouchers, meals, holidays etc – to suit different situations and differing employee needs; the Rolex watch won by the car salesman in each of the last three years for being the top salesperson is one of the worst examples of recognition, for him and the other sales staff, I have come across!

McDonald's recently revamped its recognition schemes in the UK with these aims in mind and has found a correlation between their rate of use and incidence of awards, and the financial performance of its restaurants.

The strategic framework of different recognition schemes now operating in a service organisation is shown in Table 6. A small number of competitive schemes are operated nationally to recognise exceptional performance, for example by the best project teams. But there is now a whole range of low-cost ways of recognising the contribution and performance of all staff at the local level, with a diverse and shifting mix of schemes.

‹ There are few better examples
of the need for an evolving
strategic approach to reward
than recognition schemes ›

Table 6

RECOGNITION POLICY IN A SERVICE-SECTOR ORGANISATION

	Corporate level	Local level
Distribution	To highest performers against key criteria	To as many as possible, so long as criteria met
Frequency	Annual	Fast and as frequent as possible, so long as criteria met
Size	Significant, but with non-financial as well as financial recognition	Low value but still meaningful, eg letters, vouchers
Currency	Reasonable financial reward with high recognition attached	As varied as possible to address individual motivations
Purpose	Reinforce importance of demonstrating core values and achieving key goals, illustrate highest performance possible, eg best team performance, best customer service award, etc	Provide general broad-based recognition and thanks for good performance and significant efforts beyond the norm
Operation	Organisation-wide, centrally controlled	Devolved as far as possible
Proportion of spend	20%	80%

There are in fact few better examples of the need for a 'light' and an evolving strategic approach to reward than these recognition schemes. The research demonstrates that their impact is best when they are highly targeted and operated over a short time frame. Hence they need to be regularly changed, but always within a framework of support and direction to ensure that their business impact is retained.

So to sum up on total rewards:

- *ⓘ* your rewards strategy needs to encompass all aspects of rewards, to maximise its business impact and leverage on employee behaviour
- *ⓘ* you should take an integrated approach to all of your reward

practices, with each other, and with your other HR programmes, to best support a clear employment 'deal' and coherent set of HR goals

- you need to assess and measure the cost, perceived value and impact of rewards policies in all four quadrants of the framework and focus your attention and activities in those areas that potentially can add the greatest value.

Key design choices: moving from control to flexibility

Some of the most commonly listed strategic reward ambitions in UK organisations include the desire to:

- 'loosen up'
- reduce the overwhelming emphasis on control that, as Makinson (2000) describes it, has defeated attempts to introduce greater diversity and creativity in reward management in the Civil Service
- attack the trappings of status and authority, irrespective of personal value or contribution, which many of our reward schemes still reinforce, from the company Jag in its reserved space to the grade-based allocation of share options.

Many standard features of the reward schemes in most large UK organisations today – job evaluation, multiple grade structures, differentiated benefits plans – originated when the bureaucratic organisation structure was the norm and the 'commander' model of business strategy in vogue.

Today it is a very different setting. Our organisations are delayered and devolved. They need speed to market and of response, with effective front-line service and wholesale innovation. They preach a gospel of empowerment, personal accountability and investing in their most important asset. Flexibility is the overriding reward aim, whether in terms of relating pay to the market and performance, to meet personal employee needs or to adapt over time. Interestingly, the Towers Perrin (1999b) European rewards study found a high level of satisfaction that the first two of these were being achieved by recent reforms, but a much less favourable verdict on the latter two goals.

That research demonstrated the changes in scheme designs that are being driven by the flexibility objective, including:

- ❷ the move towards simpler job evaluation schemes
- ❷ the introduction of fewer grades and broader pay bands, by half of participants in the last three years
- ❷ the use of job-family-based pay and development structures, by 20 per cent
- ❷ the just-described growth in flexible benefits programmes.

Yet as we saw in Chapter 3 in respect of the internal devolvement of reward management, one person's flexibility can be another person's loss of accountability and budgetary control, and a recipe for general confusion and disarray. As the mobile phone company with 4,000 staff and no organised pay systems found, an element of structure and control is desirable if managers want to spend time doing anything other than negotiating personal deals and arguing over pay issues raised by their staff.

The skill of the reward professional here – and in respect of the majority of other significant design considerations – is to select the appropriate balance of flexibility and control, structure and freedom, uniformity and variation, to suit the needs, character and goals of their organisation. This is well illustrated if we consider the market trend towards broadbanded pay structures, one of the most widespread and visible reforms designed in pursuit of the flexibility agenda.

Broadbanding

According to Carol Braddick (1992), 'Pay grades have straitjacketed many organisations: to escape, companies are adopting broadbanding, which is more compatible with the needs of a flexible working environment.' Greater job, career, market and performance pay flexibility were indeed the primary objectives for the 50 per cent of organisations that had delayered their grade structures in the previous three years in the Towers Perrin (1999b) research. As one participant told me, 'We wanted the emphasis to be on personal development and contribution, rather than on points-scoring to get a promotion.' The CIPD's latest research found a majority of companies now claiming to operate these flexible structures.

But both of these studies demonstrated a situation that is very different from the radical pay management approach recommended in some of the US literature, with the removal of job evaluation and the free movement of staff pay levels in three or four bands of 100 per cent to 200 per cent in width. Instead, we found that, 'broader-banding would be a more accurate characterisation of the movement', with:

- three-quarters of organisations continuing to evaluate jobs
- a median of three management and five to eight non-management grades
- median range widths of 30–50 per cent for non-management and 50–80 per cent for managers
- fewer than one in 10 organisations managing with ranges of over 80 per cent from minimum to maximum
- a majority of organisations operating some form of intermediate control points or zoning within their broader pay ranges.

So why the conservative approach? Is this another example of HR managers failing to take a lead in driving through what the business really needs, constrained by history, their lack of vision and the enormity of any redesign exercise?

Experience shows that this is not the case, but rather it represents a measured and realistic assessment of the plusses and minuses of pay restructuring and of the importance of pay management processes rather than simply scheme designs. A study carried out in a sample of organisations who had moved to broadbanding at least three years ago found that most felt that the intended benefits of an increased emphasis on contribution rather than status and the flexibility to reflect different market and functional needs were being realised. Interestingly, a number of them also spoke of the exercise raising the profile and perceived contribution to the business of the HR function.

But these structural changes had also placed tremendous pressures on other aspects of pay and HR management, and in many cases this had caused implementation and operating problems. Staff communications on pay issues, the quality of market data, the capabilities of line managers to appraise and adjust the pay of their staff were all found wanting, as the traditional promotion and status-seeking attitudes were confronted. As one compensation manager told me, 'We are seeking a transformation in mindset that has to be pursued over

many years. It doesn't just happen overnight after the grading structure is redesigned.'

We will consider the change management processes involved in
Chapter 7, but the key point to make here is that most organisations
recognise that they need to maintain an appropriate balance in their
reward management approach – see Figure 13. Budgets need to be
adhered to and staff need to clearly understand and trust how their
pay is managed, what their progression opportunities are and how
fairness and consistency will be achieved, alongside the goals of
greater flexibility. The strategic business needs of most organisations
are driving them to move this balance in the direction of flexibility,
but, as with a real set of scales, push it too far and too fast and everything falls off.

Take the example of a UK bank. The newly installed chief executive
spoke of the need for a 'meritocracy' and a 'gradeless society' to
achieve his business goals. The HR department rapidly delivered a
change from 15 grades with incremental progression to five broad
bands with fully flexible merit increases.

Yet it soon became evident that much of the HR and cultural infrastructure was insufficiently developed to support this pay structure.
Union opposition and industrial action led the bank to reconsider,
and after a much more thorough review of needs, further changes
were made to deliver a more balanced solution. Distinct job family
structures of between four and nine bands were introduced, supported by improved market data. More structure was put around the
performance review process, with guaranteed progression to band
mid-points for effective performers.

Flexible benefits schemes

The same evolution to greater flexibility but maintaining a
sensible balance in the reward management approach is evident
if we look at flexible benefits schemes. Sixty per cent of UK organisations may operate them, but the majority are not designed
to deliver the full 'spending-account'-type flexibility of US
companies. Even there, companies such as Motorola have experienced problems when employees have used their new freedoms to

Figure 13

THE REQUIRED BALANCE IN THE PAY MANAGEMENT APPROACH

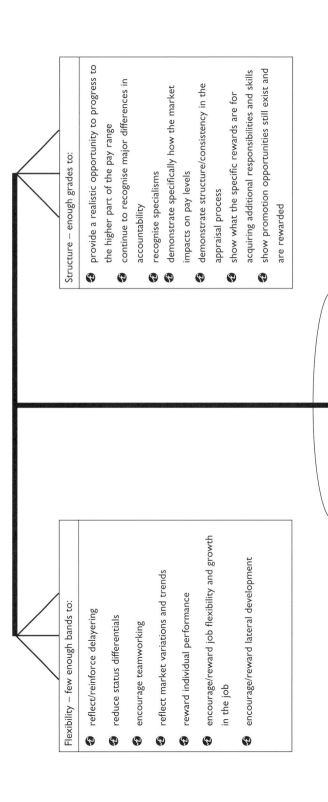

Flexibility – few enough bands to:

- reflect/reinforce delayering
- reduce status differentials
- encourage teamworking
- reflect market variations and trends
- reward individual performance
- encourage/reward job flexibility and growth in the job
- encourage/reward lateral development

Structure – enough grades to:

- provide a realistic opportunity to progress to the higher part of the pay range
- continue to recognise major differences in accountability
- recognise specialisms
- demonstrate specifically how the market impacts on pay levels
- demonstrate structure/consistency in the appraisal process
- show what the specific rewards are for acquiring additional responsibilities and skills
- show promotion opportunities still exist and are rewarded

make unwise investment decisions and destroy their pensions savings.

In the UK we are seeing a range of flexible schemes emerging relating to the organisation's ability to manage that flexibility and the diversity of employee needs and their ability to understand and benefit from it. Some companies offer choice only within particular benefits, such as a higher- or lower-value car. Moving along the scale, the cafeteria or menu approach is the design that seems at the moment to deliver the best balance of flexibility and structure for most companies. The choice from a menu with a restricted range of options on each benefit makes for easier administration and communication and helps avoid sudden major changes that can disrupt supplier relationships and put an employee's own future security at risk. Full choice across many reward items offers the maximum gains in terms of flexibility and employee added value, but requires high levels of employee diversity and understanding.

‘Balance and speed of change need to be tailor-made to your own organisation’

So, balancing the reward goals of flexibility and structure, and evolving at an appropriate rate in the direction of the former, are important components of the reward strategies in many organisations at the moment. But it is a balance and speed of change that need to be tailor-made to your own organisation. As Armstrong and Brown (2001) explain in respect of pay structuring, 'Broadbanding only has real meaning in respect of the context in which it operates ... the concept of "best fit" is thankfully replacing that of "best" practice.'

Key design choices: paying for internal equity versus paying for market worth

The weekly wages of Premier League footballers in England, which soared on average by over 30 per cent in the last 12 months, may be taken as a demonstration of either the complete triumph, or the ultimate failure, of a totally market-driven approach to rewards. Few clubs are now able to maintain any semblance of a pay structure. 'Farewell to internal equity' was how one personnel journal headlined the current trend. Professor Keith Bradley recently described how the labour markets in many sectors are coming to resemble professional sports, with key skill shortages, increasing rates of staff transfers and the disproportionate impact of a few 'stars' on organisational performance. In the USA, executives are apparently hiring agents to advertise their wares and negotiate new contracts.

Rates of market increase in pay levels undoubtedly are becoming more diverse and unpredictable in an environment of rapid change and staff shortages, with the median pay levels of website designers increasing by 46 per cent in one year and declining by 22 per cent the next. Even in Ireland, where a national wage agreement has been in force, two-thirds of companies admit breaking the annual pay award ceiling to retain staff in particular functions such as IT.

A majority of participants in the Towers Perrin (1999b) European research rated external market alignment as one of their top three reward objectives, so as to recruit and retain the talented staff needed to implement their business strategy. Ninety-seven per cent regarded external market surveys as being essential components of their reward strategies, and there has been a huge growth in the number of pay surveys in the UK, assisted by the introduction of online and interactive databases such as PayNet and Insite.

Correspondingly, the goal of internal equity has moved well down these companies' hierarchy of objectives in the last six years. Seventy-three per cent of European employers make separate arrangements for staff in areas of high market demand, with the use of market supplements now common in both public and private sectors and currently being widely extended in the National Health Service.

Over a fifth of organisations now operate job-family-based pay structures – that is, they have different, market-based pay ranges and sometimes totally separate pay structures for jobs of a similar size but in different functions or occupational groupings. Explaining the introduction of job families and removal of common job evaluation, one financial services company told its staff that 'the market pressures and needs so clearly evident for many years in IT are now apparent in many of our functions and specialisations.' Why should the pay of, say, treasury staff in a bank's headquarters bear any relationship to that of service assistants out in the branches?

An example of the market-related zones that now operate in the two of the five broad bands that an insurance company recently introduced are shown in Figure 14. The higher market rates for jobs in the claims function compared to those in the customer services area mean that the former have a higher pay range at each grade level.

Twenty-five per cent of organisations in the Towers Perrin (1999b) study now operate without any internal system of job evaluation. The obituary of these schemes has been written many times by pay

Figure 14

AN EXAMPLE OF MARKET ZONING AT AN INSURANCE COMPANY

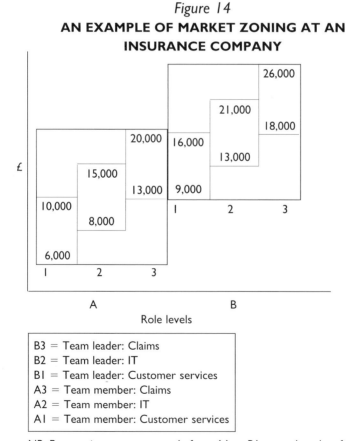

B3 = Team leader: Claims
B2 = Team leader: IT
B1 = Team leader: Customer services
A3 = Team member: Claims
A2 = Team member: IT
A1 = Team member: Customer services

NB: Progression most commonly from A1 to B1 etc rather than from A1 to A2.

commentators in recent years, who write them off as 'inflexible barriers to excellence', and 'paying for the wrong things' (Emerson 1991). Remove these rigid obstructions to pay flexibility in relation to the market and performance, and all apparently will be well with your reward strategy.

Yet is an exclusively market-driven approach really a problem-free, flexible route to strategic realisation? Is job evaluation really dying? Indeed, are these two objectives of internal equity and market competitiveness, with their respective design artillery of job evaluation and market surveys, really in conflict and mutually exclusive? My answer to all three questions, for the majority of organisations of all types, would be strongly in the negative.

As Nicky Demby pointed out at the 2000 IPD Compensation Forum conference in London, 'the proliferation in the quantity of market data has been matched by the decline in much of its quality'. Such concerns may partly explain why a majority of HR staff do not share market data with line managers or employees, even though it may underpin their pay decisions, and when such secrecy hardly seems a recipe for developing an understood and supported reward strategy.

There is no single market rate of pay out there for a given job, which you could set if only you had perfect information. There is a range of pay evident in the market and each organisation needs to decide where to position its job-holders within that range. This is dependent on a number of factors, including the market position you want and can afford to adopt, the relative size of the job, and the background and contribution of the individual.

Yet in a number of companies pursuing this route, the inflexibility of job evaluation points is replaced by the practice of paying virtually everyone at 100 per cent of their market rate, with no account taken of their personal performance. Another problem for some organisations adopting an aggressive market-focused employment deal is that with no other reward ties into the organisation, their stars are more likely to leave if someone in the market offers them more. Indeed, ultimately the logic of totally market-driven pay for free agents falls in on itself, for as in the Premier League, how can you ever establish a true market rate for a position, with such massive variations depending on the individual player concerned?

And job evaluation certainly is not dying out, with only 5 per cent of companies planning to remove their systems. Some of the reasons why companies retain their evaluation systems to underpin a common pay management framework include:

- the requirements to comply with equal value legislation
- the desire to retain the flexibility across an organisation to restructure and to provide broad career development opportunities
- the need to value unique and organisation-specific jobs
- the need for a solid starting point from which to vary pay in relation to the market and performance.

But job evaluation is changing, with a majority of the three-quarters of companies who retain such schemes having adapted them in the last three years. Common changes to make job evaluation systems more flexible, business-aligned and market-driven include:

- abandoning fixed pounds-for-points linkages in favour of placement into fewer bands with market-aligned ranges
- moving to simpler job classification approaches, which are the fastest growing variant now used by almost a third of companies
- removing traditional job input factors such as qualifications and emphasising measures of job accountability and impact.

The majority of organisations are pursuing both objectives, of external and internal 'fit', because both can contribute to improved staff retention and motivation, furthering the achievement of business goals. Montemayor (1999) highlights a raft of research showing that employee satisfaction with pay depends as much on a sense of fair and consistent administration as on the absolute level, and that in many companies internal relativities are still a vital determinant of perceived equity.

The two goals are not opposites nor contradictory, and we are seeing hybrid designs emerging as organisations pursue both ends. The same job family definitions in some sectors are being used both as the basis for internal pay structures and external pay benchmarking. In other organisations, the points weighting for particular internal evaluation factors now relate to their correlation with market data, while some use market value as a factor in itself.

<blockquote>

‹Job evaluation is playing a more supportive, defensive role in many situations›

</blockquote>

So, defining a policy on market definition and stance, monitoring and maintaining that position, and reflecting labour market variations are all important components of an effective reward strategy. But the increasing impact of the external market has not removed the requirement in many settings to maintain a flexible but robust foundation for equitable pay management across the organisation. Job evaluation is playing a more supportive, defensive but still important role in many situations.

Key design choices: paying for the job or paying for the person and their competence

Very similar arguments have been made by advocates of pay driven by personal competence, as a replacement for job evaluation, at the foundation of reward strategies in the new knowledge-based economy. Lawler (2000a), for example, sees market-, performance- and person-based pay as the three 'strategic thrusts' required in the new century. Job-based pay, he argues, made sense in bureaucratic organisations with a high division of labour:

> In a world in which individuals do not have traditional jobs and where people are able to add considerable value because of their high levels of skill, it is dangerous to pay them according to job rather than individual worth . . . it fails to encourage individuals to develop the right skills and knowledge.

The compensation director of Guinness described competency pay as the replacement for job evaluation, 'the way tomorrow's organisations will pay', while Pilkington Optronics moved to competency-related pay and performance management to create 'a more focused workforce that understands the pay system and can develop themselves in ways that provide the necessary competitive advantage'.

Others have advocated a competency pay route as an alternative to performance pay, seeing it as a more effective way of assessing the contribution of knowledge workers than relating pay increases to five SMART (Specific, Measurable, Achievable, Relevant, Timely) management-type objectives. 'Anything is better than performance pay', one HR director of a company introducing competency pay told me. Thirty-six per cent of US companies in an American Compensation Association (1996) study cited this switch from a performance pay to a competence approach as an important motivation.

These arguments are having a practical impact. Two-thirds of companies now include competencies in their performance management systems. In a Towers Perrin (1997) European study, 13 per cent of organisations were linking competence and pay, and an amazing 70 per cent were planning to reinforce the link between competence and reward. In the ACA study, 14 per cent of the sample had competency pay already operating, with a similar proportion of schemes under development. Users in the UK include well-known companies across all sectors of the economy: Glaxo Wellcome and ICL; NatWest Bank and the Woolwich; Scottish & Newcastle and Volkswagen.

Paying knowledge workers according to the development of their personal skills and competence is not a new phenomenon. Companies such as BP, BT and ICI have operated technical ladders for their research staff, generally with broader bands and person-rather than job-based 'promotions', for many years. And the increasing professionalisation of the workforce and wider need for creativity and innovation outside the research and development lab has undoubtedly encouraged its application. In certain extreme cases we have seen companies drop job-based pay altogether and relate pay wholly to the growth of personal competence, as in a technology division of SmithKline Beecham, and at solicitors Mills and Reeve. Both instead use a personal career life cycle model to structure pay.

Yet these extreme examples are unusual and typically only apply to a relatively small proportion of the total staff in the organisation. The SmithKline Beecham example covered 400 employees in a division with serious question marks over its future and did not encompass the administrative staff.

Here again, wholly personal competency-based pay is in reality far from being the visionary, problem-free solution to our strategic reward issues in the new millennium. In the right settings it has contributed to improved productivity and quality and is generally very popular with staff. But Lawler (1996) himself points out the difficulties in defining and measuring competencies in practice, and it was the complexity of doing this that led the AA to abandon its scheme. ICL and Bass both moved back from a totally competency-based system of pay increases, in the latter case because it encouraged a lack of focus on results. Other organisations have experienced pay cost escalation, primarily because they ignored the true meaning of competence, which is the application of required skills and behaviours, not just their acquisition. Sparrow (1996) opposes the linkage as conflicting with the development aims of competencies and sees the 'headlong rush' into competency pay as being driven by fads and fashion rather than strategic business need.

Sparrow's concerns are exaggerated, because the rate of growth is actually relatively slow, with 18 per cent of European organisations linking pay with skills and competence by 1999 according to the Towers Perrin (1999b) study. The majority of organisations with competency pay are well aware of the dangers, recognise the need for a well-established competency framework and its use for other HR purposes prior to making the link to pay, and in our survey they were taking an average of one to two years to implement it. Yet it is the way in which competency pay is actually being implemented and operated that is most revealing. Here again, the importance of growth in personal competence as an influence on reward decisions is increasing, but this is merely shifting the balance of factors affecting reward, not replacing the other considerations such as job size and internal relativities. It is competency-related, not competency-based, pay.

Hybrid approaches

In practice, companies are incorporating competencies into their existing job evaluation and performance-related pay systems and creating hybrid approaches to best fit their strategic and structural needs, avoiding the risks of radical upheavals in reward systems and processes. The predominant method of linking competencies and pay in the UK is actually through job evaluation, using competencies either wholly (as at ICL), or in conjunction with traditional accountability factors, as at Thomas Cook and Triplex, to place jobs in grades.

Similarly in respect of pay progression, most companies are like Bass, paying for a combination of what results are achieved, as well as the competence displayed, and how they were achieved. At Coutts, base pay increases depend on growth in required competencies, and results are rewarded with an individual or team bonus. More commonly, base pay increases relate to both criteria. In a water company, for example, the pay of a newly recruited technician increases in steps up to his or her range mid-point, in line with the acquisition of skills modules. But progression any higher in the range is dependent on personal performance.

In an electricity company, competencies have been grafted onto its pay-for-performance system. Half of the overall performance rating that individuals receive is based on their personal objectives (eg achieve financial targets) and half on the achievement of agreed competency targets (eg teamworking). Emphasising the links, at Land Registry, each personal competency growth goal has to relate to a strategic business goal, such as improving service, to ensure that personal development really does support the business direction.

❛Many organisations find their traditional reward systems rigid and inflexible❜

A simple framework illustrates the alternatives for companies – see Table 7. Many organisations, strategically and structurally, have moved out of the left-hand columns of a narrow cost and job focus, and hence find their traditional reward systems rigid and inflexible.

But while employers want us to develop our skills, grow our jobs, think out of the box, and do what the business needs rather than stick rigidly to our job description, in most cases we do still have a defined area of responsibility and have to uphold certain disciplines – adhere to budgets, carry out quality control procedures and so on. Using Plachy's (1998) definition, we are carrying out flexible roles, which can be varied to suit our personal competence, but not operating in a totally unstructured environment where we do personally what best suits us. And interestingly, as we have seen, small rapidly growing organisations in the right-hand column on that chart

Table 7

VARIATIONS IN REWARD APPROACHES, FROM JOB- THROUGH TO PERSON-BASED

	Job	Role	Person
Organisation features	❷ High division of labour ❷ High specialisation ❷ Tight, narrow, detailed job definitions ❷ Large number of distinct jobs	❷ Fewer, broader role profiles ❷ Reduced hierarchy ❷ Roles flex as individual develops ❷ Multi- and up-skilling	❷ Work tailored to suit individual capabilities ❷ Fluid network of personal responsibilities ❷ Project working
Business strategy	❷ Cost leadership ❷ Economies of scale ❷ Synergies	❷ Mixture, eg think global, act local approach	❷ Quality/service differentiation ❷ High margins
HR approach	❷ Instrumentalist or paternal deal	❷ Commitment-based deal	❷ Competence/leased-talent deal
Development approach	❷ Technical and functional/disciplines, short-term focus	❷ Technical and behavioural ❷ Short-term and career development	❷ Life skills, total work experience, employability
Reward approach	❷ Points-factor job evaluation: emphasis on tasks and inputs ❷ Many grades, narrow bands ❷ Promotion as significant reward ❷ General pay reviews, possibly with increments ❷ Strong central/HR control of pay practices and budgets	❷ Simpler evaluation, eg slotting roles ❷ Fewer grades, broader ranges ❷ Increases for movement into bigger role ❷ Pay reviews based on contribution in the role, ie competence and results ❷ Looser reward management by line, with central/HR guidelines	❷ Market-driven pay, no/little internal evaluation, competency-based ❷ Few broad ranges ❷ Personal development/growth-based pay increases ❷ Individual pay reviews based on personal competence ❷ Line-manager-driven
Performance appraisal	❷ Top down ❷ Past results and rating focus	❷ Two-way ❷ Past and future, results and competence, pay and development focus	❷ Informal ❷ 360-degree ❷ Development focus

generally find that at a certain size, a wholly personal approach to pay becomes very tough to manage.

So many organisations are now evolving to a balanced, hybrid de-based approach to reward and organisation structuring in the middle column, with:

- fewer, broader role profiles
- simpler evaluation schemes
- broader pay bands
- looser performance management schemes, with an equal emphasis on the reward and development aspects
- pay progression based on personal contribution – that is, a combination of competence displayed and results achieved
- flexible working hours and arrangements
- personal choice from a menu of benefits.

The balance of job- and person-based reward systems, of course, varies between organisations, and there is still enormous design choice and challenge within this broad approach. But hopefully we have demonstrated both the need for an integrating logic of approach and the need to get underneath simplistic, generalised and extreme recommendations to develop schemes that really do fit with what your organisation needs, and what can be delivered in practice.

Key design choices: paying for performance – not whether to but how to

Nobody today can operate an effective reward strategy that does not embody a clear position and approach to performance pay. The competitive pressures on our organisations and the necessity of using our pay budgets more effectively, as well as the controversial nature of the topic highlighted by the Barclays Bank and teachers' pay disputes, all make such a position essential. But what position should it be?

Is it an essential tool to reinforce improved performance in the global economy, necessary, as the CBI's director general explained, 'to control unit labour costs, keep economic growth on track and secure jobs', and, as the Government continues to insist, in the public sector? The managing director of Yorkshire Water Services described the introduction of merit pay to replace service increments 'not as a threat but as a necessity'. The Towers Perrin (1999b) European study did find a correlation between the use of performance pay schemes and corporate performance, and a number of other research studies have found such correlations (Wallace Bell (1989), for example, in respect of profit-sharing schemes).

Or is performance pay by nature, as Kohn (1993) asserts, demotivational in its impact and impossible to manage in practice, a dying remnant of the individualistic 'greed is good' 1980s, out of place in our team- and knowledge-based, high-trust and flexible organisations of today? According to an OECD study of performance pay in the public sector, 'managers said schemes did not work, were difficult to understand, and did not deliver a clear pay–performance link'.

Types of scheme

Here, perhaps most of all, the extreme views tend to get the headlines and these bear little relation to what is going on in the majority of UK organisations. Throughout Europe, and increasingly in Asia, the incidence of schemes to relate pay in some way to performance continues to grow. The Towers Perrin (1999b) European study demonstrates that as far as base pay is concerned, wholly merit-based increases now predominate for management and professional staff, and only a quarter of participating organisations still use across-the-board general increases for non-management staff. Almost three-quarters of the 44 per cent making changes to their pay review practices in the past three years had extended merit pay, and only 2 per cent removed it. The UK has the highest incidence in Europe.

More radically, perhaps, we are also witnessing a rapid growth in the incidence of bonus schemes and variable pay, as companies attempt to obtain more variability in their total pay costs and endeavour to create a stronger 'line of sight' between what employees do and are rewarded for, and the strategic goals and performance of the organisation. The level of variable pay in the total cash package for the average European employee has increased by between 3 per cent and 5 per cent in the last three years – see Table 8. A similar growth is anticipated in the next three years, so that a typical employee can expect to have a bonus opportunity of over 10 per cent of base pay.

Table 8
THE INCREASING LEVELS OF VARIABLE
PAY IN EUROPE

	Mix of base pay and variable pay		
Staff category	*1996*	*1999*	*Forecast 2002*
Senior executives	80 : 20	75 : 25	69 : 31
Management/professional staff	88 : 12	84 : 16	79 : 21
Non-management staff	96 : 4	93 : 7	89 : 11

Source: Towers Perrin

Over 90 per cent of organisations already operate bonus schemes, with the majority having three or more. Seventy-two per cent of these organisations are planning to introduce new bonus schemes, with higher payment opportunities and extended membership in approximately a third of them. In the public sector, five of the main UK government departments have committed to introducing bonus schemes with at least a 5 per cent maximum for all staff, with HM Customs and Excise leading the way.

It is the diversity of these newer performance-related base pay and bonus schemes that is their most evident feature. Companies are no longer, as Hunt (1998) describes, trying to force fit every staff group and performance pay issue into a single, individual merit pay scheme model. This was a major failing of many of those who, as Brown and Hudson (1997) describe, jumped 'lemming-like' on to the performance pay bandwagon in the late 1980s and early 1990s.

Multiple scheme designs and approaches are being introduced to suit different needs and audiences. Brown and Armstrong (1999) detail this plethora of new and amended schemes, combining considerations of results and competence; profits, service and quality; company, unit, team and individual contribution. Two-thirds of companies now operate individual bonus plans, 61 per cent merit pay schemes, 46 per cent profit-sharing, 28 per cent project bonuses, 23 per cent team rewards and 11 per cent gainsharing.

Thus a computer company, which has expanded its range of products and services and now has a number of reasonably independent divisions, recently dismantled the uniform sales commission scheme it had operated for many years. Some divisions complained that it was discouraging a focus on long-term relationship-building and that it was too high. Others said that it did not reward their best performers highly enough.

So in response, the company introduced a number of different schemes. Salespeople selling high-volume products in fast-growth markets retain a relatively low base pay, with an uncapped individual commission scheme. But sales staff selling complex systems and solutions, which may take many months to organise and negotiate, are on a higher base pay, with competency-based increases, and a capped, objective-based bonus plan. A clear case of best fit replacing typical market and assumed 'best' practice.

‘Classifications between different types of reward scheme are being torn down’

Indeed, as companies craft design solutions to their own particular needs, the classifications between different types of reward scheme, and even between base pay and bonus approaches, are being torn down. Forty-one per cent of companies have introduced combination or tiered incentive plans that attempt both to provide local incentive and reward broader co-operation. Thus a French retailer now modifies its overall profit-sharing payments according to the performance of each store against four key strategic targets: sales growth, costs, quality and service levels. In a UK power group, staff may obtain a bonus funded according to the financial performance of their location, modified by the performance of their immediate work team, and adjusted to reflect their individual contribution.

In a UK retailer, money is being diverted from future base pay increases to help to fund a store-based gainsharing scheme, which will offer a maximum bonus opportunity of up to 15 per cent in three years' time. And in a major bank, all employees get a similar percentage pay increase if they have performed well, but the higher up their pay range and against the market they are, the smaller the proportion of this increase that is consolidated in base pay, and the larger the proportion that is paid out as a lump sum bonus.

The prize

Are these new types of performance pay working and driving the achievement of strategic business goals? The overly simplistic nature of the traditional question 'Does performance pay work?' partly explains the failure of many early schemes. They were simply borrowed from elsewhere on the assumption that they could be installed and run indefinitely thereafter, like a piece of machinery, and without any thought given to supporting processes such as objective- and target-setting.

The research is certainly much more mixed than the negative headlines on PRP might lead one to believe. While there have been a number of failures, there are enough studies and cases now to convince all but the most ardent critics that performance pay schemes are an option that most organisations need to consider, and that they are successful in achieving their goals in the appropriate conditions. For example:

- Katzell (1993) found a positive correlation between the motivation of knowledge workers and the use of individual performance pay.
- Bullock and Lawler (1984) found that three-quarters of a sample of 33 companies with gainsharing plans reported productivity gains, ranging from 4 per cent to 25 per cent per annum.
- An ACA (1997) study of team rewards found an average return to the business of twice the amount paid out to employees in bonuses.
- Bonus schemes were the highest-rated reward practice in terms of effectiveness in the Towers Perrin (1999b) European research, and their use correlated positively with high levels of total shareholder return.
- At Scottish Nuclear Electric, the use of a gainsharing plan co-incided with a 46 per cent improvement in productivity over two years, while at Sun Life Assurance, team bonuses supported a reduction in controllable costs of 30 per cent, and a 45 per cent improvement in service levels.

The approach

But if you cannot just implement an off-the-shelf scheme, how then do you determine the type of performance pay that is required in your own organisation? Follow the reward strategy pathway outlined in this book and ask yourself a series of questions:

- What performance goals is the organisation trying to achieve, and how and how well do these cascade down the organisation?
- What capabilities do we need to have and how do we organise ourselves to achieve these goals? Will profit-sharing, for example, reinforce our integrated business model and structure or, in a devolved setting, be seen as an irrelevant give-away?
- How do staff contribute to these goals and what is our culture and HR strategy to further their achievement? What behaviours and achievements do we need to reinforce, and how prominent is, and should be, the role of rewards in this reinforcement? How and how well do we develop, grow and manage the contribution of staff?
- What, therefore, should our reward objectives be and to what extent do our current reward schemes reinforce their achievement? What sorts of performance pay schemes could better contribute to the achievement of these goals in the various parts of our organisation? What would be the strengths and the risks of introducing them? What support processes and resources would be required to make them work effectively?
- And only then, with the answers to all of the above questions can you answer: What do the detailed scheme designs need to be? What levels in the organisation should they be operated at? What measures should be employed? What payment opportunities and levels available, over what timescale, with what control and operating arrangements? And so on.

In following this process with performance pay, three other pieces of advice will help maintain a strategic direction and impact in what in many cases will involve a range of different schemes and designs. First, be crystal clear about your performance pay scheme objectives. Some early individual performance pay schemes damaged organisational effectiveness precisely because they achieved their goal of reinforcing individual performance too well. The trouble was that they led people to ignore important aspects of performance not measured in their pay plan, such as helping colleagues to achieve their goals.

No scheme is perfect and therefore each alternative needs to be analysed closely against your objectives, and particularly in respect of bonus schemes, the relative emphasis on collective reward and individual incentive. An analysis was carried out with the directors of a manufacturing company to determine the suitability of the following reward schemes:

- ❷ profit-sharing
- ❷ gainsharing
- ❷ small team bonus
- ❷ individual performance bonus
- ❷ individual base pay movement.

In a very competitive product market, they felt they needed to get a better return on their pay budget, but were not sure which scheme offered the best route for them. They wanted on the one hand to drive individual performance improvement, supporting the introduction of individual merit pay and bonuses. But on the other hand they were also doing a lot of work on culture change and building effective teams, and this pointed towards a collective approach.

In the end they introduced a combination of schemes to achieve these various goals: individual merit pay for managers; team gainsharing in the plants; and a profit share for support staff. Here again, while schemes now display great diversity in design, all but 2 per cent of those companies with team reward schemes also operate individual performance pay. The two are being introduced to complement each other and achieve different goals, not to conflict and with one replacing the other.

Second, make sure that you consider the full range of alternative designs in order to achieve your goals. Table 9 gives a brief categorisation of all of the different reward methods that can be used to reinforce the achievement of strategic goals, and even this ignores the numerous types of multi-level and hybrid schemes that are emerging.

Third, do not forget the processes. Whatever the reward plan design, as we consider in more detail in Chapters 6 and 7, the supporting processes – of performance management, communications, involvement and so on – generally explain a large part of the success of performance pay schemes.

Table 9

A CATEGORISATION OF DIFFERENT TYPES OF PERFORMANCE-RELATED REWARD

Reward method	Organisation level		
	Individual	*Team*	*Organisation*
Base pay adjustment	● Merit pay ● Pay at risk	● Team adjustment to base pay funding	● Varying pay budget according to organisation performance
Variable pay and bonuses	● Executive bonus ● Individual bonus ● Piecework ● Sales commission	● Team bonuses ● Project bonuses ● Gain-sharing ● Location bonus	● Profit-sharing ● Gainsharing
Other forms of reward	● Individual non-cash recognition, eg holidays ● Learning opportunities ● Executive share options	● Team non-cash recognition	● Corporate events ● All-employee share options

The design process

The information and examples we have looked at in this chapter present a fairly authoritative demonstration that the days of following the herd, universal 'best' practice and standard off-the-consultant's-shelf solutions are well and truly over in UK reward management. This may make our lives initially more difficult, in diagnosing our situation and designing schemes tailored to address our own needs, but it is in itself a demonstration that reward management has genuinely become more strategic and is having a greater impact on the achievement of business goals.

'Effective reward management is about making this strategic impact'

Effective reward management is not therefore just about sound and robust scheme design and efficient scheme administration and operation, but about making this strategic impact. Reward strategy is far from being all about grand business plans, major strategic changes and boardroom meetings. While we have seen a wide diversity of reward issues and schemes illustrated in this chapter, we can discern a fairly consistent, broad direction and pattern in the huge amount of design and redesign work that is currently under way.

Yes, occasionally in situations of business crisis or major structural change, such as a merger, we are seeing radical changes in reward scheme design introduced in relatively short time frames. In one retailer, as part of the plan to avoid the receivers, base pay levels were reduced by around 25 per cent and bonus schemes introduced in a matter of weeks.

Yet we have seen that far more typical of the reward change and redesign experience of many organisations has been a process of incremental 'tinkering' and improvement:

● improving the design of traditional and tested reward schemes, such as job evaluation and recognition schemes, to focus more directly on reinforcing what will make the business a success

● evolving tailored hybrid schemes, often with distinct origins in different sectors and geographies, but now being brought together to meet the unique challenges our organisations face today; tiered incentive plans, role evaluation using competencies, merit pay schemes rewarding the what and the how of performance, broader pay bands, bonus schemes combining team and individual performance considerations – these are all examples of this melding process at work, underneath the extremist views and rhetoric that reward schemes generally seem to attract

● making a series of changes over a number of years rather than risking one-hit 'big bang' changes; in many organisations, for example, broadbanding has been introduced over a number of years, with the BBC moving progressively from over 40 grades, to 20 and then to 12; similarly, many multi-tiered incentives began as company profit shares and were then extended down, or have emerged 'bottom up' through a series of local initiatives and trials, the positive outcomes of which have been taken up and more systematically extended throughout the organisation; this phased process of evolution allows the organisation to build its capability to manage the new approach, test new schemes, and build staff understanding and support, and we shall consider it in more detail in the next two chapters; it also encourages the organisation to review and adapt its schemes as needs change in the future, with Tim Wilson of Lloyds TSB a proponent of the concept of short, overlapping reward product life cycles, rather than allowing policies to disintegrate in crisis before they are replaced.

Reward management design work today is therefore a much more challenging, varied and difficult process than it has been in the past. But thereby it has the potential to be considerably more satisfying and fulfilling, with our reward schemes making a far more powerful contribution to the performance and success of our employers, and the motivation and satisfaction of our people.

Case study

A NEW AND COMPREHENSIVE REWARD STRATEGY DESIGN IN A UK BANK

Strategic change

The strategic decision to abandon its status as a mutual building society and convert into a quoted plc intensified the process already under way in this organisation to review all aspects of its structure and operation, so as to succeed in the fiercely competitive retail financial services market. For example, a wholesale restructuring of the branch network was set under way, centralising back-office operations in regional centres, devolving more authority to operations managers, reducing the number of layers in the organisation, and increasing the numbers and skills of customer service staff.

The new corporate business strategy to prepare for and operate as a quoted bank focused on expanding non-housing income while continuing to increase share of the mortgage market, through improved distribution and the use of new technology, enabling the company to simultaneously reduce costs, improve service and introduce new products.

HR and reward audit

The HR function undertook a wholesale review of its practices and processes as a result of these business and structural changes, in order to improve the value it added to the business and to produce a more co-ordinated approach. The bank was by no means a laggard in terms of its pay and reward approaches, having moved all staff into a harmonised pay structure of 12 grades in 1990, and related pay increases to performance against agreed personal objectives and required competencies since then.

However, this in-depth review highlighted a series of issues with the existing pay and rewards practices, and a mismatch between the requirements and demands placed on staff by the business strategy and what they were actually being rewarded for. In particular:

- the merit pay system was seen as producing too little differentiation for the considerable efforts involved, while the very complex and detailed appraisal system was generally regarded as a once-a-year points-scoring exercise
- the general staff bonus scheme, paying out a common amount to all staff, was seen as providing no incentive and as uncompetitive in some functions
- the grade structure, with highly differentiated, fixed, grade-related benefits, was felt to reinforce a traditional status-based organisation and offer no element of personal choice.

The new reward strategy

A new and evolving reward approach was therefore implemented as part of a much broader re-engineering of the HR function, which involved giving businesses much greater freedom and accountability for their own HR policies, including rewards.

Key principles of the new approach reflected many of the themes raised in this chapter and included:

- increasing the flexibility to relate rewards to personal achievement and development, and to specific market value, and to reflect varying business needs, individual motivations and patterns of employment
- building and rewarding staff commitment
- continuing to operate equitable reward practices, in line with good practice outside
- giving line managers greater freedom and support to operate reward practices in the way that best suits their business.

The intended shift in policy direction is illustrated below:

- *from* job/task focus *to* broader roles and personal contribution
- *from* internal evaluation/points focus *to* greater external market focus
- *from* 'How can I get promoted?' *to* 'How can I grow, develop and contribute more?'
- *from* rigid, uniform rewards approach *to* more choice and flexibility, within a common framework
- *from* HR function controls/administers pay reviews *to* line managers flexibly and actively manage reward in support of business goals.

The reward changes introduced as a result of the new strategy have included:

- briefer and more flexible role profiles for all staff; in the branch network, for example, there are now just eight roles, ruling out the need to continue with detailed points-factor job evaluation
- moving all staff into a flatter pay structure of six broad bands, with market-related pay ranges varying for the different functional families
- a simplified classification system for placing jobs in bands
- a simpler and more devolved performance management process, abandoning detailed points ratings and emphasising the two-way communication between managers and staff
- pay increases influenced by a briefer and more business-

focused competency framework, using a flexible pay increase matrix in each business

- the introduction of executive and all-employee share schemes – the Sharesave scheme reinforces the importance of shareholder returns and is designed to act as a common 'glue' to reinforce co-operation and retention across the organisation
- the removal of many status- and grade-based differentiations, for example in holidays and car parking, and work is currently under way to introduce a cafeteria benefits scheme
- most radically, a range of new bonus schemes – all branch staff now have the opportunity to earn an annual bonus of up to 25 per cent of base pay, using a common framework of corporate performance criteria, but with individual measures and payments determined in each business; in addition, specific market and performance-related bonus schemes have been established in different businesses and functions, such as treasury.

The base pay aspects of the changes were introduced by 40 line managers who had helped HR staff with their design, emphasising their business-driven nature and illustrating the importance of the design and operating processes. They also led the intensive communications programme that the bank undertook, which involved the bank's trade union at all key stages.

The impact
The reward changes at this bank have been designed to provide a powerful cultural message in terms of the importance of personal and team contribution and to facilitate greater flexibility in people's work, so as to maximise and reward their development and contribution. The new systems are simpler to understand, and more efficient to operate, providing a common framework for schemes that are tailored to suit the needs of the different parts of a more diversified organisation.

The bank has deliberately eschewed grand strategic plans and extravagant technical designs or terminology, such as competency-based pay. As the head of HR puts it, 'We have progressed and learned as we go, step by step.' Only recently has a formal people strategy document been drafted. This, he believes, has allowed the changes to 'develop in line with the grain of the business' and really address local needs and issues. Their success, he concludes, is down to local manager, staff and HR function support.

The reward agenda continues to move on, with flexible benefits on the way and greater flexibility in terms and conditions under negotiation, to deliver improved service and efficiency levels. The change process has not been without its hiccups and problems. Staff concerns at the lack of pensionability of bonus have led to the introduction of a pensionable bonus waiver, so people can use part of their bonus to boost their pension contributions in a tax-effective way. And the bank constantly seeks to improve the quality of its reward communications and has targeted line manager training on this.

Nonetheless, the bank's reward approach has genuinely become more strategic: focusing on the real business and organisational drivers; re-engineering the HR and compensation function to support the new organisation structure; providing links between pay and performance through a variety of tailored vehicles; addressing a whole variety of cultural and developmental issues; and supporting the operating and performance management processes at the sharp end, where the reward strategy becomes a reality for staff.

A recent opinion survey found the bank's staff to have very high relative scores in terms of commitment to serving their customers and recognising the need for continuous change, as well as high levels of understanding and acceptance of their new rewards package – a powerful and mutually reinforcing combination. Despite the negative predictions in the financial press at the time of the bank's flotation, they continue to pursue a successful and independent, customer-oriented business strategy in the UK market.

Chapter summary

● Reward scheme designs have to be guided by a clear, integrated and prioritised set of objectives if they are to genuinely add value to a business and provide consistent messages to employees about what is rewarded and recognised in the organisation. These objectives act as the parameters against which existing schemes can be assessed and new or modified schemes introduced.

● Without clear reward strategy and individual scheme objectives, the temptation is simply to follow external fads and fashions in reward design work and lose the essential requirement of tailoring policies and practices to suit your own business goals, circumstances and culture.

● A total rewards framework is also an important means of strategically integrating and relating the range of reward schemes in an organisation. Developing and integrating a 'bundle' of rewards programmes that apply across all four quadrants of a total rewards approach – pay, benefits, environment and development – helps to maximise the motivational impact of your reward strategy.

● Current trends in reward policy goals in UK organisations include moves towards more flexible person- and competency-based rewards, a stronger emphasis on the external market as a determinant of reward levels, greater pay variability and more attention to rewarding contribution.

● In responding to these trends, extreme and radical changes are often described by commentators as being necessary and occurring. In reality, organisations are generally shifting the balance in their scheme goals and designs, rather than replacing one objective with another, and evolving a wide variety of tailored and often hybrid scheme designs so as to achieve multiple reward objectives.

● Thus the balance in scheme designs is moving from highly structured and controlled arrangements to more flexible broad bands and benefits schemes, providing greater scope to recognise individual differences. Yet an element of structure, through broader bands and a menu of benefits choices, is generally retained, to ensure an underlying goal of fairness and integrity and to simplify the communication and operation of schemes.

● The external market is becoming more influential as a determinant of reward levels, as evidenced by the growth in job-family-related pay ranges. It is important therefore to include a policy on market pay in your reward strategy. But internal equity and relativities remain important factors in most organisations, influencing staff motivation and the patterns of career development. Thus we are seeing hybrid schemes being used, such as job evaluation, which include market-related factors.

● Similarly in respect of rewarding personal competence, organisations are introducing competencies into job evaluation and performance pay schemes, rather than replacing them. This ensures that the 'how' as well as the 'what' of someone's personal contribution to the organisation is recognised, but avoids the risks of a wholly competency-driven approach, such as a lack of attention to results. It is largely competency-related rather than competency-based pay.

● Competitive pressures make some form of performance-related pay and reward a necessity in most organisations, and the majority now relate base pay increases to performance and operate variable bonus schemes. But the traditional focus on individual merit pay as the sole means to achieve this goal has been replaced with a much wider variety of scheme designs, evident both within and between organisations. Combined base pay and bonus approaches and multi-tiered bonus schemes demonstrate the new emphasis on business fit and creativity in scheme design.

● To develop the most appropriate performance-related rewards in your organisation you need to ask: What performance goals is the organisation seeking? How do employees contribute to those goals? What reward schemes can best reinforce that contribution? You need to specify clear objectives for each scheme, consider the full range of design alternatives and ensure appropriate supporting processes are in place.

● In all of these areas we are seeing a process of incremental and evolutionary change in reward practices now occurring.

Chapter 6

Reward strategy as process – alignment with employment needs

Chapter objectives

- demonstrate why the process aspects of reward strategies and changes are so critical to making them an effective and operating reality
- show that the alignment of reward strategies with employee needs is at least as important as that with business requirements
- describe how the concept of the psychological contract can be used in practice by your organisation to help frame an effective, two-way reward and employment strategy.

The importance of two-way reward strategies

Winnie the Pooh's annoyed response to Rabbit's clever observations on his predicament in getting stuck in the entrance to his burrow was 'It's not the "what" I am having trouble with, it's the "how".' It is a comment I have heard over the years from many line managers, struggling to implement and operate the wonderful new reward schemes that their HR department has, often with very little notice, foisted onto them and their employees. Michael Armstrong's observation that many so-called reward strategies amount to no more than 'composing a list of policy goals and schemes, and then forgetting how they work' may be somewhat cruel, but has more than a grain of truth in it. As the HR director of The Prince's Trust put it to him, 'It's relatively easy to design the (pay) system; it's getting it to work that matters.'

Of course, the critics of planned business strategies have always highlighted the implementation problems. As *The Times* observed after the managing director of Altavista UK resigned – having failed

to deliver the promised free Internet access to 250,000 subscribers –
'The only problem was that while Mr Mitchell knew what was
required, he was not so clear about how to provide it.' But there
cannot be a better example of the importance of abandoning what
Ghoshal and Bartlett (1999) label as our corporate obsession with the
'what' of strategy, structure and systems in favour of a new focus on
the 'how' of purpose, people and processes, than HR and reward
management.

‘ People and process have been at best relegated and at worst ignored ’

But surely that is what HR management is all about, right – people?
Ironically, at least in reward management, the traditional comfort of
compensation and benefits professionals in design detail and their
historical reticence on pay issues, combined with the new and overwhelming emphasis on business-driven HR and reward strategies,
has meant that considerations of people and process have been at best
relegated and at worst ignored. At a recent IBC conference on reward
strategy, the talks and case studies were all about strategic direction,
business alignment, value creation and goal reinforcement, without
a single mention of the word *motivation*. And the subject of
implementation was only raised briefly, in the last session.

As well as being an issue of poor and misaligned processes, which we
consider in more detail in the next chapter, this is fundamentally a
matter of mindset and the 'top-down' model of reward strategy that
has been predominantly adopted. I witnessed the effects of this
emphasis in contemporary reward strategies while doing some work
on attitudes and culture in a manufacturing plant of a European car
company. Two years before, they had introduced a new bonus plan
with seven performance targets, each derived from one of the strategic
business goals of the company after an exhaustive analysis by management consultants. The directors were delighted at the degree of
strategic business alignment. Yet they had missed out that vital
second step in the reward strategy pathway (see Chapter 2) – identifying the required employee capabilities and contribution to business
success – and failed to consider the whole right-hand perspective, of

employees, attitudes and culture, in the Towers Perrin reward strategy model. As a result, we found that two-thirds of employees felt unable to influence the measures in the plan and a majority would have preferred to return to their previous pay arrangements.

According to Professor Lynda Grattan (1997), therefore, 'the challenge we face in HR is not one of content – the "what" – but rather the process – the "how".' But just why are these processes so important, and why is the re-orientation required in the concept of what a reward strategy is? Contemporary management theory emphasises the benefits of an empowered and high-involvement management approach, but what is the return on adopting this more people- and process-oriented style, particularly in respect of reward management? This chapter focuses on addressing these questions and setting out an alternative, more balanced and workable concept. In the next chapter we then look at how this can be delivered in practice.

There are three sets of reasons for asserting the significance of these reward processes:

- the difficulties in implementing contemporary reward strategies
- the business returns that can be achieved
- the increasing importance of human capital.

Implementation issues

First, as we saw in Chapter 1, the majority of organisations now have a defined reward strategy but are experiencing difficulties in implementing it and making it an operating reality. Lack of employee understanding and support, poor performance management, inadequate line management skills and training, weak supporting processes – these were what the participants in the Towers Perrin (1999b) European study told us were frustrating the practical implementation of their strategic reward goals, and our equivalent study in North America paints exactly the same picture. While better reinforcing the achievement of business goals and performance, and more successfully recruiting and retaining staff, reward policies and changes as a whole across Europe were rated as least effective in the areas of increasing employee understanding of reward, improving the ability of line managers to use rewards as a business tool and flexing in response to organisational change. The assessments of their impact in terms of employee motivation were also decidedly mixed.

Exactly the same pattern emerges from the study of virtually any individual reward practice. Kessler and Purcell (1992), for example, found that problems with performance pay schemes in the companies they studied related to 'the lack of support systems, the lack of management training, and the highly subjective nature of assessments'.

In our time- and resource-constrained organisations, the temptation is to respond to these process issues quickly and usually ineffectually, blaming employees and line managers for the problems: communicate the same message but louder, commission a new brochure, design systems that minimise the reliance on line managers, return to a uniform scheme design with central control. Yet the era in which the HR manager could claim to have designed an excellent appraisal system, but that line managers had fouled up its implementation, are thankfully well and truly over, even if the difficulties with performance management are not. Hopefully you will gain ideas and examples of more positive responses to such difficulties in the next chapter.

Correspondingly, there is a whole raft of research studies demonstrating that the success of reward schemes correlates more strongly with these process factors than any design or environmental variable. Table 10 provides some examples. Take the study by Angela Bowey (1983). She was actually trying to find out which type of performance pay scheme was the most successful to operate. What she in fact found was that any type of scheme stood a similar chance of success or failure. What actually differentiated the most successful schemes was the attention paid to related processes when they were being developed and operated, most notably employee communications and involvement.

Whether employees and line managers were involved in the design process, whether employees supported and trusted the plan, and the amount of effort put into related communications and training were the things that really mattered. De Matteo (1997) similarly found that the success of team reward schemes was most strongly correlated with the levels of communication and staff understanding.

Table 10

SUCCESSFUL PAY CHANGES CORRELATE STRONGLY WITH INVOLVEMENT AND COMMUNICATIONS

Study	Factors correlating with success of incentives	Factors where no correlation found
Bullock and Tubbs (1990) n = 330	❷ Formal plan involvement structure ❷ Staff involved in plan design ❷ Employee favourability ❷ Participative management style ❷ Controllability of targets* ❷ Productivity rather than profit orientation* ❷ Shorter payout periods*	❷ Size of organisation/plan membership ❷ Union presence ❷ Industry ❷ Technology
Bowey and Thorpe (1982) n = 63	❷ Extent of consultation – involvement – amount of communication ❷ Supervisory skills/spans of control ❷ Market/sales growth ❷ Shorter payout periods* ❷ Smaller size of membership*	❷ Plan design in terms of: – performance measures – level of measurement – type of staff covered
Towers Perrin (1990) n = 177	❷ Senior management commitment ❷ Employee support/involvement ❷ Emphasis on communications ❷ Related HR activities, eg training ❷ Performance measurement at levels below corporate ❷ Shorter payout periods* ❷ Operational or blended rather than wholly financial measures	❷ Organisation size ❷ Union presence ❷ Age of plan ❷ Industry

*Weak correlation

Business returns

Second, therefore, operating with effective reward and HR processes, particularly in respect of communications and involvement, not only makes for effective pay and reward schemes but also has a positive payoff to the business. In North America, a University of California (1998) study, for example, rated 216 companies according to their level of staff participation. It found that the average rate of return in the high-participation companies was 21 per cent, compared to 14 per cent for those with the lowest levels of involvement. Wallace Bell (1989) found a similar differentiation in the financial perform-ance of companies with profit-sharing schemes compared to those without.

The Workplace Employee Relations Survey (Culley 1998) of 300 organisations in the UK found positive correlations between busi-ness performance, employee involvement and a range of HR and reward practices, including performance pay. Towers Perrin's (1999a, 1999b) reward studies covering over 1,000 organisations in Europe and North America found that the companies with the high-est total shareholder returns made wider use of bonus and share plans, were more open in communicating on reward issues and rated their performance management schemes more highly than the other companies in the research. We look at each of these processes in the next chapter.

Human capital investment in the new economy

This is a fairly powerful battery of evidence, but even more signifi-cant is the third point, which is that future developments in the new economy will render these associations and their business impact even more powerful in the future. The rapid rate of change in our organisations means that we will have to get better at continually improving and adapting our reward schemes, which as we saw in the last chapter is the predominant pattern of change already evident. We address this requirement in the final section of the next chapter.

But it is another factor that has been regularly emphasised through-out this book – the rising numbers, power and influence of the pro-fessional knowledge workers – that will really force us to address the process and perception issues, and quite literally turn our reward strategies upside down, or at least from a predominantly left-brain to a right-brain concept.

❛People really are becoming the most important asset for competitive success❜

The announcement of a £10,000 'golden hello' being offered by Accenture (formerly Andersen Consulting) to new graduate recruits may not be a great example of long-term strategic reward thinking, but it provides further evidence that the 'talent war' is well and truly under way and that people really are becoming the most important asset for competitive success in many markets and organisations.

Tom Davenport (1999) best captures the impact of this change in competitive business dynamics and the labour market on the way we need to manage and reward our people. As the bargaining power of professional employees increases, he argues that the 'people as assets', cost-based model of using financial reward policies to 'buy and sell' staff is becoming increasingly outdated and misguided. Instead, he argues we are being forced to adopt a human capital model, in which an employer's investment in its staff is matched by the employees' investment of their own human capital in the organisation. As he explains, 'their capital is the ability, behaviour, effort and time they contribute to a company', and, 'like an investor in any market, they expect a healthy return on that investment'.

As we shall see, the expected return is in many cases different from the traditional fixed pay and benefits package that prevailed in large Western multinationals for much of the post-war period, or even a £10,000 welcome. If they fail to receive an adequate return, they will leave and invest their capital in another of the numerous market opportunities they find elsewhere.

In the new economy in the new century, therefore, the challenge is 'to attract, develop and retain people who get so much value from the organisation, and give so much in return, that they create sustained competitive advantage'. And so the role of the HR and reward specialist is to help 'win this race for human capital' by 'crafting a return on investment array that attracts the most talented, creative and motivated workers'.

And of course, the value of the reward package and the return on investment is not an absolute sum – it is a perception, a subjective judgement of the balance between what I give as an employee and what I get back. Towers Perrin's giving me time off to spend with the family and write this book is not just done out of the goodness of their heart. They know that I value such time very highly and that it should in return strengthen my investment back in the organisation.

Conversely, if like a dozen well-known UK companies who Towers Perrin recently surveyed, you as an employer are investing on average a sum equivalent to 30 per cent of base payroll in a generous benefits package, yet two-thirds of employees believe the value of that package to be worth less than 20 per cent of pay, then you are making a poor investment and their perceived value of the return they are getting is less than it should be. In response, employees may even up the balance by reducing their investment of time and effort or decide to invest it elsewhere.

And so, however wonderful your new bonus or recognition scheme looks on paper and whatever the rewards on offer, if an employee suggests an improvement and gets told to shut up and get on with his or her job, it is probably not going to be a very effective nor highly valued incentive. It is here that so many reward strategies and schemes fail: in the gap between policy and practice, rhetoric and reality, saying and doing, intention and perception.

So this is why, somewhat paradoxically, this book argues that to help our organisations succeed in the new economy, we need to downplay the 'top-down' focus on strategic business goals and reward scheme designs and pay more attention to what employees require and the processes to deliver it. Or as Davenport (1999) puts it, 'focus less on the cost of the individual to the organisation, and more on the value of the organisation to the individual'.

The rest of this chapter illustrates how the idea of the psychological contract can be used to help realign your reward strategies in a more balanced and mutually beneficial manner for employers and employees. The next chapter looks in more detail at the specific processes that serve to maximise and further this type of relationship, and really move your reward strategy on from intent to implementation and impact. We first consider the sort of rewards at work that can serve to create this sort of highly valuable, mutual relationship, and then look at the specific processes that serve to maximise and further it.

Using rewards to create a positive psychological contract

Many UK organisations have a hard time trying to make sense of the concept of the psychological contract, and so beyond a few general statements about providing 'employability' and a 'mutually beneficial relationship' in recruitment literature, its practical impact is still somewhat limited. Funnily enough, this is not a difficulty shared by their employees. Whenever I ask groups of staff in a company to 'define their deal', or more fun, draw a picture of their employment relationship, the results are always informative and surprisingly consistent between groups. Images of sailors lost at sea with sharks swimming around them often seem to feature!

In the future, however, because of the changes just described, it is going to become increasingly important to think through what sort of employment relationship you need to create in your organisation, and how reward policies and practices can build and further that relationship. Incorporating the totality of this relationship, and the employee perspective on it, are going to be vital ingredients in effective reward strategies in the future.

A definition

The psychological contract or employment 'deal' is not a new idea and it basically refers to the mix of formal and informal obligations and commitments that employers and employees make with each other and believe should and do exist. Historically in this country, beyond legal employment requirements, it has often been a largely unspoken and assumed relationship, whereas in North America employers tend to be more up front about it. I can remember well my mixture of surprise and support when I listened to the then CEO of Apple, John Sculley, in the mid-1980s refer to his firm's contract to an audience of potential MBA recruits:

> We'll offer you the opportunity to express yourself and grow, if you promise to leash yourself to our dream, at least for a while.

It was the breakdown of the traditional post-war employment deal with many large employers in the 1980s and 1990s that really brought the issue to the fore. Downsizing, outsourcing and re-engineering in many cases shattered the unspoken trade-off of employee effort, discipline and loyalty, in return for a job-for-life and an array of service- and status-related rewards. It led to more employers explicitly addressing the employment relationship and specifying the mutual obligations and returns.

At Hewlett-Packard, as part of an explicit 'new deal', in return for flexibility, commitment and contribution, employees receive challenge and development in their roles, a stake in the business and a variety of market- and performance-related rewards. Every Southwest Airlines employee receives a 'personal flight plan' listing the obligations and personal freedoms that characterise the employment experience in the company.

Now it has reached the stage where an accounting-focused and fairly traditionally run UK government agency has just spent a lot of time with its staff going through a process of defining what values and behaviours will support the achievement of its goals and what they and their employees must do for each other in order to live these values and achieve their goals. The mutual commitments that the organisation and its staff have taken on in relation to their goals have been organised into four categories, as follows: commitment to the organisation and its goals; being a learning organisation; caring for staff; and equal opportunities. These commitments were summarised in a document that was shared with all staff. For example, as part of being committed to the organisation:

- the employer agrees to provide challenging work and access to influential people
- employees agree to provide high-quality work and to stretch their own boundaries.

In the open, learning organisation category, meanwhile:

❷ the employer agrees to give the space and opportunities necessary for employees to develop

❷ employees agree to seek out feedback and to network.

The high proportion of professional employees who are highly marketable to the private sector is a revealing feature of this body and explains why it has recognised the importance of doing this in order to retain a highly skilled and committed workforce.

But why is the psychological contract so generally important in today's business environment, and why is it so critical to the operation of effective reward strategies? There are three critical sets of factors:

❷ one from the perspective of the organisation

❷ one more from the perspective of its people

❷ the third of mutual significance.

Importance to the business

From the business angle, the relationship between effective HR and reward practices and organisation performance documented in Chapter 1 is not automatic – the practices do not themselves produce the results. It operates through and is mediated by the psychological contract, and what employees perceive and believe they will receive from the organisation through the operation of these practices and the achievement of the corporate goals – see Figure 15. As Guest and Conway (1998) explain, 'The link between HR practices and how the business performs depends on the quality, trust and commitment of the workers.'

‘Create this positive employment relationship and achieve higher productivity’

It is what Cox and Purcell (1998) refer to as this 'holy grail' of trust, motivation and commitment that lies at the heart of the psychological contract and of the reinforcement that your HR and reward practices can provide to the achievement of your business goals. Create this positive employment relationship, supported by your pay and

Figure 15

THE SIGNIFICANT RELATIONSHIPS REVEALED BY THE CIPD AND WERS RESEARCH

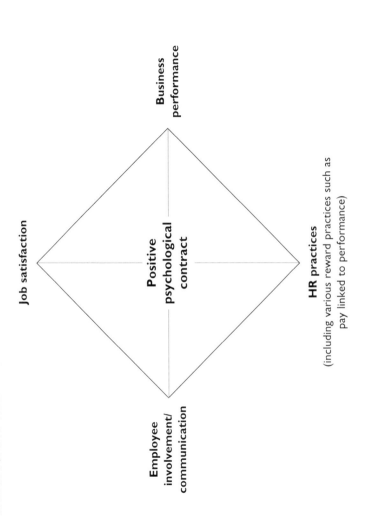

Job satisfaction

Business performance

Positive psychological contract

Employee involvement/ communication

HR practices
(including various reward practices such as pay linked to performance)

reward practices, and Guest and Conway's (1998) research implies that you are likely to achieve higher productivity and performance and competitive advantage.

This research for the CIPD demonstrates that this positive relationship, in turn, depends on three sets of factors:

- employee perceptions of fairness
- trust in their employer, their management and HR practices
- the delivery of the 'deal' in practice.

Davenport (1999) similarly found that employees would most productively maximise their investment in an employer if three elements are in place:

- clear and openly shared business goals
- a clear understanding of job requirements and contractual expectations
- mutual acceptance that 'both parties must trust that they will willingly live up to the stated and implied tenets of the deal'.

Towers Perrin's (1997) biannual Workplace Index, a telephone survey of the attitudes of over 5,000 employees, appears to confirm the importance of trust and mutuality. It found significant differences between employees' commitment to the success of their organisation and intentions to stay and advance there according to the degree to which they believed that they would share in that success.

Devolving more responsibility to staff and establishing a positive and trusting contract, in an environment where top-down planning and management has become increasingly obsolete, has been a crucial part of the business turnaround at drinks company Bulmers. As Director Nigel Rudd explains, 'Now we recognise that there will be a lot we can't predict, so we invest time in building the vision and making people truly responsive.' Management has 'become much more about listening and explaining, developing understanding, and making commitments jointly with staff, so that we can meet our commitments to customers'.

So mutual understanding, real reciprocity and trust appear to lie at the core of a positive psychological contract, which underpins the strategic success of organisations in our knowledge- and service-based economy. Even in traditional 'smokestack' sectors it is vital. Explaining the success of a gainsharing bonus scheme in four US steel mills, where it was associated with significant improvements in productivity and performance, Dan Duncan (1998) of Ameristeel emphasised that 'there needs to be openness and mutual trust' to make 'employees willing to contribute, which in turn improves productivity and their pay'.

It is in the areas of reciprocity and delivery of the deal that a number of organisations appear to be experiencing problems, and it is in just such organisations that the implementation of new reward strategies proves particularly problematic and employee cynicism and opposition most difficult to overcome. It is not so much a problem of staff pining for a return to the old, paternal employment relationship and job-for-life deal. There are now many different types of workplace deal on offer from employers, and while some are more attractive than others, the evidence suggests that each can be satisfying and rewarding for different types of people.

A characterisation of three deals that we found amongst UK employers while carrying out a competitive study for a financial services organisation is shown in Table 11. Many pundits have championed the leased-talent-type deal of a company such as Pepsi as the 'best' approach in our new competitive economy. Yet many well-known organisations are continuing to succeed with a modified form of paternalism, while a commitment-based ownership relationship is now being claimed by a large number of companies.

Problems emerge, however, if the deal promised or implied by the company is not delivered in practice. Take the example of performance-related pay and employee perceptions of it revealed by the Workplace Index (Towers Perrin 1997a). Over 90 per cent of employees in companies where they perceived that outstanding performance was rewarded said that they were motivated to help their company achieve its strategic goals, compared to 60 per cent of employees who did not perceive this to be the case. This confirms Guest and Conway's (1998) findings that the use of some type of pay for performance correlated with the existence of a positive

Table 11

A VARIETY OF EMPLOYMENT RELATIONSHIPS
EVIDENT AMONG UK EMPLOYERS

	Leased talent	New paternalism	'Employee owners'
Key message	'We will give you a great CV'	'We will take care of you'	'We will build a great success together'
Employee self-concept	'Mercenary' professional	Family members	Partner in the business
Work organisation	Flexible Segmented Emphasis on process/expertise	Hierarchical Structured Emphasis on procedures	Empowered, regular change Emphasis on initiative, shared values
Value measured by	Assignment challenge	Job size	Role impact and value added
Key reward tools	Competency-based applications Job families Individual incentives Personal contracts	Job evaluation Profit-sharing Good benefits Promotions	Broad bands Team-based pay Share schemes Personal development
Outcomes	Competence	Loyalty	Commitment

Source: Towers Perrin.

psychological contract. Yet although a majority of these companies had PRP schemes in place, fewer than 40 per cent of employees felt that their employers really did reward outstanding performance or that they would share in the company's success. Here we have a classic instance of the rhetoric/reality gap, and of the deal not being delivered in practice. Towers Perrin's Workplace Index (1997) concludes on this basis that:

> Employees appear to accept the messages that employers have been giving them: that there is no job for life, that their pay is performance-related, that they are responsible for their own career development. But they don't believe that management is now delivering on its side of the bargain, and that they are likely to share in the success of the business.

A variety of studies point to declining levels of trust in UK companies, which are not seen by their employees to be delivering on their side of these new, more flexible employment relationships. Between 1996 and 1998, Guest and Conway (1998), for example, found a declining proportion of employees feeling that they were kept well informed and seeing employee/management relations as positive. From a reward perspective, the rapid growth occurring now in all-employee share schemes in North America and forecast in Europe could be interpreted as a very positive trend to help create this mutuality. But if these types of misunderstandings and low levels of employee trust exist in your organisation, not only is business performance likely to be affected, but a share scheme on its own may have little impact in addressing the real problems, and you still may be unable to attract and motivate staff of the calibre you need to achieve your business's strategic goals.

Attraction is the third area of importance. As we saw in Chapter 4, new economy companies operating in competitive markets are being forced to spell out and to actively 'sell' the deal they offer to their target employment audience, just as a company might research, market and sell to its targeted customer base. The analogy of markets is a good one, for as David Lewis (2000) explains, 'In an era of affluence, consumers have largely exhausted the things they need to buy, and now concentrate on what they want to buy: shopping has become not merely the acquisition of things but the buying of identity.' With unemployment at a 25-year low in the UK, and 80 per cent of employers reporting skill shortages, the discerning people in today's labour market are making similar choices.

Thus the employee deal has evolved into the company brand in the recruitment market, and again, I have seen some very different employment relationships and rewards work extremely effectively in securing the sort of employees the organisation needs to succeed. In one case a stronger emphasis on employee development and 'fun' helped to recruit call centre employees in a very competitive East Midlands labour market, and in another, a start-up energy company successfully drew employees from larger competitors with the promise of high levels of challenge and responsibility at an early age. But here again, the reality of the employee's experience has to live up to the recruiter's promises.

Rewards and the relevance of the psychological contract

‘Employee perceptions mediate the relationship between pay practices and business performance’

So what is the relevance of the psychological contract to your reward strategy, and what should you be doing about it in your work on reward policies and practices? The relationship between the two is mutually reinforcing. As we have seen, employee perceptions mediate the relationship between pay practices and business performance and have a major impact on the success of reward changes.

On the other hand, pay and formal reward and employment practices are one of the most tangible symbols of a company's culture and employment offering, inextricably intertwined with them. Therefore they are critical to demonstrating that the employer is delivering on its side of the employment bargain. The use of certain pay practices does relate to the existence of a positive psychological contract. Conversely, both Guest and Conway (1998) and the WERS research (Culley 1998) found that dissatisfaction with pay (by 41 per cent of employers in the latter) was the most significant contributor to employee mistrust and a negative and unproductive contract.

The Towers Perrin (1999a, 1999b) reward studies in Europe and the USA demonstrated some interesting common features of the reward strategies in high-performing companies, and these are summarised below.

- *Pay:*
    - significantly disproportionate share of all pay programmes for high-performing employees
    - shift from fixed to variable pay
    - broader use of stock and/or stock options
    - differences in deals based on employee contribution
    - emphasis on rewarding results, not tenure, at all levels.

- *Learning and development:*
    - career enhancement programmes for all employees, with an emphasis on top performers

- performance management supporting vision and business strategy
- emphasis on development among key employees and future leaders
- performance goals that directly link the individual's actions to the organisation's business objectives.

- *Benefits:*
  - flexibility and portability
  - emphasis on non-traditional benefits
  - focus on shared responsibility/funding
  - designed and communicated to reflect employees' life-stage needs
  - use of cost-effective delivery mechanisms.

- *Environment:*
  - continued efforts to inform employees of the vision; visible leadership and ongoing commitment to attaining the vision
  - consistent, regular communication about the business and performance expectations
  - alignment of all HR systems with company goals
  - greater employee involvement in business decisions.

Please note that this is not claiming any spurious relationship between the existence of certain reward practices and the various aspects of corporate performance we analysed, although greater use of variable pay and share schemes is evident in these companies. Rather, through the reward, HR and management processes these organisations create a positive and mutually beneficial employment relationship, what Ghoshal and Bartlett (1999) call 'competitive advantage through context', a highly productive and motivating internal environment. It is an environment characterised by:

- a strong emphasis on performance management, clarifying goals, regular feedback, and rewarding individual and collective achievement
- investment in staff development
- encouraging and rewarding through multiple means the behaviours that drive strategic success
- using a flexible and broad range of rewards to, as Angela Baron (2000) explains, 'cater for the needs of the full spectrum of employees and their needs'.

Individual practices can be borrowed by competitors but copying this positive environment and the employment relationship as a whole is much more difficult.

Practical actions

So in respect of your reward strategy and its relationship to the psychological contract:

1   Recognise the importance of aligning the reward strategy with employee values and needs.
2   Define the current employment relationship and the relationships that need to exist to ensure future success and identify how reward practices can contribute to delivering the required deal.
3   Create your own tailored contract and ensure that all your reward practices are aligned with this.

First recognise, as Angela Baron (2000) goes on to describe in her review of HR practices and the bottom line, that 'it is not only the business and organisational factors that influence the effectiveness of practices, but also the diverse needs and expectations of the workforce'. Recognise therefore that alignment of your reward practices with employee values and needs is every bit as important as alignment with business goals, and critical to the realisation of the latter.

In one sense, you do not need complex concepts from psychology to do this, but simply to change the reward strategy mindset. In one very down-to-earth company, we simply thought through how we wanted the reward changes we had planned to help improve business results to be experienced and to feel for their employees. The descriptions are summarised as follows:

⦿ *For the company:*
  ⦿ It is a win/win situation.
  ⦿ Rewards genuinely support our business goals and values.
  ⦿ We get a good return on our investment in reward.
  ⦿ We grow our people and maximise our return on the investment in them.
  ⦿ We can recruit and retain high performers: staff turnover is appropriate.

- ❷ We can change/amend policies and practices when we need to.
- ❷ The company/situation is well administered and under control.
- ❷ We know what is going on.
- ❷ We know how well it is working.
- ❷ *For our people:*
  - ❷ It is a win/win situation: I will share in the success of this business.
  - ❷ It is worth going the extra mile.
  - ❷ I am paid fairly for what I do and the skills I apply.
  - ❷ Exceptional performance is rewarded and recognised: the best performers get the most reward.
  - ❷ It is worth developing myself and maximising my contribution to the full.
  - ❷ I am well looked after: the rewards meet my personal needs.
  - ❷ It is stretching but fun and exciting.
  - ❷ I understand our reward approach and its components.
  - ❷ We celebrate success.

This led them to go and discuss the proposed changes with employee groups, and a number of alterations were made as a result, which greatly assisted implementation.

Systematically try to define the deal that exists in your organisation at present, the sort of employment relationship that needs to exist for you to succeed in the future, and how reward practices can contribute to achieving and delivering that deal. Then systematically assess the extent to which your reward practices and changes to them do fit the required employment relationship, because serious mis-alignment can be every bit as damaging as the 'misfits' with business strategy that we highlighted in Chapter 1.

Do not for example try introducing a uniform team bonus plan design or a general profit-sharing scheme in an organisation with the type of individualistic leased-talent employment relationship pictured in Table 11. Or worse still, make a proposal to call all staff in this type of organisation 'associates' and see the reaction you get. The relationship here is based on success through innovation and individual competence and growth. It is rewarded by challenging work, an individually focused pay and development approach, valuing and recognising 'stars', and building people's CVs in return for their immediate contribution to the business. A number of research studies demonstrate the dislike of these types of professionals for collective reward approaches. If, as in one consultancy, the globalisation of business calls for stronger international co-ordination, then the team rewards to encourage this need to be built up gradually and in a well-argued fashion.

Motivation under the new paternalism-type relationship is provided in a more long-term and caring framework, with clearly defined career paths and a continuing focus on internal development and promotion and a strong emphasis on internal equity in rewards. Whatever the futurists and gurus might say, it is a model that still works very well for companies such as Unilever and Shell, even if they have moved to recognise the importance of more internal differentiation and market-related flexibility.

The employee-owner type of relationship tends to operate in non-hierarchical and high-involvement organisations, characterised by HR and reward systems such as in-depth and bottom-up goal-setting, 360-degree appraisal, share schemes and team bonus arrangements, with a high use of recognition programmes.

Table 12 summarises the types of pay schemes that we found associated with these types of employment deal that we researched. Of course, these are overgeneralised and simplistic models, and aspects of all of them may be present in large organisations. Nonetheless, as with the generic strategy models we considered in Chapter 2, they are helpful in starting to think through the relationship. Each organisation, however, needs to create its own special relationship and align its reward practices, in their totality, with it.

A television company recently went through this process and defined its deal in terms of the four aspects of total rewards. Creative programming and fast response to technological changes were at the core of its business strategy. The principles of its reward strategy emphasised:

- ❷ recruiting and retaining educated, mobile, professional staff
- ❷ workforce flexibility to meet variable programming requirements
- ❷ an informal, 'learning' environment.

Table 12

REWARD STRATEGY IMPLICATIONS OF PARTICULAR EMPLOYMENT RELATIONSHIPS

Rewards	Leased talent deal	New paternalism deal	Employee-owner deal
Focus of pay system	Replacement value in market	Job value in career structure	Business value in flat hierarchy
Focus of pay competitive-ness	Retaining key talent	Entry-level recruitment	All staff, aggressive total pay
Pay mix	Varies by job family	Average	Highly leveraged
Pay structure	Market rates, job family structures	Broad grades	Broad bands
Reward for high performers	High base pay for stars	Through promotion	High bonuses
Variable pay	Individual and project incentives	Corporate, eg profit-sharing	Value-based, business challenge, and team incentives
Communi-cations on pay	Need-to-know basis	Open opportunity structure	Open, as a business process
Recognition	Individual cash awards	Trash/trinkets and public ceremonies	Team awards
Focus of performance management	Results	Goal and task achievement	Contribution
Development	Challenging work	Career paths	Coaching and goal-setting
Preventing burnout	Sabbaticals	Parties	Varied work

Their deal, therefore, demanded intense, creative input from staff in a regularly changing context. In return for applying their talents, the rewards offered included:

❷ fully competitive base pay levels, related to individual contribution; bonuses were little used, not being highly valued by staff, and with few simple financial or productivity measures available

❂ flexible benefits, with portable pensions and an emphasis on 'lifestyle' benefits

❂ self-development within a strong and well-funded support structure, and considerable scope to grow personal roles

❂ an attractive, status-free, open, 'cool' environment to work in.

‹ Defining and aligning with your own deal is one universal requirement of a successful reward strategy ›

And finally, this is not just a requirement for 'cool' organisations. While the form of expression and components differ, defining and aligning with your own deal is one universal requirement of a successful reward strategy. As the case study below illustrates, even in one of the most traditional and consultant-fad-resistant charitable organisations, a group of employees developing their own picture of how the employment relationship needed to change if the charity was to succeed for another century was one of the most critical components in the successful implementation of a wide-ranging reward change programme.

Case study

USING REWARDS TO REINFORCE THE REQUIRED CULTURE CHANGES IN A MAJOR CHARITY

Background
This leading UK institution, funded entirely by charitable donations through a long history stretching back over 100 years, is regarded as a sector leader in many aspects of its work, including the quality of its services and the professionalism of its fund-raising activity. It employs approximately 1,000 staff across a range of technical, professional and administrative activities.

However, in its HR and reward practices, the organisation definitely could not have been described as leading-edge. Under a new director, high priority has been given to building an organisation and culture capable of delivering on the increasing expectations and demands of its trustees, donors, volunteers and the people receiving its services.

The organisation's culture is described by its head of human resources as one of contrasts, combining the modern and the traditional: innovation in its services with a general conservatism and suspicion of internal changes; a strong volunteer and not-for-profit ethos, with a professional drive for perfection and hard commercial 'edge' to its activities. He has been making a series of changes in the HR function to move it from its traditional 'rule-making' and administrative role, towards making a clearer contribution to organisation goals and enabling and supporting line managers in achieving them.

The reward changes that the charity has been undertaking in the last few years demonstrate both the contribution that these can make in reinforcing a much broader culture-change process, as well as the need to move at a manageable pace, which reflects both the realities of the existing situation and the vision of where it is heading. In fact, in many ways the scale of the reward changes now evident might surprise even the architects of those changes themselves.

Initial reward changes

The initial stimulus for change came from a staff opinion survey that revealed surprisingly widespread and strong criticism in two areas: communication and involvement, in what was perceived to be a top-down, autocratic culture (with the existing performance appraisal system, for example, being criticised for being a once-a-year one-way exercise); and pay and rewards, which were felt to be generally low and operated in an inconsistent manner across the organisation.

The work on reward began fairly tactically in direct response to this, with the design and introduction of a new job evaluation scheme to support a move towards a simpler and more harmonised set of reward arrangements. Existing arrangements were a complex mix of different pay structures and systems for the various staff groups, with many historical allowances and anomalies. The exercise took two years, rather than the planned six months, to achieve, but on completion all but the manual staff were moved into a common pay structure of 12 grades, on the basis of their job evaluation scores.

Parallel to this work, a number of initiatives to improve communications throughout the organisation, including the introduction of regular team briefings, were undertaken.

The diagnostic review

However, in many ways the job evaluation exercise raised as many questions as it answered, and so a second phase of work was then begun, with a review of all pay, grading and allowance arrangements. The review involved meetings with senior managers and staff groups, a study of market trends amongst other charities and an analysis of the current schemes. An internal advisory group reviewed the findings and the changes that were recommended to address the issues raised.

The study's findings revealed some major variations in perceptions between, for example, long-serving administrative staff in headquarters and the generally younger specialist engineering and IT professionals. However, three consistent issues emerged:

- Although employee turnover was low, staff generally felt that their efforts and effectiveness in a period of rapid change for the organisation and its services were not being adequately recognised and rewarded.
- Strong perceptions of inequality and inconsistencies in pay arrangements, which the job evaluation exercise had raised, were still widespread.
- A general lack of understanding of reward systems was evident, and more broadly of how the culture and employment relationship in the organisation was changing.

Some typical comments from the staff groups were as follows:

- *On change:*
  - 'Will the restructuring mean I am out of a job?'
  - 'There used to be a family feel ... job security, but the organisation's changing so much now.'
  - 'The young people don't care about the pension.'

- *On communication:*
    - 'We receive newsletters but there's no communication.'
    - 'We evaluated all the jobs and got regraded ... so what?'
    - 'I didn't know I had got a bonus until it got paid.'

- *On pay and progression:*
    - 'There's no incentive at the top of the grade.'
    - 'The system rewards you for stagnating.'
    - 'There's nowhere to go.'

- *On performance pay:*
    - 'They don't know how to be good managers.'
    - 'I don't think you can measure performance in certain jobs.'
    - 'We work as a team: how could you differentiate?'

- *On allowances:*
    - 'The mileage payment is absurd.'
    - 'Base pay is low and you make up the difference with your subsistence.'

The external analysis demonstrated that many of the major charities were facing similar business-style pressures to become more efficient and performance-oriented organisations. The relatively high size of pay awards given by the charity in recent years, with a large portion accounted for by service increments, was becoming increasingly difficult to justify to the organisation's governing body, and was not fully appreciated by staff.

Twenty per cent of them were already on the pay ceiling for their grade, and so market supplements and an *ex gratia* bonus scheme had been used to provide more flexibility to reward high contributors and those in areas of high market demand. However, the bonuses and supplements were not generally communicated and the criteria for their allocation were not clear. They therefore reinforced staff perceptions of unfair and inconsistent treatment.

A relatively archaic system of subsistence allowances and expenses, heavily differentiated by grade, also operated and accounted for a comparatively high proportion of the earnings of front-line staff.

The advisory group summarised the current reward approach and culture it reinforced, and contrasted them with the necessary changes (see Table 13). Their reward systems suited a steady-state, paternal and autocratic organisation with a uniform, passive workforce, rather than meeting the needs of a modern, highly dispersed charitable organisation with demanding service and efficiency goals. And despite a generally competitive reward package, particularly in respect of benefits and conditions, the impact on staff motivations and their sense of recognition and commitment to the success of the organisation was relatively small.

The new reward strategy and its detailing

Supported by this analysis, the senior management team agreed to a wide range of reward changes, as part of a clear, communicated strategy to staff. The aims included:

- clearly setting out the goals for reward practices
- recognising the contribution and development of all staff
- providing greater flexibility to meet the needs of the different parts of the organisation
- improving the management of pay and rewards
- continuing to maintain equitable and competitive practices.

The importance of these reward changes to reinforce the broader change process under way in the organisation and the corresponding significance of management and communications processes to the successful implementation of these reward changes was recognised by the way in which the charity carried out the detailing work phase over the next two months, and then the preparatory phase for a further three months prior to implementation.

Members of the HR function led small 'virtual' teams working on each aspect of redesign. But all staff were given a detailed briefing in a series of meetings held by the director regarding the outline nature of the changes, and then given regular written updates as the design work progressed. The teams consulted regularly in detailing their designs. The pay banding team, for example, worked up a seven- and eight-band structure, and then sat down individually with each functional head to see which would best fit his or her own structure and needs.

Table 13
THE CHANGING EMPLOYMENT RELATIONSHIP
AT THE CHARITY

Old deal	New deal
Employer expects: if you	**Employer expects: if you**
🏵 Are diligent, nose to the grindstone, do your tasks	🏵 Work to targets
🏵 Are loyal and accrue long service	🏵 Respect our core values
🏵 Respect our traditions	🏵 Develop your skills
🏵 Give high attention to detail, are reliable	🏵 Contribute beyond the minimum acceptable
	🏵 Are open and responsive to change
	🏵 Contribute ideas/suggestions/ improvements
Employees receive: we'll provide	**Employees receive: we'll provide**
🏵 No great work pressure, and job security	🏵 Training and career opportunities
🏵 Incremental increases and promotions	🏵 Competitive pay
🏵 Not great pay	🏵 Rewards for effort, achievement and growth
🏵 Good benefits of a caring, paternal organisation	🏵 A sense of being valued, recognised and contributing to a worthwhile cause
And you'll be part of:	**And you'll be part of:**
🏵 A male-dominated, somewhat paternalistic family	🏵 A more modern, efficient organisation that combines its best traditions with innovation and efficiency
🏵 A traditional, well-respected organisation	
🏵 But one that is falling behind the times	

A series of half-day workshops was held with the top 100 managers in the organisation, in whom the development of a more integrated, professional and participative approach to management was seen as a major priority by the charity's director. The first meeting explained the rationale and outline of changes, the second the details of changes once they were worked up, and the third covered the communication of the changes to their staff, for which they had the primary responsibility. A lot of thought was put into planning the transition from existing to new arrangements, which included the preparation of new contracts for all staff and the offer of a cash incentive for them to accept.

The package of detailed changes that were implemented the following April included the following:

- moving all staff into a flatter structure of eight bands, with wider market-related pay ranges
- replacing the subsistence and allowance systems with a much simpler single disturbance allowance, which was differentiated according to the level of disturbance and unsocial hours worked rather than grade; they also moved to pay expenses on receipt
- formalising the *ex gratia* bonus scheme to recognise specific and defined achievements and behaviours by staff throughout the year, with a review process to ensure consistent standards were applied
- harmonising working hours, involving an increase in the basic working week for all administrative staff
- introducing a number of new benefits that employees could purchase at a company-negotiated discount.

April also saw the start of implementing a new performance development and review scheme, again supported by relevant management and staff workshops. This acted as the basis for the new system of pay adjustment that was to be implemented 12 months later. In the higher bands, pay increases would be entirely merit-related. But displaying their sensitivity to the need to build trust and understanding amongst staff, a general inflation-linked increase was retained for staff in the lower grades. But there would then be the flexibility to reward high-performing staff with an additional sum at these levels.

Also illustrating the evolving nature of their reward strategy, despite a brief to detail a flexible benefits scheme as part of the new strategy, the benefits design team came to the conclusion that such a scheme was a step too far for the organisation to manage and administer and for staff to understand at this stage. Therefore outline intentions were put forward and a number of new employee-purchased benefits proposed. The development of a fuller flexible benefits approach is seen as the next item on the reward agenda.

Outcomes and learning points

Despite the breadth of reward changes proposed, virtually 100 per cent of staff accepted the move onto their new contracts of employment within the sign-up period. The whole review, redesign and implementation process took less than half the time that the job evaluation exercise had previously taken.

The charity's head of personnel attributed this success to two factors: first, the new director's arrival, and second, his use of the reward agenda to help support a necessary change in the whole approach to management and culture in the organisation. 'We had considered reducing the number of grades at the time of the evaluation work but it was generally agreed to be a step too far.'

Many managers consulted individually at the start of the exercise saw little need to change pay arrangements and feared considerable staff disruption from doing so. Yet according to the head of personnel, the diagnostic work demonstrated clearly that much of the pay infrastructure (grade differences in allowances, incremental progression and so on) 'were driven by the militaristic-style organisation of the past' rather than 'the modern, efficient, merit-based organisation of the future'. The necessity of change was obvious, and subsequent help with the development of managers' skills to manage rewards and other processes in a more open and participative way helped to secure their widespread support for the programme.

This commitment, along with the involvement of staff throughout the project and extensive communication and discussion with them – again led from the very top of the organisation – was the critical factor in making such a comprehensive programme of reward reform work. As the director put it in the main document given to staff detailing the final package:

This is not a cost-cutting exercise. It is a carefully considered pay and benefits strategy which will support our vision for the organisation and help us reward staff appropriately for their contribution to the success of the Institution. The management team and I fully endorse the new package as the right way for the organisation to move ahead in the 21st century.

Chapter summary

- The overwhelming focus in the reward strategy literature and practice is on business goals and alignment. Yet without a much stronger emphasis on meeting employee needs and having the reward processes in place to do that, the potential returns of a more strategic approach to reward management will not be realised.

- Effective implementation and operating processes, particularly in the areas of employee communications and involvement and performance management, are vital because they:

  - do much to explain the success or failure of individual reward schemes
  - have positive business returns in their own right
  - are becoming even more important in our knowledge-based and human-resource-constrained economy, where employees want to see a practical return delivered on the investment that they make in their employer.

- The key to meeting both business and employee needs successfully is the definition and delivery of a positive psychological contract, defining the mutual obligations, contributions and rewards for each party. This can also serve as an effective brand and differentiator in the recruitment market, which is much more difficult for competitors to replicate than individual pay practices.

- There are many different types of 'deal' evident in today's organisations, and reward policies are an important and concrete representation of them. It is vital that reward practices are aligned with the stated deal, in order that it is seen to be delivered in practice and to build trust and commitment amongst employees.

Chapter 7

Reward strategy as process – making it happen

Chapter objectives

- ❂ highlight the key processes to address in effectively implementing and operating your reward strategy: communications and involvement, performance management, and change and transition management
- ❂ list the main requirements and provide tools and examples to help successfully manage each of these processes in support of your reward goals.

The importance of implementation and operating processes

However well-designed and business-aligned your reward schemes, employees will judge the value of their rewards and the return on the investment of their capital in your organisation through the operating processes: the example their managers set and what they read about their directors' pay in the newspaper, what their colleagues relate to them, their experiences in the workplace on a day-to-day basis, their perceptions of the fairness with which reward schemes are operated and administered. As Thompson (1998) observes, 'There is a popular belief that performance pay is a powerful motivator, yet a neglect of the conditions that must exist for pay to have any motivational impact.'

I fell into this trap when presenting a proposal for a new gainsharing plan to the board of a company in Ireland, focusing exclusively on the technical design details and business performance improvements we were seeking. 'Where', asked the HR director pointedly as we finished our material, 'are these business improvements going to come from?'

In this chapter, therefore, we examine the three sets of processes that are key to implementing and operating your reward strategy effectively:

- ❷ communications and involvement
- ❷ performance management
- ❷ the management of change.

❛ These processes have a universally powerful impact on the delivery of reward strategies in practice ❜

Somewhat paradoxically, they are so important that while this book argues throughout against the use of generic 'best practice' reward strategies and scheme designs, these processes do have a universally powerful impact on the delivery of reward strategies in practice, and in creating the type of high-performing and valued employment relationship that was profiled in the last chapter.

Communications and involvement

The importance

These are the processes that are the universally most important determinants of an effective reward strategy, and yet I always find writing about them in a reward context difficult, avoiding generalisations, clichés and repeating the blindingly obvious. Partly, it is because one always seems to be preaching to the converted, and partly precisely because it is so self-evident. A reward strategy can only work in practice if effective 'top-down' communications means that people understand the focus of the strategy and the rationale for its components, what each scheme is meant to do, how each works, and the actions, behaviours and results that they are meant to reward (hopefully linked to the business goals). Then, in a 'bottom-up' sense, it can only be effective if people actually are motivated by the rewards on offer to do these things and really get involved and committed to achieving the strategic business goals.

We have already seen many examples in this book that demonstrate that the success of reward strategies and any particular design component of them – be it broadbanding, flexible benefits or incentives – appears to relate to the investment in and quality of these processes more than any other design or environmental variable. An ACA study (MacAdams and Hawk 1994) of 663 bonus plans found that 40 per cent of companies used non-management employees to help develop the plans. These employee task forces were associated with better business performance and stronger perceived links between performance and reward by staff. As Angela Bowey (1983) found in her study of different bonus schemes, 'the degree of involvement and communications during the process of design and operation was far more important than the type of plan'.

The Towers Perrin (1999b) and various other macro-reward studies do appear to suggest that higher-performing companies are more open in their communications on reward issues and devote more effort to training first-line managers on pay and performance management. Perhaps most convincingly of all, it is a factor emphasised by the organisations in virtually every reward strategy case study in this book, whatever their size, age or sector, and however large or small the reward issues they were dealing with. As Martin Neville told me in respect of a very successful gainsharing plan that he helped to introduce in Eli Lilly's Basingstoke plant, 'Nobody has told me that we are overcommunicating.' Neville attributes a lot of the success of that scheme and related changes to a heavy emphasis on communications and involvement, with directors giving monthly staff briefings and an employee team communicating performance and plan progress to their colleagues.

This type of openness and involvement contributes to the success of reward schemes through many channels – see Figure 16. It is not just enough to fire information at people and expect them to comprehend and commit. People like to be involved, even if any resulting programmes do not align exactly with their personal wishes, so you often get a Hawthorne-type effect, with an improvement in performance brought about simply because we all respond to this sense of being involved and attended to. Your employees also develop a better understanding of what your reward strategy and its components are about, their purpose and how they work, building understanding and trust.

Figure 16
THE IMPORTANCE OF EMPLOYEE COMMUNICATIONS AND INVOLVEMENT

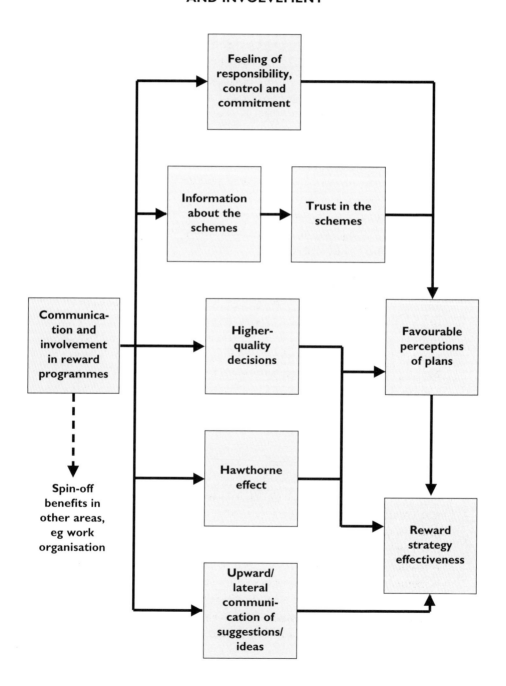

Involvement also improves the design of schemes. While running focus groups to help a professional institute reform its grade structure, its HR manager remarked that she could not see how we could have done the work without understanding the views of staff on the current grades and the alternatives we presented. Focus groups often also lead to suggestions for improvement in other areas. In a recent case I was soliciting views on the introduction of a new bonus scheme in a manufacturing plant, yet the shift arrangements were raised as an issue by every staff group. The subsequent changes that were made to them had a significant effect on employee morale and productivity.

And once a reward scheme is operational, performance improvements, as my Irish HR director friend pointed out, can only come from the 'upward' efforts, suggestions and input of staff. All in all, the realisation of your reward strategy can become something of a self-fulfilling prophecy if you openly involve staff in its development, operation and evolution.

The communications pathway breakdown

Yet while it may be starkly obvious, many UK organisations appear to continue to be oblivious to this in the manner in which they communicate with and involve staff and their line managers in reward issues. They simply are not doing it enough, or well enough. Despite our apparently enlightened age of multimedia communications, empowerment, partnerships, open book leadership, management by walking around and the ubiquitous focus groups, it is in this arena that we see the greatest gap between rhetoric and reality in reward management.

Evidence

In the course of follow-up interviews for the Towers Perrin (1999b) European rewards study, one HR director told me, 'the reward strategies I like are the ones that work'. A reward strategy cannot possibly work if you do not tell anybody about it. Yet that study revealed an astonishingly prevalent 'black hole' in the area of reward communications and involvement. Fewer than one in 10 organisations actually consulted with employees before implementing their new or amended reward strategies (compared to over a third who involved outside consultants), and only 50 per cent of them actually share the strategy even with line managers. Hardly surprising then that most participants admit that the impact of their reward strategies is confined to senior management and HR staff, with only 16 per cent feeling that they are widely used throughout the organisation. Are these real strategies, without a life beyond the document they are written on?

Only 17 per cent of the 460 organisations in the study regarded improving employee understanding of their pay and rewards as one of their five most important reward strategy goals; only 9 per cent gave building a broad-based employee ownership mentality a similar emphasis; and only 22 per cent saw increasing employee involvement as a strategic reward priority. Yet the 82 per cent aiming to use rewards to improve their employees' focus on key business goals will only do so if employees understand and buy in to those goals, and fully appreciate the links with their rewards. A recent Investors in People (2000) report drew a similar conclusion of companies 'paying lip service' to employee involvement and satisfaction, with only 6 per cent of the senior managers questioned rating it as a principal business objective.

In many organisations at the moment, employees are very well informed on their employer's business strategy and market dynamics, and they can describe the reward schemes in operation, designed to reinforce these. Yet many employees – see Figure 17 – cannot see the connection between the two. They do not understand how what they are doing does actually affect strategic performance, and they therefore are often less than committed to achieving those goals, and feel they cannot influence the measures used in their reward schemes, which therefore fail to motivate them. Your own corporate reward strategy pathway cannot possibly operate if employees' own perception of it, as illustrated in Figure 17, is not in place. As Nigel Rudd at Bulmers explains, 'We had to show how each individual's job contributed towards achieving our vision, if we wanted people to be really committed.'

Perhaps the lack of strategic emphasis given to reward communications and involvement reflects a high level of existing employee understanding of reward programmes. Our study found, unfortunately, precisely the reverse situation, with the most astonishing statistics in this area of lack of employee understanding of some of the

Figure 17

THE REWARD STRATEGY PATHWAY FOR EMPLOYEES

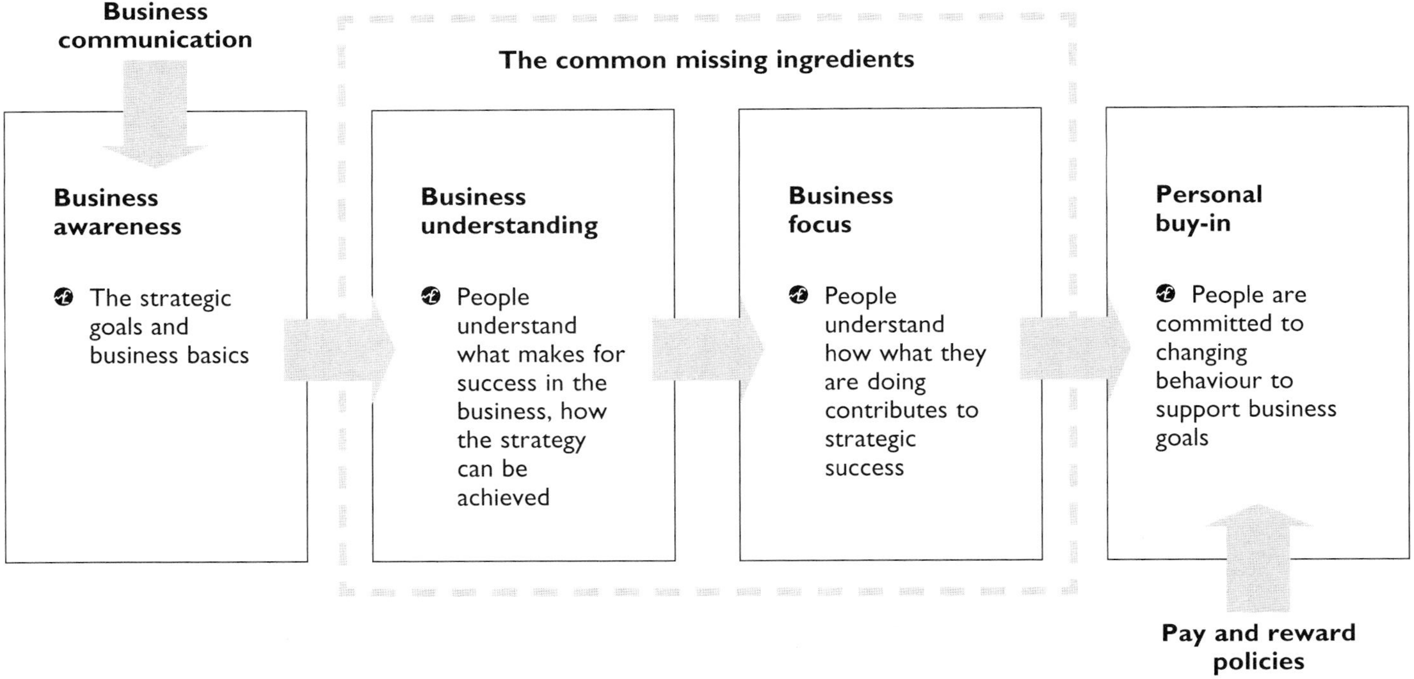

Business communication

The common missing ingredients

Business awareness

- The strategic goals and business basics

Business understanding

- People understand what makes for success in the business, how the strategy can be achieved

Business focus

- People understand how what they are doing contributes to strategic success

Personal buy-in

- People are committed to changing behaviour to support business goals

Pay and reward policies

most basic pay and reward systems. Only 8 per cent of these organisations felt that employees had a strong understanding of how their job evaluation scheme works, only 4 per cent how their pay levels are set in relation to the market, and only 12 per cent how their pay increases are determined each year. How can the full value of the total rewards package – which as we have seen is an important component of many contemporary reward strategies – ever be realised when over 90 per cent of employees in these organisations are not made aware of it? And how can the bonus schemes that operate in over 90 per cent of them be effective when fewer than a third estimate that their employees have a strong understanding of them and, remarkably, only 7 per cent involved employees in their development?

Causation

The reasons for this situation are not hard to fathom. They focus on:

- the lack of attention given to communications and involvement
- a reliance on traditional and often ineffectual channels
- a long-held fear of opening a Pandora's box of issues and grievances.

Despite all of the reward changes going on in the last three years, which we described in Chapter 4, the activities, emphasis and spend on employee communications has remained flat in almost two-thirds of these organisations. Eighty per cent of the participants in Towers Perrin's earlier 1996 study forecast major changes in reward communications to support the implementation of their reward strategies, yet only a quarter of them actually implemented them.

It is a common situation. You intellectually acknowledge the importance of communications, but with all the design work and preparation required to implement and operate your new reward schemes, it somehow gets left out.

Despite the opportunities offered by the new technologies – 26 per cent of organisations are using e-mail and intranets for communicating reward information – the predominant channels remain:

- 'top-down' information provided to staff by their first line manager; this may be the form that most staff generally indicate to be their preferred one for rewards information, and with the devolvement of reward strategies in many organisations, its significance has increased; yet only half of them provide any training in reward communications to their line managers, and almost two-thirds of HR staff have concerns over their line colleagues' reward management understanding and capabilities

- ❷ one-way written handbooks and memos, often in the dry format of your typical pensions guidebook, and with an overwhelming emphasis on the technical design details rather than the strategic reward goals or vision; unfortunately this is the manner in which much reward information currently appears to be being transferred online, with the notable exception of some excellent comprehensive and interactive reward information systems at organisations such as the BBC.

> ‹ The traditional UK approach of using reward as a rigid control mechanism is very much alive and well ›

Reticence rather than incompetence seems to be the major contributor to this situation, however. As one director of compensation participating in our European study told me, 'Our employees aren't getting the information, [so] they don't understand or trust decisions on pay.' Over 40 per cent of organisations do not provide employees with their job's salary range, under 20 per cent allow access to the job evaluation methodology, and half refuse to disclose the distribution of performance ratings and the size of merit pay awards at each performance level. Here the traditional UK pay and reward approach of using reward as a narrowly-focused and rigid control mechanism, rather than as a visionary and motivating, strategic business enabler, is very much alive and well.

I have heard the arguments many times as I have encouraged companies to be more open in their approach: staff would not understand the technical details, we would set off unrealistic expectations, they would fear we were going to cut pay, we cannot consult until we know what we are going to do, etc. Hence the typical pattern of a UK reward management project is as follows:

- ❷ get the specialists to investigate the issue and come up with the fully detailed solution
- ❷ then get it approved by directors, work on the administration and get the PR people to put the communications together
- ❷ then blast staff with an avalanche of material about the changes the day before their launch.

It is about as effective as many crash language courses: two weeks later, most people cannot even remember what the new programmes are called, never mind comprehend them.

Yet as Davenport (1999) says, 'employees are not stupid' – they know that there is no huge pot of gold to allocate. Generally employees in the focus groups I run are much better informed on personal financial matters than used to be the case, and typically with sensible and well-thought-through views on their reward programmes.

But people are understandably often concerned when changes to their reward package are proposed and made. While I am rarely advocating the total openness of everyone knowing every one else's package, as is the case at computer company CMG (although like nudity, the surprise and shock soon appears to fade), the scope for misunderstanding of many reward changes is large, and the naivety of companies who assume people will not draw their own conclusions if they are not consulted with sometimes beggars belief.

Some common initial employee reactions to some of the most wide-spread components of contemporary reward strategies include the following:

- ❷ *broadbanding:* 'they're taking away my promotion opportunities'
- ❷ *competency pay:* 'so you are saying I am not competent'
- ❷ *merit pay:* 'you're robbing Peter to pay Paul'
- ❷ *flexible benefits:* 'they're worsening our package'.

Such perceptions simply have to be addressed before any of these initiatives are implemented if they are to have any hope of success.

So while reward management in Europe has moved beyond a narrow design focus to encompass strategic business agendas, the general failure of HR and compensation specialists to enter into a more open and participative relationship with staff and their line managers is, in many instances, frustrating the achievement of their reward strategy goals in practice.

Opening the reward strategy box

The Towers Perrin (1999b) European study does, however, paint a more positive picture for the future, in that many organisations recognise their process failings and are resolved to address them. In high-growth sectors, such as information, communications and technology, much higher levels of openness and employee involvement on reward issues are already evident. More generally, an explosion of information and improved media on reward issues is forecast in the next three years, with a pleasing emphasis on the goals and purpose of rewards, and on involvement rather than one-way information giving:

- 97 per cent of organisations plan to communicate the links between business goals and reward programmes
- 74 per cent plan to be more open in sharing market data with line managers and staff
- 93 per cent intend to communicate the value of the total rewards package to staff
- 41 per cent plan to increase their investment in training managers on reward issues.

Some of the best communications material on reward change programmes has emerged from line manager workshops, where after briefing them on the outline changes, they analyse the communications needs of their staff and produce the materials to address them themselves, as in the case study at the end of Chapter 6. Martin Neville of Eli Lilly would say that the best he has seen has been produced by the staff themselves, with a bit of desk-top publishing assistance.

Finally on this topic, what should you do then if you recognise any of these failings in your own reward communications and involvement processes, and are witnessing the damaging effects on your reward strategy? This is not rocket science, whatever the media and communications consultants might say.

Some simple models are useful for analysing, thinking through and addressing these areas. The application of one very simple pathway model to a flexible benefits project I worked on is based on the idea that people only commit to something if they go through prior stages of awareness and understanding. Having found a positive employee reaction to the idea of benefits flexibility early in the project, we still had to deliver this understanding and commitment in practice. A phased series of communications, using different media at different stages, and with some variations for different employee groups, was therefore used. The results were very positive in terms of employee take-up and subsequent ratings of the value of their reward package.

Practical actions

Generally, however, the following fairly basic recommendations are useful:

- make a commitment
- audit the situation
- involve the staff.

First, commit personally and gain the commitment of your colleagues to the benefits of openly sharing reward information with staff and involving them directly when considering and making changes. Plan out just how far you want this openness to go and the stages you will need to go through to get there. And in many cases it needs to be given due priority in your reward principles and activities. It needs to be up there as a primary goal and one of the first considerations to be addressed when you are starting to think through and plan changes to reward programmes.

Second, audit the state of reward communications in your organisation at present, so that you understand how far you have to go to achieve the desired situation. Only 16 per cent of the organisations in our European reward study (Towers Perrin 1999b) did this, and only 18 per cent made any attempt to assess their line managers' skills in this area, despite the increasingly heavy reliance on them. Yet one of the first principles taught in the business strategy classes of my MBA was that people who do not know where they are will never find their way to where they want to be.

Third, involve staff themselves in that process of investigation and consult with them regularly during any reward change exercise. This does not mean advocating total industrial democracy and a vote on the reward change options that you have in every situation, (although in my experience, a workplace ballot that delivers a major vote in favour of changes to terms and conditions invariably is followed by successful implementation and operation of those changes). You need to take other considerations into account in the design of your reward schemes, such as legal requirements, market practice, affordability and so on. But again, employee opinions should be given a high weighting in most settings. Some more ideas and examples of how to do this are provided in the next chapter.

Fourth, learn from your marketing colleagues and their techniques. At the specific level, do your market research before you design your new reward 'product', test market it, and do a detailed customer segmentation and media/message analysis as part of a comprehensive market and launch planning exercise. Produce your materials attractively and professionally and to suit the needs of your audiences.

And at the more general level, draw out the key themes in your reward strategy and regularly communicate and reinforce them, so that people can see them in practice in the operation of schemes. Effective branding of reward strategies and designs, giving them a clear and attractive vision and meaning, is something that an increasing number of organisations are successfully doing. Performance reporting and appraisal schemes are being replaced by titles such as 'Excel' and 'Grow', performance pay by rewarding contribution, productivity bonus schemes by 'Sharing in Success' and 'Partners in Performance'. Of course, the reality of these schemes has to live up to the titles, but the chances of this will be much greater anyway if you adopt a participative approach.

Just as business strategies today are necessarily less about complex and detailed plans and forecasts, and more about setting a direction and equipping people to act and respond in that direction in a rapidly changing world, so reward strategies cannot be just an amalgam of detailed, heavily engineered and control-oriented schemes. They have to be about setting a broad direction and vision for reward, and enthusing and enabling people to follow that direction.

‹ Minor improvements could put you well ahead of the competition ›

Finally, remember that the main sources of communications about reward issues are not just the media you use. The behaviour in practice of managers and leaders, and the systems themselves of pay adjustment and performance management in particular, in many senses speak louder than words. But again, this is where the benefits of an integrated, strategic approach to reward and HR management, underpinned by effective processes, can really pay off and differentiate your organisation in the labour and business markets. Here is a setting where minor improvements could put you well ahead of the competition.

Performance management
More process problems

'Improving the management of performance is the most difficult challenge we face', was how one operations director in our European rewards study (Towers Perrin 1999b) saw the future obstacles to enacting their fledgling HR and reward strategy and making it a business-contributing reality. Many of the other participants were in agreement with him. The study revealed a similar pattern to that on communications and involvement, which is scarcely surprising when the performance management process offers such significant opportunities to establish the pathways illustrated in Figure 17. It can provide the vehicle to translate the business goals into meaningful employee objectives and requirements, and the forum to specifically plan and support the improved contribution of everyone to those goals.

But the pattern is depressingly alike: verbal recognition of the importance, but a lack of attention in practice to it, and even more so here, a focus on technical systems, rather than process solutions to the evident problems.

Importance

Performance management is widely practised by European organisations, present in well over 90 per cent of them, and now covers all staff in the majority. Three-quarters of the 460 participants in the Towers Perrin study had introduced new, extended or altered their performance management approaches in the last three years. Popular changes included the incorporation of competencies and of perform-ance metrics, such as the balanced scorecard, aspects of 360-degree appraisal and a strengthening of the links both to reward and development.

Jeff Skilling, the CEO of international utility Enron, believes that 'the changes that we made to performance evaluation were the most important thing for forging a new strategy and culture at Enron – it is the glue that holds the company together'. Rather than being assessed directly by their boss, the workforce is divided into pools, and staff in each pool are judged individually by a committee of executives from across the company.

Academic research generally supports the contention that it is a process that is critical to the effective implementation of HR and reward strategies. It universally emerges as one of the 'bundle' of progressive and high performance HR practices in the research work carried out by Guest and Conway (1998), the WERS (Culley 1998), Sundridge Park, and Becker and Huselid (1996). And on the down-side, the numerous studies into the difficulties of operating perform-ance pay schemes demonstrate that these are typically performance management and measurement, rather than pay problems. As Charles Cochrane, Secretary of the Council of Civil Service Unions puts it, in the public sector 'it's not performance pay that is the prob-lem, it is the appraisals and how they have been used'.

Yet 84 per cent of the organisations in the Towers Perrin (1999b) research were still dissatisfied with their performance management schemes and therefore had further changes planned. The main reported problems were in terms of the operating process, with:

- 45 per cent highlighting a lack of good appraisal practice, such as failing to hold meetings and an unwillingness to differentiate between employees, with a lack of training for reviewing man-agers (42 per cent) contributing to this
- 38 per cent lamenting a lack of funding for resulting pay increases and development actions

❷ 29 per cent blaming lack of employee understanding – 'it's a great appraisal scheme: they just don't understand it'.

Many of us experience and empathise with such operating difficulties in this country. As an employee in a pharmaceutical company told me recently, 'My manager always seems to be uncomfortable in the meetings, like it's a relief to get it over with.' But the academic research suggests such experiences are globally widespread.

Evidence

Hendry, Bradley and Perkins (2000) emphasise that 'performance management gives the HR professional an unrivalled opportunity to engage in a debate at the heart of the business'. But Grint's (1993) damning verdict based on a review of 40 years of research is that 'rarely in the history of management can a system have promised so much and delivered so little'. In the 1950s, Renesis Likert (1959) observed that 'the aim of performance review is to increase effectiveness, not to punish ... [yet] interviews as a rule are seriously deflating to employees and can do irreparable harm'. He would probably be justified in holding a similar opinion today.

Causation

Exaggerated expectations and promises appear to be one of the problems. It is all very well to talk about fully integrated HR systems and processes, yet in many companies performance management is now intended to be part business planning and monitoring, part employee and career development, part succession planning, part performance pay and part multidirectional communications system. No wonder it is often perceived to be failing, and no wonder many systems have now become incredibly detailed and complex accoutrements to what is basically a fairly simple process of an employee and the manager sitting down and planning what to do, how well things are going and how to improve. As Hendry, Bradley and Perkins (2000) observe, 'Performance management is about people and motivation, yet the system often gets in the way.' Twenty-five per cent of participants in the Towers Perrin (1999b) research felt that the results did not justify the effort involved.

Ironically, while performance management is critical to the delivery of many contemporary reward strategies, an overemphasis on the reward and review aspects and a lack of attention to, or conflict with, the future improvement and development aims is also a finding that has consistently emerged from the research. Seventy-three per cent of the companies in the Towers Perrin (1999b) study linked their appraisal system to pay increases and rewards, with 81 per cent using it for personal development needs and the majority using the same system to try to address both goals. It is a dilemma many organisations have faced over the years: don't link it to pay and it doesn't get done and your pay system is then not meeting a performance linkage goal; but link it to pay and the development component gets ignored, as employees seek to prove their perfection to their managers, rather than openly discussing their weaknesses and development needs.

Another common dilemma is the immediacy issue. Many companies complain that their system is a once-a-year ritual, with objectives being set that, because of the rapid rates of structural and business change, have become irrelevant by the time at which the level of their achievement is due to be assessed. Around a third have introduced more frequent appraisal meetings and incorporated the input of additional sources of information to improve the quality of the performance discussion. Yet managers often appear to complain about the time that is then incurred, and a number of the companies interviewed in the study doubted whether the intended higher frequency of meetings is actually being achieved.

Whether and how to rate performance is a continuing source of debate and change in performance management systems, with a five-fold rating scale remaining the most popular, but a significant number of organisations are moving to simpler methods of agreeing performance levels. Sir Michael Bichard's (2000) recent report on performance management in the Civil Service proposed a move to a three-fold categorisation.

Twenty per cent of companies are now not using a rating scale at all in an attempt to avoid the 'appraisal as school report' problem, which one public sector agency's HR director told me about. These include well-known companies such as Astra Zeneca and Bristol Myers Squibb. Again, the process should be about people and motivation, yet as Winstanley and Stuart-Smith (1996) observe, too often the focus is on rating and 'appraisal is a form of control, used to "police" performance'.

Solutions and actions

There is not the space here to go into lengthy explanations of the answers to all of your performance management problems and the detailed designs of contemporary systems. Partly this is because the subject is so well covered in other publications, notably by Armstrong and Baron (1998). But largely it is because performance management is perhaps the best illustration of Becker and Huselid's (1996) conclusion that 'high performance work systems are highly idiosyncratic and must be tailored to each firm's individual situation', a point that has been reinforced in relation to all aspects of effective reward strategies.

For example, BP Exploration and the AA both successfully link performance management to pay without any rating scales, yet the removal of ratings led to confusion and eventually the removal of any link to pay in a professional institute that I worked with. Similarly, Nuffield Hospitals and Bristol Myers Squibb operate with two separate systems, one focused on short-term performance and pay, and the other on longer-term improvement and development. One major accounting firm has quarterly meetings, each focusing on a different aspect of planning, developing, reviewing and rewarding. Yet many organisations would find it impossible to operate with two schemes or quarterly meetings, and some of the best examples of performance management have been in small businesses with no formal scheme in place at all.

Rather, we will briefly illustrate the predominant trends for the future and highlight the key actions that you need to take to ensure that your performance management approach is aligned with your HR and reward strategy. The main actions are:

- focus on the process aspects
- prioritise performance management goals and focus on the main ones
- allow for flexibility
- involve employees more
- focus on achievable improvement and allow sufficient time.

Process focus

‘Recognise that process is all-important in performance management’

First, as emphasised throughout this chapter, recognise that process is all-important in performance management, not the systems or the designs. Far too often, companies concern themselves with the design details and classically the paperwork, rather than addressing what performance management is really aiming to do in the organisation and how in practice it can do that. Some of the common changes planned by the organisations in the Towers Perrin (1999b) research indicate that the penny is finally dropping, and that companies are increasingly trying to build quality into the process, rather than imposing it top-down through detailed control, rating and review mechanisms. Fifty-one per cent, for example, have plans to introduce or improve their reviewing manager training, and an increasing minority are also running training for employees in the new processes, emphasising the mutual responsibilities and benefits. Thirty-six per cent were moving to multi-rater appraisal.

More will also join the minority who are simplifying their 'all-singing, all-dancing' systems to help with the process of performance improvement, and as Hendry, Bradley and Perkins (2000) put it, 'focus on a few key activities which really make a difference'. Fletcher (1997) believes that 'companies are abandoning more complex systems and the fruitless search for objectivity: accepting both the imperfections and the necessity of appraisal, they are focusing on areas of achievable improvement'. My own preference is for simple open paperwork, as in BOC where the forms consist of fairly blank sheets. One is for employees to rate their own performance and set out their personal aspirations and goals, and another for the reviewing manager to do the same from their department's perspective.

Armstrong and Baron's (2000) research points to this transformation in performance management occurring, paralleling the changes in reward approaches we have described. There is increasingly a more holistic and process emphasis, broader consideration of performance inputs and outputs, and much stronger local line management ownership and staff involvement. As they express it, performance management is coming 'out of the tick box'.

Second, clearly spell out and prioritise the performance objectives and goals of your schemes and then focus on delivering these few key priorities in practice. The emphasis may be, as at the AA, on business goal alignment and employee development, with pay driven more by the market and personal competence. In which case the budgeting and business planning processes need to be highly participative, and line management skills in identifying development opportunities for their staff, rather than simply recommending training programmes, relatively advanced.

Or the emphasis may be on the reward and reinforcement aspects, in which case the rewards really do need to differentiate exceptional performance, as at one of my client's where the pay increases for the highest performers have recently doubled to as much as four times the overall pay budget increase. They have achieved this partly by simplifying the performance rating system to focus on the few truly outstanding staff and the small minority of unsatisfactory performers.

In most cases performance management in the future will need to involve aspects of both personal development and reward. I have never been convinced by the argument that discussions about pay can ever be totally divorced from discussions about performance, particularly in open and fast-moving knowledge-based organisations. But you need to ensure that the two aspects are fully understood and that they do not come into conflict. Bristol Myers nicely sets out the objectives of the two complementary components of their Performance Partnerships system:

1 Performance review is concerned with:
   - reviewing past performance
   - agreeing specific short-term objectives and standards
   - supporting the achievement of business goals and short-term performance
   - providing an equitable means of linking pay to performance.

2 Training, education and development (TED) is a developmentally focused process aimed at:

- maximising individual development and the achievement of potential
- longer-term performance improvement and growth
- establishing and implementing individual development plans.

Interestingly, their research director believes that the two systems will come together in the future, but for now the distinct emphasis is required to deliver on both sets of reward and development goals. Another point that this example illustrates is the very basic need to set out clearly the content and timing of each stage in the process, and who has what responsibilities in it. It is amazing how often people are not actually aware of this.

Focusing on the few key goals and components provides an effective platform for greater diversity in performance management practice within organisations, which is a third consideration and requirement for many of us, mirroring the same evolution in reward practices that we covered in Chapter 3. As Kessler and Purcell (1992) observe, performance management should be a natural process, and as such, cannot be confined within a corporate straitjacket if it is to be truly effective. In one NHS unit, for example, a common performance management framework was drawn up after a detailed review of current practice involving consultations with staff. This framework included common principles such as genuine two-way communication, and components, such as that the 'hows' and 'whats' of performance had in all cases to be addressed.

But in phase 2 of the work, different staff groups tailored this template to suit the needs of their own occupations, paralleling the trend towards job family pay structures. This ensured a high level of ownership and face validity in the new system. The paperwork now looks very different for the various staff groups, but the common principles and framework are adhered to and are evident in practice.

'Opening up' your approach to performance management to achieve this greater understanding and ownership is another key recommendation. The growth in 360-degree appraisal is one formal manifestation of this trend, with generally positive, although some mixed, experiences. The growth in self-appraisal and the use of employee log books and portfolios is another. However, there are a myriad simpler ways of achieving this, many of them related to developing the sort of openness and mindset that we discussed in the previous section. Rackham, for example, found that managers with an open, encouraging style were far more effective in appraisal meetings

As Egan (1995) says, many bad experiences are 'due less to any glitch in the programme design than to the inadequacy of the assumptions underlying such programmes'. The aim must be to achieve the situation of the accountancy firm mentioned above, where staff push their managers to hold regular meetings, to ensure that their performance is recognised and their development plans agreed, rather than the current situation in many organisations where staff view it as a process 'done' to them.

Finally, take Fletcher's (1997) advice and focus on manageable improvement, giving sufficient time for this to occur. I learnt this from my work in a car company, where a rapid implementation timetable meant that we did not have time to run a fully comprehensive training and briefing programme for managers and staff on the new performance and pay management programmes. So instead we adopted a 'just-in-time' approach to implementation and the training support. After giving everyone an overview of the whole process, the initial short workshops concentrated on effective objective-setting. In mid-year we ran some further workshops on ongoing coaching and continuous development, as well as surveying and reviewing the effectiveness of the objective-setting that had occurred. Only towards the end of the year did we detail the pay linkage aspects and focus our training on developing performance review skills in managers.

This approach allowed the car company to build up its capability to manage the new process, as well as developing a momentum behind it and a trust in it amongst staff, who gave a positive response to the initial objective-setting and development planning. This made the potentially more contentious issue of the pay link much easier to address later in the year.

Reward strategy as a change process
Achievable improvement

> ‘Change management and evolution are an integral part of reward strategies’

This car company example illustrates a critical and much more general point about the required change in the mindset that we have traditionally adopted in developing and operating our reward strategies. We need to look at these strategies from an employee as well as a business perspective, and in terms of processes and operation, rather than just objectives and designs. But we also need to recognise and accept the concepts of change management and evolution as being an integral part of our reward strategies if we are to make them truly effective in contributing to business performance over the long term.

A lot of my early reward strategy work involved describing the current 'as is' situation in a firm and then contrasting this with the desirable future reward state there, the 'to be'. The reward strategy was a statement of this future nirvana, contrasting current rigidity with future flexibility, lack of a market and performance link in a status culture with a strongly contribution-driven set of arrangements, and an HR-administered set of pay plans with a line-owned and employee-involved set of schemes. This future state was painted in detailed and attractive terms, such that the directors would invariably buy in to it. Yet what we failed to give sufficient attention to was how to actually get from 'A' to 'B', and how big the jump required was.

Now I realise that reward strategy is actually much more about setting the broad direction and actually addressing how to make that journey. Indeed, as the managing director of a power company put it to the first meeting of a joint management/staff study group he had set up to review the level and direction of reward change required, 'We may not need to change very much, but a lot of the benefit will come from the process itself, of asking the "why" and "how" questions which we have never addressed before.'

Thankfully, many other people appear to be making the same realisation. Consider these descriptions of reward strategies provided by two HR directors, the first in a major bank and the second in a pharmaceutical company:

- ❷ 'We take a graduated approach, learning as we go, moving step-by-step, developing understanding and agreement before we move forward again.'
- ❷ 'Changing, evolving, testing, improving as we go, as part of a continuing long-term process – this is the key to successful reward management, just as it is to our research and development activities.'

This is the essence of real reward strategies and the approach that is required and which is now being applied far more widely. This pattern of changes that is becoming evident was characterised in our European study (Towers Perrin 1999b) as 'regular incremental "tinkering", evolving at a speed to suit the needs and capability of each organisational setting'. Trevor Blackman represented the Royal Bank of Scotland's reward strategy journey as progression up a snakes-and-ladders board, thankfully with more and larger ladders than snakes!

The practical implications of this more realistic and process-oriented concept of reward strategy are essentially twofold.

1   Develop capacity, competence and commitment in your reward strategy.
2   Treat the implementation of the reward strategy as a major change management exercise.

Developing capacity, competence and commitment

First, you have to plan and enable your organisation to progress along its own particular reward strategy pathway, allowing sufficient time and making sufficient resource available to successfully make the transition. As we saw in Chapter 5, big bang changes rarely succeed in reward management. In flexible benefits, broadbanding or whatever, organisations are progressing in appropriate stages towards their desired goals. This is developing three critical 'C's in your organisation:

- ✪ the *capacity* to make changes, particularly given the plethora of change programmes and initiatives under way in most companies
- ✪ the *capability* of managers and administrators to deliver the changes as intended
- ✪ the *commitment* of staff to the changes and their effects.

Too often in the past, organisations have given the priority to changes that were strongly aligned with their goals, such as performance pay, but failed to consider the amount of effort that would be required to operate them and gain staff acceptance. Lower-profile changes, to working conditions and recognition schemes for example, have often achieved more in practice because they have been far easier to implement and operate.

The importance of an evolutionary approach is best illustrated with an example. A newly privatised water company, with a new HR director from the private sector, rapidly made a series of changes to the reward schemes of its managers, with flexibility and performance as the main objectives. The hierarchical industry-wide arrangements were replaced reasonably successfully with broader bands, performance pay and incentive schemes. In the following 12 months, the organisation attempted to apply the same approach to all remaining staff, with a new evaluation and grading structure, new appraisal system and merit pay scheme, and new collective bargaining structure developed and introduced.

In a sense, the new reward strategy had been too attractive and the directors had given insufficient thought as to how the reward goals would be achieved across a much larger population of staff, with a very different set of views and experiences. Not surprisingly, the implementation of such a major change programme over such a short timescale went badly, with the effects including industrial action and the breakdown of the company's payroll system.

Subsequently, a more gradual series of changes were planned and negotiated with the trade unions, following extensive consultation with staff. The desired end state was thereby largely achieved within the following three years by moving along a clear, staged, evolutionary pathway.

Reward as change management

Second, as in this case, treat the implementation of your reward strategy and its components and changes as a major change management exercise in its own right. Putting new reward plans in place represents a significant change management challenge, with typical sources of resistance including self-interest, conflicts of interest, fears of pay reductions, power and political battles, cynicism and the demands of other initiatives and priorities. The reward strategy cynics are right in this regard; the answer is not to abandon our strategies, but to plan and achieve progress given these realities and constraints. We need to use all of the tools and techniques of the change management experts in doing so, a number of which we have already mentioned in this chapter: open and early communications and involvement, employee needs analysis and audience segmentation.

A few of the disciplines I typically go through as part of thinking through the reward change process include the following:

- considering the process implications of any proposed reward scheme changes at an early stage, as to what will be the level and nature of changes required in pay budgeting, pay administration and systems and so on, and the work that needs to be done to achieve them
- thinking about the various audiences for the changes – managers, professionals, unions etc – and the level of support that we need from them to make the changes happen, and how we are going to achieve that support; who we need to make the change happen, who we need to help it happen and who to not oppose it happening – too often the focus falls on winning over the arch opponents and cynics, whereas research suggests that building up support first amongst the typically agnostic majority is a much more effective change-realisation strategy
- conducting a rigorous analysis of the gains and losses, costs and benefits of the changes from the perspective of all of these different groups involved and affected.

Nobody would argue that making reward changes is not a difficult and time-consuming process. But by paying greater attention to that process, we will improve our chances of realising the substantial gains that a strategic approach to reward management offers. Only then will we see Grattan's (2000a) 'living' strategies evident in rewards.

Chapter summary

- Open and effective, two-way communications and involvement processes contribute to the success of organisations and their reward practices in many different ways: building understanding and trust in them, demonstrating the links between business performance and rewards, and providing channels for performance improvement.

- Remarkably high levels of secrecy and misunderstanding on reward issues are prevalent in UK companies, frustrating the effective implementation of reward changes. Communications and involvement has generally been given a low priority in reward strategy goals, and the use of traditional channels and line managers' skills have often been found wanting.

- Practice does now seem to be changing, with more organisations committed to addressing these problems. Companies need to commit to being more open on reward issues and give communications a higher priority in their strategic goals. They need to audit the current situation and take steps to improve it, such as training managers and involving employees directly in redesign work. They also need to brand and 'sell' any changes more effectively and attractively to their staff.

- Performance management schemes present a similar picture, with a general recognition of their importance and potential, but widespread dissatisfaction with their failings in practice. The problems appear to relate to confused and overambitious objectives, complexity, an excessive focus on the pay link, and operating problems in our fast-changing organisations.

- Actions to address these issues include:
    - focusing on the process rather than the systems and the paperwork, for example through improved manager and staff training and support
    - defining a few clear goals and priorities, setting realistic and manageable targets for improvement, and ensuring that the reward and developmental objectives do not come into conflict
    - allowing for diversity within the organisation in terms of how these goals are achieved, with local tailoring and flexibility
    - heavily involving staff in the redesign and operating process.

- ❷ Reward strategies need not only to specify principles and goals, but also to set out and manage the process of moving from the current to the desired reward situation. This transition generally takes place in stages. It needs to be planned and enabled with sufficient time and resource, while change management techniques need to be employed to facilitate it.

Chapter 8

A pathway for developing your own reward strategy, step by step

Chapter objectives

- describe an effective approach to diagnosing, designing, implementing and operating a reward strategy in your own organisation
- highlight the key work phases and stages involved
- illustrate the process with specific tools and case examples.

The importance of the process

This book has emphasised that there are no universally successful pay and reward schemes and that you cannot effectively import an 'off-the-consultant's-shelf' reward strategy. Nonetheless, some consistent themes and components of these strategies have emerged.

- Effective reward strategies are heavily concerned with process, not just practices and principles, in order to make them an operating reality and to successfully confront the difficult change management issues that are often involved.
- Reward strategies need to be tailored and evolve to match the unique goals and characteristics of your own organisation and its staff, and the changes in them.

But just how do you do that? How do you assess which of the almost infinite range of reward schemes and variations will suit the characteristics of your employer? How do you keep pace with the rapid shifts in your organisation, when some schemes can take months to develop and install? And how do you reconcile all of the different demands and pressures – from the marketplace, from directors, from staff and unions – even in just agreeing what change is needed and what should be in the strategy, never mind making it a working reality?

In many cases, where reward practices have become obsolete and failed to respond to changed business and organisational priorities (as illustrated in the case study in Chapter 1), the problem has been recognised. But there is no agreement as to how to address it, nor often even where to start in such an apparently complex and contentious field. So it is deemed easier to leave it alone, letting the problems of misalignment multiply and become increasingly serious.

‹An effective reward strategy is a living process›

An effective reward strategy is a living process and the way in which you develop, change, implement and operate it is absolutely critical to its success and one of the most important parts of that process. This was brought home to me once when I attended one of the traditional consulting 'beauty parades' with a motor industry client, in order to decide who should assist them in implementing a new points-factor job evaluation scheme. I emphasised in my pitch that while Towers Perrin has a wonderful computerised points-factor evaluation system, I felt that we should spend some time first investigating the organisation, its needs, the current reward schemes, and what managers and staff felt. We could then assess the key reward issues they needed to address, and if points-factor evaluation was indeed a solution to some of these issues, then we would have gathered in the process all of the information we needed to tailor the scheme to suit their company. While the directors were resistant to the fee implications of all this investigation, they nonetheless agreed to my proposal. I later found out why.

Twelve months before they had gone through exactly the same procedure and a consultancy had been selected. The consultants essentially sat in an office for a month with the firm's HR manager. They analysed and produced piles of information and paperwork: job descriptions, pay information, factor descriptions, job scores and gradings. I discovered a large box with much of the work in it. But despite the agreement of the directors, in the box was where it had stayed. Line managers and staff had no understanding and awareness of the new scheme. Managers saw no need for such a complex approach and continued to set pay levels based on their views of market worth, while staff saw it as pseudo-science and HR mumbo-jumbo that they did not trust.

After we had subsequently reviewed the situation, the emphasis in the changes they made was much more towards creating stronger links between business and individual performance and pay. A simple evaluation system of slotting jobs into four broad bands was implemented and operated subsequently.

This process of developing and implementing the strategy is therefore critical to the effectiveness of your reward policies and practices. As the managing director of the energy trading company recounted in Chapter 7, even if not much change occurs, the process itself is valuable in developing a better understanding of what reward practices are aiming to do and how this can be better delivered in practice.

In addition, it is essential to tailor this process to the needs and character of the organisation. A fast-growing entrepreneurial company is not going to want you to spend six months diagnosing the situation, even though in my experience it is vital in these settings to consult widely and achieve high levels of buy-in to any new approach. Correspondingly, we recently delayed the introduction of a new reward strategy in a local authority to provide more time to build the capability and confidence in the changes that were proposed.

While it is ideal to progress in sequence along the reward strategy pathway from business needs, through capabilities required and employee needs, to rewards practices – as emphasised in Chapter 2 – the relationships are in fact multi-directional and overlapping. Quite often I find myself working in the other direction, helping to solve an immediate operating problem by working back up to define what the business really needs. Thus for a utility that had implemented a new sales incentive plan that was producing incredibly high monthly commission payments for sales staff, we identified that while they did indeed want a stronger pay-for-performance relationship, they had not thought enough about the electricity market dynamics and their organisation structure in designing their scheme.

Predicting prices in this market that had been recently opened to competition was very difficult, while teamwork was vital to securing the often long-term power contracts. We therefore redesigned the scheme to have a team component and be based on a mix of personal objectives rather than simply the contract price.

Designing reward strategies and their components needs to be an ongoing dynamic and multidirectional process and there is no one best way of doing it, no 'typical' timescale or always-included components. The content and components, even the extent to which you define and structure the strategy and the work as a formal project, will need to vary to suit your situation.

However, there is an overall approach to designing and operating your reward strategy that is consistently effective. Throughout this book, examples are provided of some of the techniques and tools that we use at Towers Perrin to help companies make these kinds of assessments, define their reward goals and tailor their scheme designs, as well as case studies illustrating this process in action. In this chapter, however, all of this is brought together so as to provide a reward strategy development pathway, your own step-by-step guide to doing it in your own particular organisation setting. The utility company case study at the end then gives a detailed illustration of the pathway in action and its outcomes in one specific setting.

A phased process
The four phases
If you are going to build a real pathway, or better a motorway, you do not immediately jump in and start laying the concrete and the tarmac, painting the directional arrows and yellow lines and putting in the signposts. No, the work progresses through a series of phases.

First there is a huge amount of preparatory and planning work to be done. The best route needs to be assessed and surveyed, the usage forecast, the materials and design planned, and a consortium of land and construction companies and funding agencies formed. Local authorities, residents and government all need to be consulted and involved – all this before the first sod is cut.

Then the design work follows a detailed work plan and schedule, involving the co-ordination of many different suppliers and contractors. Unexpected problems emerge and have to be dealt with, and even the route changed in some cases. Before traffic can use the motorway, it then has to be rigorously tested and certified. And finally, once it is open and operational, regular checks and maintenance work needs to be undertaken. Start one phase of the work before the prior one is properly completed and you have major problems: cracks appear in the road, the streetlights don't work, or whatever.

Yet nowadays, with such significant rates of change occurring in reward practices, I encounter at least as many difficulties caused by a failure to follow this type of systematic process when introducing new schemes as I do problems resulting from a failure to modify reward schemes so as to align them with changes in the business. In fact, I probably spend almost as much time dissuading companies from implementing unsuitable, ill-thought-through and over-hastily designed schemes as I do persuading them to make essential reward changes.

Your reward strategy has to follow a similar development and construction process if it is to be anything other than a five-minute wonder and if it is to have a genuinely effective life beyond any written strategy document or reward policy manual. It is generally recommended that you progress through four phases in this process:

- an initial diagnostic phase, when the current business, cultural and reward context is reviewed, and the goals, principles and direction for your future reward strategy is set and agreed
- the detailed design and development phase, when the reward changes and practices to deliver on your principles and goals are detailed and initially tested and costed
- third, a period of preparation involving more detailed testing and building the capability of the organisation to operate the reward practices as intended, as well as planning the transition from the current reward schemes
- finally implementation, which with any major set of reward changes is itself likely to be phased, followed, importantly, by ongoing review, modification and adaptation of your schemes and processes.

Table 14 summarises the main components and elements that are typically required in each phase. The rest of the chapter describes and illustrates each of them in turn in more detail.

Table 14

A PHASED PROJECT PATHWAY TO CREATING A LIVING REWARD STRATEGY

	Phase 1
Purpose	Diagnosis of current situation, setting the future direction and principles, development of the future reward architecture
Outputs	❷ Full understanding of current reward situation ❷ Identification of key reward issues ❷ Future reward strategy definition and components ❷ Defined employment 'deal' ❷ Prioritisation of schemes and changes ❷ Detailing and communication plan ❷ Buy-in and support of relevant interest groups
Typical stages	❷ Planning ❷ Formation of project teams ❷ Interviews and group discussions ❷ Market analysis ❷ Internal data review ❷ Workshops

	Phase 2
Purpose	Detailed design of the components of the future reward approach

Outputs	❷ Detailed scheme designs, eg:
	  ❷ pay structures and levels
	  ❷ base pay reviews
	  ❷ incentive and bonus plans
	  ❷ share schemes
	  ❷ benefits
	❷ Schemes initially modelled and tested
	❷ Preparation plan
	❷ Senior management approval

Typical stages	❷ Design team meetings ❷ Drafting of scheme designs ❷ Testing of new schemes on sample of jobs ❷ Further consultation ❷ Staff updates and briefings

	Phase 3
Purpose	**Preparation and testing, building the capability to deliver**
Outputs	❷ Agreed, finalised changes/schemes ❷ Fully tested and costed reward schemes ❷ Trained managers and staff with clear understanding of reward strategy and changes ❷ Defined implementation and operating responsibilities and policies ❷ Appropriate, phased implementation plan ❷ Branded reward strategy with clear themes and components
Typical stages	❷ Further testing of designs, eg pilots ❷ Analysis of transition from current situation ❷ Detailed modelling and costing ❷ Development and delivery of communications and training support ❷ Trade union negotiation ❷ Design of operating, administration and control procedures

	Phase 4
Purpose	**Implementation and ongoing review and adjustment**
Outputs	❷ Detailed implementation communication ❷ Effectively implemented reward schemes ❷ Effectively operating reward processes ❷ Operation of review mechanisms and modifications as required ❷ Further development of management skills and staff understanding
Typical stages	❷ Full and possibly phased implementation ❷ Regular audits of effectiveness ❷ Design of any modifications to schemes

The benefits

‘Having clear and agreed objectives is essential’

Following this type of phased process has a number of significant benefits. First, it is critical for ensuring that your reward approach is strategic, that you have some clear goals and principles in place, related to business and employee needs, which your reward schemes can then be designed to deliver. We have seen many examples in this book already to illustrate that having clear and agreed objectives is essential for the successful operation of any reward scheme, and indeed defines what success actually is.

In addition, it ensures that these goals are in place before the most resource-intensive and costly detailed design work is undertaken. I have on a number of occasions seen problems emerging well into the design detailing phase because senior management suddenly question important aspects of the approach – such as feeling that individual rather than team performance should be rewarded, or job evaluation removed altogether rather than simplified – when the design of these schemes is all but completed.

Agreeing the rationale, goals and outline components of your reward strategy in phase 1 avoids such problems, or rather confronts them early in the process so that they can be debated and addressed without wasting unnecessary resources on designing inappropriate schemes.

For those of you looking at Table 14 and thinking what a major and costly exercise it is, this does not mean that there are no 'quick wins' in reward, nor that everything, wagon-train-like, has to move at the speed of the slowest new practice to develop or most recalcitrant division to adopt it. In reality, as we shall see, the phases shown are interactive and overlapping, and often certain changes can be implemented fairly quickly and painlessly.

But even with these faster changes, it is essential to ensure that they are supporting the direction your business has chosen to go in, that people understand them, and that you can operate them effectively before you implement them. Many of those companies who implemented 'employee of the month' recognition schemes borrowed straight from their competitors – and found employee cynicism and demotivation in response – probably wished they had reflected in more detail on the need for them and form they needed to take.

Third, this phased progression allows you to progressively build up the capability of the organisation to ensure that the operation and experience of your reward practices is in line with the stated goals, which as we have seen is where so many reward strategies fall down. Phase 3 is when the formal systems and procedures to administer and operate schemes are finalised – transition arrangements, appeals processes, budgeting controls and so on. But throughout the whole process, the understanding of the strategy and its implications is being developed, and champions and agents of the change process being identified and trained.

Building understanding, support and commitment to the reward strategy and its components – which as we saw in the last chapter is probably the most critical factor of all in making your reward strategy real – is a fourth benefit of this approach. Views and agendas can be identified and brought out in the first phase, and then understanding and support built up for the selected strategic direction and goals thereafter, with progressively higher and more detailed levels of communications and involvement occurring.

This is a question not just of getting unions and staff on board and supportive, but also of ensuring that all the senior managers fully buy in to the process. Kessler and Purcell's (1992) research found managers, for example, agreeing with the introduction of performance pay in meetings and then rubbishing it to their colleagues and staff outside. And as the case study at the end of the chapter illustrates, if any unforeseen difficulties do subsequently emerge in implementation, senior management needs to be seen to be fully supportive, rather than leading a hasty retreat.

Roles and responsibilities

As well as regular consultation and communication through these work phases, you should specify work roles and particularly decision-making responsibilities on any reward strategy project. Reward work combines major business and cultural impact with incredibly detailed and intricate design and operating issues (how do we treat people on maternity leave? what is the impact of the working time regulations on our shift patterns and payments? do we pay bonuses to those on long-term absence? etc). Having clearly defined roles and responsibilities is essential to ensuring that one does not come into conflict with the other and that your strategy addresses both the 'wood' and the 'trees' of reward management.

Often when I am engaged on this type of work in an organisation, we form both a policy or steering group and a project or design team at the outset. The policy group would be formed of executives responsible for managing the organisation and for signing off the reward strategy, changes and any related costs. They would meet at the start and end of each phase to agree key outcomes and subsequent work plans. Their time commitment is not typically very significant, but their understanding and buy-in is essential for reward schemes to have strategic impact, and as the Towers Perrin (1999b) European study shows, compensation and HR managers are increasingly involving directors in this way. The group also plays a key facilitation and overseeing role throughout the project.

The project design team obviously comprises relevant HR staff and undertakes the bulk of analysis, design and preparatory work on the project. Typically the project is led by the head of compensation and benefits, who would devote a significant part of his or her working time to it. But I am a keen advocate of also involving line managers directly on the team in order to build credibility and support for any subsequent changes. This also ensures that any new designs reflect the realities of operating life in the organisation, which failure to take account of in the past has often frustrated the successful introduction of reward changes. The pressures on their time are always great and getting them on the team is difficult, but the returns are even greater. Sometimes we have a core membership of the design team who can devote more time to the project, lessening the time demands on line managers involved.

One of the most successful project teams I was involved in, at a vehicle importer, was actually led by the dealer development manager. His knowledge and credibility in the company were critical to our success. Scottish Amicable similarly used a design team comprising HR, line managers and staff members to detail a new competence- and results-oriented rewards approach.

One of the questions I am most frequently asked is whether trade unions and members of staff should be directly involved on these teams. British Energy, for example, used a mixture of line managers, HR and trade union staff on a number of separate design teams during phase 2 of their reward change work, and full-time union officials were represented on the steering group.

The answer is: it depends. While maximum levels of involvement on the project should be endorsed, this has to be balanced with creating a project team of an appropriate size who can deliver on their goals.

I have worked on design teams with up to 20 members and I have found this to be too large a group to actually get the work done on time collectively.

In the foods division of a large UK group, members of staff from all the main functions were represented on the initial project team of a dozen members and then on the sub-teams who took on the detailed design work in each area in phase 2. They were not unionised.

However, in a large local authority I worked with earlier this year, with a huge diversity of functions and types of staff, there was a core project team of eight, including union officials, line managers and HR staff. In this case, we set up a number of consultation forums with the various staff groups, so that we could solicit their views on the progress of the project at key points but not have everybody trying to design the new competency framework, pay method and performance management system at the same time. Similarly, British Energy's design teams consulted with literally hundreds of staff as they carried out their phase 2 work. And as described below, it is important to get the input of all interested parties into the work at key points, whether through formally structured or more informal means.

‘Recognised trade unions need to be involved, and the earlier the better’

Recognised trade unions clearly need to be involved, and the earlier the better. Officials can bring good experience and knowledge of pay issues and designs evident in other organisations that they represent to the project. Doctrinaire objections to particular practices irrespective of the context and need are now, thankfully, rarely apparent.

However, I have seen examples where the unions feel they are put in a difficult situation by being on the project design team, in that it might appear to compromise their ability to negotiate the final details of any new or changed practices in phase 3. Again, in such cases regular consultation with them is still advisable as the work progresses. This makes it much less likely that there will be any nasty surprises late in the process for either party. If the unions are presented with a set of proposals late on in the process that they have had no input into and no understanding of, then the chances of their agreeing to them are bound to be much less.

One of the advantages of undertaking a root-and-branch review in phase 1 is that you can use this to help finalise who actually will be involved in the design work in phase 2, and how the design work will proceed. On a recent project with a county council, we used the phase 1 consultations and interviews to 'talent spot' managers and members of staff who were knowledgeable on the subject and could contribute something to the project's progress in phase 2. Generally it is helpful to have a mix of people with different backgrounds and experiences, some who have been in the organisation a long time, know its culture and how the current schemes operate, and some who have joined recently and have more knowledge of alternative practices in other organisations.

Whoever is on the project team, it is essential that they commit to the goal of producing the most appropriate reward strategy for the future success of the organisation and do not simply represent the self-interests of the group that they form a part of. Establishing this understanding and agreeing behavioural and working norms is an important part of the initial meetings of the project team.

If you involve external consultants with the project, it is important that they do not dominate the process and do all the work, because the chances of the reward strategy being tailored to your organis- ation and of it working in practice once the consultants have gone will be much lower. Agree a sharing of responsibilities with them, focusing them on where you do not have the skills and resources in your own organisation and where they can add most value. Ensure that they transfer their learning and experience to your in-house team.

The length of each phase varies considerably, depending on factors such as the size of the organisation, the scale and seriousness of the reward issues, and the resources that are devoted to addressing them. On average, however, phase 1 might take one to two months to com- plete, phase 2 six to 12 weeks, and phase 3 up to three months. Full implementation in a large organisation might take up to two years. But as illustrated later in the chapter, a much more intense and shorter exercise can be used to highlight issues and set the future direction.

Phase 1: diagnosis and direction

I was at a meeting with a company last week, discussing the reward practices that would be needed in their new customer service centre. I went with the HR manager to see the project manager who was to become the head of the new operation. 'So, where are the outline reward schemes?' was his welcome to us, and he was none too pleased when we explained that we still had the proverbial blank sheet. We explained that we wanted to get his input first, in terms of his performance priorities, how he saw the team structure operating, how much role flexibility he was anticipating, what culture he wanted to create and so on.

Fortunately, the powerful evidence of cripplingly high levels of demotivation and attrition in some call centres convinced him that maybe we did need to think this through in a bit more detail first. Reward, even with the very tight deadlines involved in getting the service centre up and running, is not an area where you want to be acting first and thinking, or probably regretting, later.

Another common feature in our resource- and time-constrained organisations is jumping to a particular reward solution very early on without being clear about what the most serious reward issues are and whether this particular scheme really is the best way to address them. I have had two briefs to develop a team reward scheme in the past year where our conclusion after the review phase was that such an approach would not produce any improvement. In one case, for example, in a research facility, teamwork was indeed vital to the achievement of its business goals. But the structure was a fluid one of changing and multiple team membership, and overlaying a formal team bonus structure on this would almost certainly have introduced damaging rigidities, impeding the free flow of staff and resources that was required. So instead, we focused more on developing team-working skills in staff and used less direct recognition awards to reward effective examples of it.

Often there tends to be a simplistic view that everything in the current situation is all bad and these new schemes will be all good, when the reality is that all reward approaches have their strengths and weaknesses. Your role is to shift the balance away from the latter to get more of the former, thereby improving staff motivation and the contribution of rewards to business success.

Phase 1 is when this thinking and analysis is done:

● when you develop a full understanding of the current reward situation, its strengths and weaknesses, and the views on it of all relevant stakeholders, in the context of the key business goals and structural and cost parameters

● when you identify the key reward issues that you have, where rewards are not effectively aligned with what the business and your staff need

● when you consider feasible alternative ways of improving the degree of alignment and decide on the relative benefits and inapplicability in your own setting

● when you set out the strategic direction and principles for rewarding people in the future, supporting the type of employment relationship that will maximise the chances of business and personal success

● when you outline the reward architecture of future schemes and processes to deliver that vision in practice which can be fully integrated and consistent with itself and with your other HR schemes and systems

● when you additionally identify the process that you plan to go through to detail and roll out the strategy: the priorities, the timing, the resources required.

Questions to answer

This phase needs to provide well-researched answers to a number of key questions about your organisation and its reward practices.

● From a business perspective, what do we need to reward our people for to make the business a success? What are the key performance goals and the essential skills, behaviours and actions? To what extent do our current reward policies and practices support the business strategy, and what we need to do to achieve it? Where are the major gaps?

- In respect of organisation structure, to what extent does the way we reward people currently support the structure of the business, of teams and of work/jobs? What are the implications of the way the organisation is changing for rewards? Do we need a corporate reward approach, a business-unit-based one or both? How consistent are and should be our reward practices across the organisation?

- From a cultural and HR perspective, what is the nature of the employment philosophy that we have and need? What are our core values and to what extent do rewards reinforce these? What is our HR strategy and how well do our reward policies mesh with our other HR systems?

- In terms of employees, what are their motivations and needs and how are these segmented? What do they think of the current reward package and about possible changes to it?

- Looking at external product/service and labour markets, how competitive is our current rewards package and what should our market stance be? What practices and changes are evident amongst competitors, and what does this tell us?

- In terms of current reward schemes, what are their major strengths and weaknesses in regard to business and staff needs alignment, flexibility, cost-effectiveness and so on?

And, finally, looking to the future:

- What should the key goals, priorities and principles of our future approach be to reinforce business goals and staff needs?

- What are alternative approaches and schemes to deliver on these principles, and their relative strengths and weaknesses in our setting? How consistent/varied do reward practices need to be across the organisation?

- What are the recommended components of our future reward strategy going to be?

- What are the likely effects of making changes, and how do we build capacity, competence and commitment in the organisation to make them successfully?

- What do we do next?

This is a very demanding agenda of questions and issues, but from the alternative perspective, do you think that you could effectively implement changes to improve your rewards approach without solid and agreed answers to the majority of them? So how do you go about getting the answers?

Work stages

The work stages in a phase 1 audit that I am currently helping a telecomms business with are shown below.

1 *Planning:*
  - agree objectives and scope
  - plan detailed content/timescales
  - agree work and decision-making responsibility; form project team and steering group
  - plan communications/involvement strategy, eg initial briefings.

2 *Internal interviews:*
  - senior managers – business needs; current pay/rewards; desired changes and direction
  - union officials and other opinion-formers.

3 *Staff group discussions:*
  - current motivations and demotivations
  - views on rewards and possible changes.

4 *Data analysis:*
  - full details of current pay and reward schemes
  - related HR systems, eg performance management competencies
  - business/organisation details.

5 *Market analysis:*
  - competitiveness of current rewards in relevant market(s)
  - external trends and implications
  - relevant example schemes and case studies.

6 *Steering group meeting:*
  - review findings
  - develop reward strategy pathway
  - agree key principles and priorities.

7 *Project team meeting(s):*
  - review detail of findings and agree major issues to address
  - identify and analyse change options to address issues
  - make selection of changes
  - plan implementation.

8 *Report/steering group meeting:*
   - findings
   - future reward strategy
   - specific proposals and changes
   - next steps
   - discussion/agreement.

This case involves a reasonably comprehensive analysis, as the organisation has grown through a number of acquisitions and nobody has really looked at all of their reward schemes in a coherent way before. It may be that you do not need to undertake all of these stages as you may have prior analyses, say, on the external market, or employee attitudes, already. However, you do need to make sure that you have current and accurate information from all of the perspectives indicated on this plan.

Typical stages, therefore, would include:

- planning
- consultation with stakeholders
- internal analysis
- market analysis
- agreement of principles
- project team meetings
- next-step planning
- board approval.

Planning

Planning involves agreeing the aims and the scope of the project and agreeing the breadth of reward schemes that you are going to consider. As already indicated, taking as wide a perspective as possible at this stage is conducive to a more strategic set of reward outcomes. You will also need to form and brief the project teams, and it is generally useful to let staff know that a review is under way, without any preconceived idea as to what the level and nature of changes might be.

Consulting with stakeholders

‘People really value being asked to contribute’

Consult with stakeholders to understand the business, work and cultural dynamics in the organisation and gain their views on the current systems and possible changes. Generally this should be done through a series of interviews, focus group discussions and workshops. If there are serious misalignment issues present, these usually emerge surprisingly quickly and with a high level of consensus from these sessions. As outlined in the last chapter, even if this is not the case, you usually learn a lot about the realities of payment and reward in the organisation and about how best to go about making changes. People really value being asked to contribute.

Internal analysis

This involves analysing the reward components and arrangements at the moment, as well as related HR systems. Directors are often amazed when we show them some simple analyses of current practices, such as the number of different grades and allowances, or the amount of money being spent on job evaluation regradings, or the total costs of employee attrition, and how the total employment costs break down across the various reward items. As in the case study at the end of this chapter, the illogicality and inconsistencies of various practices and the conflict between the reward theory and the reality can often be highlighted very simply with some select examples.

Market analysis

This involves reviewing relevant external reward trends and levels. Here the issue is not just one of competitiveness but also of digging deeper into how business and employment trends in your sector are affecting rewards practices, how your competitors are responding and what you can learn from this. While you cannot successfully copy a reward strategy from somebody else, this process can certainly give you lots of ideas as to alternatives and the sort of approach that you might adopt to differentiate yourselves from the competition.

Agreement of principles

This involves getting directors to agree to some future reward principles to support the achievement of their goals for the organisation. It is often a difficult stage. While it is easy for them to nod in agreement with a few general wishes about competitiveness and equity, it is much more difficult to develop an understanding of what this will mean in practice and to comprehend that these principles may come into conflict, so some notion of priorities needs to be agreed on. Here are three techniques that can be used to achieve this:

❶ Provide them with a list of typical reward policy objectives (recruitment, motivation, cost-effectiveness, flexibility, business fit, pay for performance relationship, understanding and support, etc) and get them to rate each in terms of the extent to which they are currently being delivered and their significance to the organisation in the future. This usually opens up a productive debate on current failings and future priorities.

❷ Carry out a gap analysis, by which you get them to assess the emphasis in current practices between competing reward goals, and then assess the direction in which the reward approach needs to move. An example of the results we got from the board of a pharmaceutical company at which we carried this out are shown in Figure 18, where X marks the average assessment of where they feel current reward practice is and O where it needs to move to. As well as demonstrating which issues they see as being key (where the gaps are largest), the exercise highlights that a reward strategy cannot do everything, but is about making choices. In the financial services company described in Chapter 2, it also demonstrated that different directors wanted to move in the opposite directions on some axes, so until that was resolved, they were never going to agree to the design proposals put forward to move the reward strategy in a particular direction.

❸ Give them some example schemes – individual, team and tiered bonus schemes, skills- and performance-related pay adjustment schemes or whatever – and then ask them which they prefer and why. This often draws out their underlying principles and needs for rewards in the organisation.

Project team meeting

This involves running a workshop with the project team to review all the findings, agree the key reward issues and then work up and analyse feasible alternatives and changes to address them and better deliver the reward strategy goals and principles. The issues need to be summarised clearly and concisely, possibly using one of the

Figure 18
AN EXAMPLE OF A GAP ANALYSIS

Our pay policies strongly reinforce the actions, results and competencies that support our strategy for business success	O X	Our pay policies essentially operate in isolation from business requirements
Our pay policies emphasise internal equity and consistency	X O	Our pay policies emphasise external market competitiveness
We pay high against the market	OX	We pay low against the market
We pay very much for the job and its defined requirements	X O	We pay for the person and his or her contribution
We pay for results, the 'whats'	O X	We pay for how results are achieved, the behaviours and competencies
Our pay arrrangements are highly structured and controlled	O X	Our pay arrangements are flexible and loosely managed
Our pay issues are determined largely by HR	XO	Our pay issues are determined largely by line managers
We maintain high levels of openness and understanding of pay systems	O X	Our pay information is largely secret and not understood
Our pay and reward systems are strongly merit-based	O X	Our pay and reward systems are hierarchical and status-based
We put emphasis on cash reward	X O	We put emphasis on non-cash rewards
We maintain harmonised, consistent reward systems for all staff	O X	Our reward systems vary for different types/groups of staff

X = current; **O** = desired

formats already illustrated in this book, such as blockages on the alignment pathway, or a summary of the situation, strengths and weaknesses in each of the four areas of total rewards. Generally you should initially consider the options in a very sketchy form to avoid unnecessary work and losing the sense of direction and coherence in the required changes. Then the selected one or possibly two designs can be fleshed out further (eg by outlining the options, advantages, disadvantages, implications and examples of each option). Continuing with the status quo should always be one of the options that you consider, however bad the current situation, in order to make an effective comparative assessment with possible changes and to ensure that these changes are likely to lead to improvement.

Next-step planning

This involves considering the implications of the selected changes for the reward and HR processes in the organisation – performance management, pay budgeting, payroll, communications and so on – and mapping out how to progress the work to implementation and operation.

Board approval

This involves securing the agreement of directors to the proposed reward strategy and the goals, practices and processes it contains, and communicating and consulting on its contents more widely in the organisation.

‘Produce a clear and brief description and brand for the strategy’

But what does the finished product of all this work actually look like? What form does it take? One of the advantages of widespread consultation at this early phase in the work is that it forces you to be brief and clear about what the reward strategy aims to do and how it intends to do it. If you are unable to produce a clear and brief description and brand for the strategy at this stage, then there is further analysis work to be done. To go into the design phase without this clarity is a recipe for confused, expensive and over-running design work, and then lengthy and difficult implementation.

Examples

In the case of the rail company whose strategic reward pathway we described in Chapter 2, the output of phase 1 was a short, four-page brief to the board, which subsequently acted as the basis for an even briefer reward policy document that went to all staff. This:

- profiled the current situation, with complex, differentiated, inherited reward systems acting as a block to the delivery of a customer- and performance-focused organisation
- illustrated some of the improvements made by other rail companies
- set out four key principles for future reward practices, based on competitiveness, harmonisation, cultural fit and flexibility
- listed proposed changes in each area of reward – moving to a single, flat pay structure and common-review-date contribution-based pay progression; the consolidation and simplification of allowances; and changes to overtime and shift pay – with the purpose and benefits of each change listed
- specified the overall benefits and analysed the risks in making the changes and how it was proposed to address these, such as allowing sufficient time to train managers and negotiate with trade unions in order to avoid the problems of poor implementation and union opposition; we also gave headline costings of the changes
- set out the next steps in the implementation process.

In a power trading business, the core principles and proposals were put onto one page (see Figure 19), and this acted as the basis for consultation with the staff working party, who subsequently also contributed to detailing the accepted changes to power them in this direction in phase 2.

Phase 2: detailed design
Questions

Returning to our road-building analogy, this is the phase in the work when the detailed construction is carried out, the trenches dug, the hard-core, gravel and sand and tarmac laid, and the whole thing initially road-tested. The questions you need to address include the following:

Figure 19

SUMMARY OF THE FUTURE REWARD APPROACH IN AN ENERGY TRADING BUSINESS

Principles	Practices	Purpose
✪ Ensure business 'fit'	✪ Broadbanded pay structure	✪ To retain scope to reflect market worth and value of the job/person
✪ Recruit, retain and motivate	✪ Job family definitions	✪ To provide development and career paths
✪ Support business and personal success	✪ Pay progression linked to growth in contribution	✪ To reward people according to their personal contribution to business success
✪ Reward growth in contribution	✪ Bonus scheme with business, team and individual components, varying by level, type of job	✪ To provide reward according to business performance
✪ Be open and understood		✪ To provide personal incentive
✪ Make it manageable		✪ To reflect the market
✪ Be fair and legal	✪ Benefits: well communicated and understood internally, moving to greater flexibility	✪ To increase perceived value to employees
	✪ Recognition: to generally recognise key goals/values	✪ To create an open and more recognition-oriented culture
	✪ Personal and career development plans	✪ To appeal to employees
		✪ To assist retention

- What are the new reward schemes to deliver our reward goals actually going to look like? What are their design features and how will they work?
- How will the changes be applied to particular jobs in the organisation?
- Are you sure that they actually will work?
- How will the changes integrate with each other, so that we deliver a consistent reward message to employees?
- How much will all these changes cost us, and what will be the benefits in return?
- What do staff and all of the stakeholders think of the proposals?
- How should we finalise and prepare to implement them?

Work stages

It is more difficult to describe the specific stages and process through this phase because it varies so much according to the scale and nature of the design and redesign work under way. In the utility case at the end of the chapter, it was a six-month exercise to construct a totally new set of rewards appropriate to their new commercial environment. In many cases it will be more focused on particular issues and practice changes.

The work tends to be more technical in this phase and so the compensation and HR specialists tend to take on the leadership role and carry out a lot of the work themselves. However, as already emphasised, it is important to keep managers and staff involved – on design teams, through updates, by testing their reactions to the emerging designs – in order to continue the vital process of progressively developing buy-in and support. In fact, the utility company in the case study at the end of this chapter set up communications activities as a separate project workstream, to ensure that all the other sub-teams gave it due prominence and gave feedback on progress in a co-ordinated way.

The stages generally required are:

- planning
- additional research
- detailed scheme design
- testing and modelling new schemes
- reporting and securing agreement.

Planning

This stage involves planning the work and briefing all of those involved with it. The phase 1 outcomes can act as the template to define the goals and deliverables from the project, but generally quite a lot of thought needs to be given as to how the work is segmented and sequenced. A key challenge is often to balance the need to get specific design work completed (answering questions, say, on a bonus redesign, such as: what are the team bonus measures? how do we set targets? how do payments vary in relation to performance? how do we treat leavers and joiners? etc) with the requirement to ensure that all of the changes and new designs do actually fit together and support the strategic goals. If, for example, the work involves a new pay structure, progression method and changes to performance management, should this be addressed by three separate design workstreams, or two, or all be done by the same design team, which might take longer but be better integrated? At the charity described in the case study in Chapter 6, there were a dozen workstreams, with a member of the HR function leading a number of small 'virtual' teams to address related sets of issues, but there were weekly meetings of the leaders to review progress and ensure consistency. In respect of timing, it may make sense to stagger the work, particularly if resources are tight, putting, say, pay structure design work before pay progression, or prioritising it in terms of significance or ease of achieving the particular design change.

Additional research

This stage involves possibly carrying out some additional research to help specify the design requirements – perhaps visiting a company who has gone down a similar route, or chatting to someone in the part of the company where the change is particularly needed, or carrying out a more structured exercise, say, to specify the competencies that can and should be linked to pay.

Detailed scheme design

Detailing the design of each of the reward changes is the most important aspect of this phase. The exact steps in this will vary, and the literature on the design of different reward schemes generally covers this pretty well. But it typically involves specifying the membership and coverage of each scheme, the specific goals of the change and how it will contribute to delivering on the reward strategy – defining the operating mechanics, and specifying how it will be managed and administered. Thus if moving into a broadbanded structure is one of the agreed changes, the work might involve determining the number of bands, designing the criteria to place jobs in each band, and using market data to establish the pay ranges to apply to each band. If the changes involve flexible benefits, the work would involve more detailed analysis of the employee demographics and current benefits costs, selection of the benefits to include and the level of choice to offer on each, and addressing the administration issue, such as who will run the scheme and how often employees will be given a chance to change their benefits selection.

Testing and modelling new schemes

The emerging designs then need to be tested in terms of their workability and impact and their coherence. Typically this takes two forms. First a sample of jobs in the organisation would be selected and the application of the new designs applied to them. So we might test the application of a new evaluation system on a benchmark sample of jobs, to see whether the new criteria did differentiate, and that the bands they came out in made sense internally and fitted well in the pay ranges from the standpoints of market competitiveness and current pay. Or we might explain the new flex scheme to a sample of employees and see whether they found it easy to understand and to make their choices.

This testing will also give a more accurate idea of the full cost impact of the changes, which is obviously an important number to be approved. It is also an aspect of strategic integration; often in my work we are aiming to create stronger business reinforcement through reward by using and re-allocating the existing spend more effectively, rather than proposing to spend a lot more money. Therefore the changes often involve reducing spending in one area, maybe overtime, in order to increase it in another, such as bonuses. The costing is usually based on applying the new approaches to a sample of staff and then building up from there to produce an estimate for the entire organisation.

‘Overall integration needs to be considered from a staff perspective’

The overall integration also needs to be considered from a staff perspective. Is the overall balance of changes one that they can understand, support and accept?

Report

Finally, the illustrated and detailed reward strategy needs to be presented to the steering group and/or directors, its components and likely impact approved and the next stage of the work agreed.

Examples

A large local authority pulled out of national pay bargaining in order to get better alignment with its own particular market and business needs and to address the threat from low-cost contractors in some areas and key skill shortages in others. Four work strands were set up, with a small team working on each and the head of each team sitting on an overall steering group.

They carried out further research in respect of:

- competency frameworks
- pay progression and bonus schemes (covered by the same team)
- performance management
- communications.

The teams produced some initial designs, which were reviewed together at a day's architecture workshop with around 30 managers from different parts of the organisation. This gave valuable feedback on the perceived likes, dislikes and gaps in design, as well as on the training and communication that would subsequently be required. The pay team simplified its approach as a result, with pay progression wholly related to growth in skills and competencies and a varying mix of team and individual bonuses developed to reward results. The schemes were subsequently 'tested' in a series of meetings with managers and staff in four different parts of the organisation, who applied them to their own jobs using budget and performance data for that year. The changes were subsequently approved by the council and implemented over the following two years.

In an Irish bank, phase 1 of the work resulted in agreement in an increasingly focused and competitive marketplace to reinforce the structural move to more independent business units with more heavily differentiated and performance-related rewards, as well as generally creating a more open and recognition-oriented culture. Changes were prioritised in terms of increasing employee shareholding and the use of individual bonuses in the short term, and introducing a new performance management system and team bonuses and recognition awards later.

The bank deliberately avoided setting up the phase 2 work as a major project, to avoid raising expectations and concerns in a very traditional culture. Each piece of work was developed and implemented separately, with one-year pilots being used in most cases to test the initial design proposals. However, a review after 12 months found – despite some individual successes – a general management perception that the changes had lost direction and a lack of understanding amongst staff of the overall change in the reward approach and employment relationship that the new designs were meant to underpin. The overall project team therefore reformed and a much clearer vision of where the bank and its reward schemes were heading was put together and communicated. Revised implementation plans were assembled and the changes were then introduced as a much more coherent package, although the specific schemes in each part of the business do now vary.

Phase 3: preparation and final testing

I was asked some years ago to come in to quality review and audit some reward changes proposed and being prepared by a major building society, in readiness for conversion to PLC status. The conversion date four months thereafter, close to the annual pay review date, was the target for implementation. My initial reactions were very positive. The rationale in terms of moving into a new competitive environment and becoming more performance- and shareholder-oriented was strong and was driving a raft of changes in organisation, business practices and related HR systems. Some of the wide-ranging reward changes proposed represented quite a radical shift, such as aiming at very high levels of employee shareholding and introducing high bonus opportunities for virtually all staff. But the proposals were detailed well and appeared to have addressed all of the design requirements, and it was, after all, a radical change in the organisation's structure and competitive environment to support.

But two days into my two-week assignment, I took the HR manager aside and gave him my view: 'You are not going to make this in time are you?' His response was one of utter relief. All of those involved in the design had apparently recognised that there was insufficient time before the scheduled launch date to get all the systems and processes and associated training in place and ready, as well as negotiated with the trade union, before flotation, but nobody had dared to risk putting an apparent spanner in the overall transformation programme. Subsequently, the directors agreed to a phasing in of the changes. They were implemented initially with a focus on senior managers (who were not in a bargaining group) and on pay, with bonus and benefits changes rolled in over the next 12 months.

Phase 3 is the most critical – and usually underemphasised and under-resourced – aspect of the reward strategy development pathway in terms of moving from intent to impact. It is here that so often the danger of a gap between reward strategy rhetoric and reality emerges and is not addressed, condemning the pristine reward changes and designs to subsequent ineffective implementation and operation. Here, using the approach described in the previous chapter, the capability and competence of your organisation to successfully make the proposed changes in the capacity available is developed.

Key questions

Questions you need to address in this phase include:

- Are we sure that the new reward schemes are robust? Do we need to test them further, on paper or in part of the organisation?
- When and how are we going to implement the changes to rewards?
- How are we going to move people from their existing to the new arrangements? How will we treat 'losers' and 'winners' in this process? Will the changes require new contracts and have we addressed all of the legal issues involved with changing terms and conditions?
- How are we going to operate and maintain the new schemes? Who is going to be responsible for decisions and administration?
- How are we going to administer the new schemes? Will this be done internally or outsourced?
- What support will managers need to operate the new schemes as

intended? What must the HR function do and what initial and ongoing training and support will be required?

❷ Will changes be required to other related HR systems and if so, how and when will these be effected?

❷ What will the final costs of introducing the reward strategy be and what are the gains we will see in return?

❷ How should we brand and communicate the changes so as to develop maximum levels of understanding and support throughout the organisation?

Work stages

Some of the normal work stages in this phase include:

❷ planning
❷ testing
❷ transition, costing and impact analysis
❷ developing operating systems
❷ communications and training
❷ negotiations.

Planning

Again, good planning is important, to check that there is sufficient time and resource available to give the new strategy the best chances of success. In the local authority described earlier, this plan was finalised after presentations to the top 60 managers in the organisation. On this basis, development and implementation was delayed to take two years and a twin-track approach was adopted.

In this way parts of the organisation where the need was greatest and the HR infrastructure already well developed could progress without being delayed by the large operating divisions, while they were given sufficient time and resources to adequately prepare. In the first year the new competency framework and performance management process were tested and implemented, then the bonus schemes rolled in, while the link to pay progression was only made at the end of the second year. British Energy similarly introduced its new reward approach in the context of a three-year pay deal, giving time to prepare for and progressively implement the principles and outline changes agreed.

In a large mutual insurer that was moving into a new flexible and job-family-based reward structure as the cornerstone of its reward strategy, we actually overlapped the introduction of the new and the continuance of the existing reward processes for a six-month period. Pay increases were awarded on the basis of the existing system and pay structure at the time of the annual review, but the new market data provision and administration processes were implemented in order to check that they could cope with the new flexibility as it was going to be applied to the tens of thousands of staff. Once these processes were fully tested and managers trained, the job families were then moved progressively into the new structures over the following six months.

Project plans should be produced at two levels: first an overview of the key work steps and stages in the transition process, which the board can sign up to and everyone can easily comprehend. An example from a UK water company is shown in Figure 20. Then below this level, for the people engaged in the project, we would produce a detailed Gantt chart breaking out the stages in each aspect of the work and showing timings and responsibilities.

Testing

‹ Staff covered by pilot tests can become change agents ›

As well as confirming on a wider basis that your new strategy can be delivered in practice, pilot tests invariably provide ideas for slight modifications to the approach to improve its operation, and particularly to the way in which the changes are communicated and presented to staff. The staff covered by pilot tests often respond positively to being involved and can become change agents themselves.

It is not recommended that you run pilot tests as a scientific trial, but select the area in the organisation where the changes are most needed and most likely to succeed. When success is the result, the rest of the organisation soon hears about it, through official and unofficial channels, and this builds a positive momentum into the roll-out process. Often, as in the IT department in both the building society and the Irish bank referenced above, the pilot just acts as the initial implementation and the tested staff carry on applying the changes, which are then extended to the rest of the organisation.

Figure 20

REWARD STRATEGY DEVELOPMENT AND
IMPLEMENTATION PLAN

1999

Q1

- Agree reward strategy principles and priorities
- Implement recognition policy
- Introduce cash for cars flexibility
- Evaluate initial sample of 50 jobs
- Draft outline descriptions of new bands and pay ranges min/max
- Consider base pay progression alternatives

Q2

- Implement 1999 pay deal
- Introduce new bonus schemes
- Provisionally slot all jobs into new pay structure
- Finalise proposals on base pay progression
- Define job-family pay markets in consultation with managers/staff/unions

Q3

- Survey defined pay markets and set actual pay ranges within bands for each job family
- Prepare to implement new base pay structure
  - modelling transfer
  - transition policies
  - training
  - advice
  - communication
- Detail, model and possibly pilot proposals on base pay progression

Q4

- Move all staff into new base pay structure

1999

Q1

- Prepare to implement new base pay progression system

Q2

- Implement 2000 pay deal
- Commence implementation of new pay progression system

Transition, costing and impact analysis

Analysing the transition of staff from existing to new arrangements is invariably an important piece of work in this phase, as well as the design of policies to manage that transition. The analysis will give you a full costing for the changes, but crucially now you also need to examine the effects of the changes on individuals and to check that the bulk of people will in all likelihood agree with you that this is a necessary set of changes towards a brighter reward future, for the company and them. How are you going to treat individuals who are made worse off, who lose overtime earnings, say, or who are now paid above the maximum of their new pay range? And what about the reverse? Can you afford to increase the pay and terms of those who have been found to be below the required level?

The analysis done for a utility introducing a new market-based pay structure showed that their initial proposals would have resulted in a third of the staff having to be red-circled and have their pay frozen because they were over the range ceiling. Yet almost 20 per cent were below the minimum of their new range and the organisation could not afford to move them up to the new minimums. So at least half of the staff were unlikely to see this new strategy as positive! The organisation therefore went back to the design drawingboard in phase 2, to produce proposals that better balanced meeting employee and business needs. They also introduced a specific appeals procedure when the revised changes were implemented to demonstrate that they were prepared to listen to any staff concerns and investigate again any problems.

Developing operating systems

The operating and administrative arrangements for the new reward strategy are not usually considered its sexiest aspect, yet this is another common area of implementation downfall. Yes we would love greater rewards flexibility, but oh dear, we can't administer it. The staff concerned should be involved with this, be it from the pay-roll and/or IT functions, as part of the project team in this work phase and, possibly, throughout. If your strategy involves major changes to rewards, then a study comparing the relative merits of internal administration compared to outsourcing may also be required.

The somewhat tedious task of drafting operating policies and guide-lines also needs to be undertaken, particularly as cost control issues have emerged from implementing some of the most popular reward changes at the moment, as described in Chapter 5. The emphasis in organisations who are devolving reward responsibilities – rather than being on control through voluminous reward policy manuals – needs to be on establishing clear principles and guidelines and building in quality in advance, at this stage, into the reward processes.

Communications and training

We emphasised the importance of communication and line manager training in the last chapter, and this needs to be a major area of attention in this phase. In the major charity mentioned already, managers were briefed on the detail of the changes (which affected their rewards, as well as those of their staff) in a two-day workshop. On the first day they developed their understanding of the new strategy and we addressed any of their concerns and those that their staff might raise. On the second day they developed the communications material to give immediately prior to the implementation to their staff, including presentations and question-and-answer sheets.

It is at this point, of course, that the benefits of a high-involvement approach throughout the project really become apparent. At the end of phase 1 the current problems and future direction can be communicated. At the end of phase 2 some detail on the actual changes can be given. And now in phase 3 preparation can be made to give staff the final personal details of how the changes will affect them. Communications can also be effectively staged during this phase leading up to launch.

At a pharmaceutical company we used a branded monthly publication. This initially gave the overview and rationale for the changes and then in subsequent editions covered the major aspects: the new band structure, the pay review process and changes to the bonus scheme. A high level of mostly positive response to the publications was received on e-mail, and through this channel we were able to tailor the questions and answers in subsequent editions to answer the queries and concerns that staff raised and also tailor the management and staff training that was provided.

In respect of training, at the large mutual insurer we ran a two-day simulation exercise with the marketing department during this phase. Using the new schemes and processes as far as they had been developed at that point, we took the managers through a series of exercises to illustrate what they would have to do under the new approach: how to set pay in the wider ranges, determine pay increases once compa-ratios had gone and so on. It taught us a huge amount about the right balance in the information and support that they needed from the HR department – how much raw market data to give them, what sort of guidelines on pay increases etc. It also served to test the administration processes in a reasonably realistic setting. A shortened and more structured version of the exercise became the training programme that we subsequently ran for all managers, and some of the marketing group became appointed coaches to advise their line colleagues on effective implementation and operation.

Union negotiations

Prior to securing final board approval and implementation, negotiations with relevant trade unions and possibly the balloting of staff on any contractual changes involved will be required in many organisations. Companies are often keen to avoid a ballot, possibly fearing a very public defeat. But in a highly unionised setting it can be a very powerful way of securing and demonstrating support for the changes. Here again, the benefits of an open and high-involvement approach should pay off at this stage. I am part-way through a project in the public sector and we have just shared the findings of our focus group discussions in phase 1 with the trade union officials. Even if the ultimate changes to pay progression do not totally match with what they wanted to see happen in every detail, they will be much more likely to agree if they understand fully the rationale and see why this set of changes has been selected over others, and that implementation will be properly resourced and managed.

Phase 4: implementation, operation and review

‘A job successfully completed? No, a journey only just started’

So now the road is finished. The local dignitary comes and cuts the ribbon, the cars stream through. Your reward strategy and its con-

stituent changes are implemented and the project team has a celebration and disbands. A job successfully completed? No, a journey
only just started. As a media company in the Towers Perrin (1999b)
European rewards research told me, changing the structures and systems is the easy bit; the hard work is getting the strategy actually
working in practice so that managers and staff are motivated to act
in the positive ways that your reward changes are designed to
encourage and reinforce. Managers and staff are often left to struggle
with the new arrangements, with little support and with little recognition in the reward strategy of the problems they experience.

I therefore disagree with the title of Zingheim and Schuster's (2000)
latest book, *Pay People Right*. You never do get it 'right', only better.
In fact, in many senses the reward strategy development pathway in
Table 14 actually comes back to the start in a circle. You need to
come back again and answer many of those questions and issues originally raised and to assess the extent to which you are in fact heading in the desired strategic direction:

- How well have the reward changes been implemented, and to
  what extent are they delivering on the reward goals we set out?
- If we are phasing them in, have we got the sequencing and ordering right: can we go faster or do we need to go slower in some
  areas?
- Given what we have learnt, will any changes in design and/or
  process improve overall effectiveness?
- How are we going to assess effectiveness on an ongoing basis, and
  perhaps in some detail after a sufficient time has elapsed to wit-
  ness the full impact of the changes?
- How is the organisational and external environment and context
  for the reward schemes changing? How might we need to modify
  our schemes and processes to continue progressing towards our
  defined goals?

The absence of review criteria and procedures has been a pervasive
Achilles heel in the reward practices of UK companies. One study of
sales incentive plans, for example, found that fewer than 10 per cent
of companies had made any attempt to evaluate their impact and
success. It is essential that you specify the reward objectives and success criteria and put some process in place to assess how well your
new systems and schemes are working. In the UK water company

mentioned earlier, each reward strategy goal has specified standards set for it, with specific measures, and businesses are audited against those standards on a periodic basis – see the box below.

The Towers Perrin (1999b) European reward study suggests, however, that this omission is starting to be rectified on a more general

Principle	Standard
Strategy-driven	✪ key business goals evident in reward policies and practices ✪ defined reward strategy and goals ✪ success criteria for reward policies established and monitored
Performance-related	✪ some type of contribution-/performance-based pay schemes in operation ✪ flexibility in total pay costs in relation to business performance ✪ employees feel that performance is recognised/rewarded
Flexible	✪ evidence of reward changes as required, and any legacy issues being addressed ✪ ability to respond to local market pressures ✪ business managers do not feel constrained
Business- and market-driven	✪ business, labour and pay markets defined and surveyed ✪ appropriate market position adopted and attained ✪ ability to recruit/retain employees of required calibre ✪ desirable employee turnover rates set and achieved ✪ each business supports and 'owns' its reward policies
Devolved	✪ businesses manage own reward budgets ✪ line/business managers trained/skilled in reward management, and feel empowered in reward matters ✪ evidence that most appropriate levels for reward decisions considered ✪ appropriate variations in practice within and between businesses

basis. Over 20 per cent of companies now have specific review or audit groups in place, and the numbers planning to extend the use of the various review criteria and methods is forecast to increase by a significant amount – see the box below.

The compensation managers in the most successful companies in this research did not sigh with relief after implementing their strategies and return to the tranquillity of their day jobs. They are instead following the process of continual evolution in their reward schemes that we described in the last chapter, responding to their learning from day-to-day experience and adjusting to the regular changes in the organisation, yet all the time maintaining that clear direction towards improved reward policies and practices. This is the adaptability and immediacy that Ulrich (1997) says is required for the HR function to make a real strategic impact through rewards management. They are also scanning the future horizon for potential external 'shocks', be it worsening labour shortages, European Monetary Union, new employment legislation or whatever. They can then start to proactively plan out responses and build understanding and support for any implied changes, rather than having to react quickly and ineffectively after the 'shock' has hit.

At another pharmaceutical company, a specific review was undertaken after a year's operation of their major reward change programme. Managers were spoken to, discussions held with samples of

Review method	Currently use %	Planning to extend/introduce %
Benchmarking with external organisations	77	67
Survey line manager views	56	54
Cost reviews	54	40
Exit interviews	54	36
Survey employee views	48	55
Employee turnover reports	46	40
Specific review groups/ committees	21	34

Source: Towers Perrin.

staff, and the pattern of actual pay changes analysed. The general conclusion was favourable, but improvements were suggested in a number of areas, particularly in relation to the process for setting objectives and competency standards, where the approach was seen as too 'loose' and unguided. Some departments had done it very well, but most were now looking for clearer guidance.

These reviews, and indeed the whole diagnostic process, do not have to be a massive exercise. My work tends to take me into large and complex situations, but in many cases quick, intensive analyses can have huge dividends. The train company we illustrated earlier drew its reward strategy pathway, at present and in the future, in a one-day session.

And the large mutual insurer carried out the bulk of the phase 1 and 2 work in two four-day workouts with a team of 20 line managers and HR staff. The first concentrated on the 'why' and the outline 'what' of the changes, while the second detailed those designs and specified the 'hows' in the process. The energy and productivity of such concentrated work was incredible, and the momentum and commitment built up has been a key factor supporting the implementation of a difficult set of changes.

‘Remember: it ain't what you do, it's the way that you do it’

As always, tailor your approach to reward strategy development, as well as the reward strategy itself, to the unique needs and characteristics of your own situation, and remember, in the words of the famous old Jimmy Lunceford song, 'It ain't what you do it's the way that you do it – that's what gets results!'

Case study

HOW THE REWARD STRATEGY WAS DEVELOPED AND DETAILED IN A UK UTILITY COMPANY

Background: the business and the strategy
Industry restructuring and the introduction of a new commercial environment led to the formation of this utility from a number

of formerly separate organisations operating in the public sector. The company's board developed a detailed strategic plan for the new company, emphasising the need to:

- provide excellent customer service
- meet demanding targets set by the industry regulator
- provide value for money through improved asset utilisation and cost efficiency.

Cultural and HR issues were given a high priority by the board in order to achieve these aims. The people strategy set out by the new HR director aimed to build a united performance-orientated culture amongst the 2,000 employees, within a much more devolved, accountable and flexible structure than had been the case in their local authority past.

Analysis and phase I findings

Pay and reward systems inherited from that past were immediately identified both as a significant barrier to moving towards these goals and as an important potential lever to reinforce their achievement. Moving managers and placing newly recruited professional staff on personal contract terms, with performance-related base pay and bonuses, was a relatively straightforward task achieved within the first year of operation. But addressing the longstanding and hugely complex reward arrangements for the rest of the unionised employees was a much more challenging project.

The HR director set up a project team to investigate the reward issues and recommend the way forward for the bulk of the employees. It consisted of HR staff, line managers and representatives drawn from the elected employee forum, which included trade union officials. The team interviewed directors, carried out staff focus groups and discussions and investigated the workings of the current arrangements, as well as visiting organisations such as Transco, which had faced and made a similar transition from a public sector past. The external comparisons highlighted the spread of simpler and more performance-focused pay arrangements and also the contrast with current methods in the utility.

The internal analysis really demonstrated the barriers that the current pay and reward systems represented to progressing along the strategic business and cultural pathway that the board had set out. They were characterised by:

- enormous complexity, divisiveness and inflexibility, with staff placed in almost 100 distinct grades through the operation of six separate evaluation systems and pay structures; there was also a confusing mix of over 50 pay supplements, applied in different ways to the various types of staff and comprising over a third of the pay for many staff and of the total employment spend; there were even four different payment cycles for different categories of staff and 11 different payroll systems; this complexity created high administrative costs, the overall pay budget was essentially not being managed, and staff had little understanding of why or how these arrangements operated

- major inconsistencies and inequities between the various groups of staff with the same jobs in different regions and on very different rates of earnings; male supervisors in some areas, for example, were earning more than anyone below the board, through the accrual of various supplements and allowances, while operators in one part of the business had lower base pay rates but higher total cash earnings than those in another

- the lack of any relationship between rewards and performance, and of any means of recognising the skills and behaviours that would support future business success; payments for manual staff were based on hours, not efficiency, and across the business 'plus payments' were attached to any aspect of skills or work flexibility; the only apparent aspects of performance pay were relatively high bonus payments for manual workers, which originated in the 1970s and were essentially fixed from week to week.

The group discussions that were held with a representative sample of staff from all areas of the business revealed a surprisingly high level of support for changes to terms and conditions and the introduction of a common reward approach for all staff. The lack of relationship between skills, job size, performance and pay, and lack of understanding and involvement in pay decisions were major sources of dissatisfaction, as was revealed by the results from a questionnaire given to these employees. The average score across all employees is given in brackets after each statement below. 1 = strongly disagree and 5 = strongly agree; the strongest levels of disagreement were:

- It would be best if we made no changes at all to current pay and reward arrangements (1.4).
- All things considered, the reward arrangements are generally good here (1.6).
- Pay here is fairly adjusted to reflect increases in job content and skills (1.7).
- The annual pay review process is managed in an effective motivating manner (1.8).
- There is a strong relationship between my performance and my pay (2.0).
- There is a clear relationship between job size, level of skill and pay (2.1).
- I feel involved in decisions that affect my pay and conditions (2.1).

The strongest levels of agreement were:

- All employees in the company should be employed on common terms and conditions (4.2).
- We should reward effective teamwork here (4.0).
- The performance of the organisation should determine part of my pay (3.5).
- Individual performance should determine part of my pay (3.3).
- I am clear about the definition of my job and the performance expected of me (3.3).
- I am highly motivated in my current job (3.1).

All in all, it was a reward system divorced from the needs of the business in which managers had to specifically pay for anything outside someone's detailed and outdated job description, and staff were encouraged to maximise their earnings through all of the complex mix of reward vehicles available: 'a game', as one employee called it . Hardly the partnership and 'win-win' employment relationship that the business was seeking.

The new reward strategy
After two months of this phase 1 analysis, the board agreed to the outline of a new reward strategy that the project team pre-

sented to them. Core reward principles and themes that they
signed up to include:

- supporting the achievement of business objectives
- reinforcing the culture and values of the organisation
- establishing a consistent framework for the management of
  reward, and generally simplifying and rationalising practices
- improving the management of reward and moving to more
  openly communicated, understood and supported practices.

A major series of changes were recommended in order to
deliver these goals, of which the following were the building
blocks of the new system:

- introducing common and more generic role profiles across
  the organisation, covering the purpose, accountabilities, key
  result areas and required competencies for each role
- developing a simple but common system of job evaluation
  based on these competencies and requirements, in order to
  place jobs in a new structure of pay bands; the new pay
  ranges would be set based on a combination of market data
  and internal value
- in terms of pay reviews, the moving of all staff onto a
  common review date and monthly payment cycle; pay movement through the ranges would be based primarily on skills
  development in the lower bands and personal performance in
  the other bands
- the removal of the existing manual worker bonuses and introduction of a new company-wide bonus, with the intention to
  move to a unit/team modifier on this in the future
- a raft of changes to allowances and conditions focusing on
  simplifying and consolidating allowances and harmonising conditions such as working hours and holidays, as well as improving customer service through means such as extended
  working hours.

Each change was illustrated with practical examples of how the
new approach would look and operate.

This was clearly a major reward agenda and change management
challenge, and the risks and resources required to make it
happen were also set out. The board agreed there was no choice

but to address these issues in the manner proposed, and agreed to the strategy, an overview of which was then presented and discussed with the employee forum. The overall principle of cost neutrality was agreed, whereby resources would be utilised and managed more effectively but without any reduction in total pay-roll costs. However, individually there would be 'winners' and 'losers' from the changes.

Phase 2: detailing

The project team initially carried out a detailed planning exercise once agreement to the principles and direction had been obtained. The challenge was to define and make a radical change in reward management in an organisation with:

- little experience of other approaches
- an underdeveloped structure of the HR processes required to make it work
- a chequered history of industrial relations.

First, the priorities and overall approach to detail and transition to a new set of conditions was set out. The priority areas were seen to be the role evaluation system and movement to a common pay structure, simplification of allowances and removal of the manual workers' bonus. Pay progression, the new bonus schemes and other terms and conditions would be addressed subsequently.

Then the broad sequencing of work over the next 18 months was set out, with:

- communication of the reward strategy and establishment of design teams in the first quarter
- the development of detailed proposals in each area in the second and third quarters, initial modelling and testing, board approval and further consultation
- phase 3 preparation occurring in the last quarter of the year and first quarter of the following year, with final financial mod-elling and costing, the setting up of administration and control procedures, delivery of roll-out training and staff negotiations
- implementation commencing on a phased basis from April the following year, which was the date chosen to harmonise pay reviews.

In order to carry out the considerable amount of detailed design work, the project team organised the following structuring of responsibilities:

- the original project team became essentially the project policy group, responsible for the overall direction and co-ordination of the work
- a member of the policy group then chaired one of six design teams that were established to do the detailing work; these covered the five main areas of reward changes, with a separate team covering communications.

The teams were briefed collectively and provided with a design template, list of required deliverables and work methodology in an initial half-day session. They then constructed a much more detailed plan of their own activities and these were all pulled together into a co-ordinated overall project plan. The teams were set off on a staggered basis, with the job evaluation and banding team working from March to July, for example, and the pay review team from June to September. This allowed one team to work with the required input from another team, as well as reducing the work pressures on people required on more than one team.

Outcomes and learning points

The work in phases 2 and 3 proceeded very much in line with this timetable. The policy group ensured that the activities of the different teams were co-ordinated with regular meetings. Another meeting of the teams was held in mid-year and this helped to demonstrate the momentum that this high involvement approach had created, and the commitment of team members to the proposals they had come up with. These were subsequently agreed by the board, virtually without change.

Full implementation was, however, subsequently delayed by nearly a year through extended negotiations with staff representatives. But the HR director is convinced that this comprehensive approach was essential, both to enable all the various changes to be addressed in a co-ordinated way and to ensure that the major 'step change' required in corporate performance and employee behaviour would receive strong reinforcement through rewards. Both the company and trade unions are now committed to achieving outcomes such as a substantial reduction in levels of overtime working, a joint effort that would have been unthinkable in the company's predecessor organisations.

The HR director describes the overall programme as 'sweeping aside the pay systems of a local authority bureaucracy and replacing them with a reward policy of a commercial, customer-facing utility'. Despite the delay in implementation, he feels the company has achieved more over a three-year period than other privatised utilities achieved in over a decade of operation in the private sector.

Chapter summary

- ❷ The process of developing, designing, implementing and operating a reward strategy and its constituent parts is critical to its success. Like the strategy itself, this process needs to be tailored to the needs and circumstances of each organisation.
- ❷ This process should generally be carried out in four phases:
  - ❷ an initial diagnosis and direction-setting phase
  - ❷ second, a period of detailed design work
  - ❷ then a preparatory phase
  - ❷ finally an implementation and ongoing review phase.
- ❷ Following this structured process ensures that the design of your reward schemes does actually address the reward issues you face and that these are aligned with the principles of your strategy. It also helps to progressively develop understanding and support for reward changes: another critical requirement of the strategy's successful operation.
- ❷ There needs to be clearly defined responsibilities for the work in this process. Typically it will involve a steering body to make decisions at key points, a project team that does the bulk of the project work, and often also some consultation structure to obtain wider line and staff input.
- ❷ Phase 1 is the analysis phase. It involves examining the current reward situation from an internal and external perspective, and soliciting the views of all the major stakeholders. Key reward issues are identified and the change alternatives to address them outlined and compared. The strategic goals and direction for

future rewards are then agreed, along with the outline scheme designs and changes to better support these goals.

- These outline changes are then detailed in the second phase of the work. Typically, separate workstreams will be established to specify each of the changes proposed and to initially test their application on a sample of jobs in the organisation. Different design teams and varying timescales may be required to address each item. However, it is important that the integrated direction of the changes is maintained.

- Phase 3 is concerned with the detailed planning of the approach to implementing the agreed changes and with building the capability of the organisation to implement them as intended and make the reward strategy an operating reality. Work stages include defining policies to manage the transition from current to new practices, modifying administrative and control processes, training line managers and progressively communicating with staff.

- Phase 4 finally involves implementation, but is really the start of the process of ongoing diagnosis, modification and review, to ensure that the reward strategy does operate as intended and evolves to reflect future shifts in the organisation and its environment.

Chapter 9

Conclusion

When a female journalist asked him to define jazz, the great exponent Duke Ellington replied, 'Honey, if you've got to ask, you ain't never going to know.' I must confess to feeling somewhat the same about reward strategy, both in the sense that it is so organisation- and context-specific, and because I believe that it has at least as much to do with feeling and meaning as it has to do with the (pound) notes, the business strategy plan or organisation structure charts. Reward strategy is the rhythm, the melody for your reward practices and processes to follow. Some of the most effective reward policies I have seen have been in companies where the reward strategy is not even written down, yet it is there, a successful and working reality nonetheless.

I accept, however, that you would probably feel short-changed after buying this book if I advised you to rely totally on your own intuition in composing your own score (although I think that this would have a much greater chance of success than simply trying to import reward practices from the market, or following 'trendy' practices, two approaches that have blighted reward management in UK organisations over the past 20 years). So I will attempt here to summarise the work in earlier chapters and arrive at a fuller definition of what an effective reward strategy is and how you can obtain and operate one.

A melody, a direction, a framework, a pathway, a pattern, organisation glue – these are all images used in this book to try to convey to you the real meaning of real reward strategies. But I accept that it is a difficult idea to grasp, and even more so to practise. I have borrowed some great ideas from leading writers and authorities – Lynda Grattan's (2000a) living HR strategy, Dave Ulrich's (1997) adaptable HR specialists, Tom Davenport's (1999) human capital investment, Kinsley Lord's (now part of Towers Perrin) change management techniques – to try and illuminate it. But just as I often find it easier to express what I do not like rather than what I do, in many ways it is easiest to start with what a reward strategy is not.

It is definitely not just a set of reward practices that, however technically expert their design, operate in splendid isolation from each other and the needs of the business and its employees. The reward training we used to give our consultants at Towers Perrin was all about design algorithms and calculations and modelling. Now we take this as a necessary given (and we described some of the essential design principles required and common practices in Chapter 5). Instead, in our training we now focus on developing skills in assessing organisational and employee needs and meeting those needs through the application of our technical and process skills.

But as we have seen, compensation and HR staff in many companies have already followed the advice of the strategic HRM advocates and come out of their technical design and administration backrooms. They have their HR and reward strategy principles explicitly defined and agreed at the boardroom table, and in some cases voluminous and attractive descriptions of the idealistic practices that are designed to underpin those principles. As demonstrated in Chapter 1, a strategic approach to rewards in this sense, of looking at the wider goals and needs of the organisation, is essential:

- to prevent the retention of practices that reward for 'A' when the organisation's needs have shifted to 'B'; to better align them with what employees need to do in pursuit of future business goals (we illustrated this alignment pathway in Chapter 2); and to respond effectively to major business changes, such as a merger (covered in Chapter 4)
- to match rewards to the structure and design of the organisation and to reinforce the degree of job and unit flexibility required in today's fluid and shifting structures, which we covered in Chapter 3.

But this is only half the story at best (see Figure 21). As Grattan (2000, 2000a) explains, in a new era when human capital really is the basis for competitive success, we have to be cognisant in our strategies of the distinctive nature of ourselves compared to financial capital and technology. There are three key differences: we search for meaning and purpose, to understand; we have a soul and emotions, and from our emotional side comes excitement, trust and commitment; and we have memory, meaning that our time frames and speed of transformation are relatively slow.

'Reward strategies are fundamentally about personal needs, experiences and emotions'

In moving from a purely technical, administrative and control focus to embrace a broader business and organisational agenda, many of us have ignored or downplayed these distinctions. This is why organisations are now experiencing difficulties in delivering on their strategic reward goals, which is bringing the whole concept into question. Reward strategies are not just about 'left-side' business plans and structures and systems. They fundamentally have to be about 'right-side' people and processes, and the reality of personal needs, experiences and emotions in the organisation.

Reward strategies, as we saw in Chapters 5, 6 and 7, have to incorporate this broad agenda if they are to work in practice and take an open, involving, employee-oriented and what at Towers Perrin we call a total rewards perspective to address it. They have to address the 'soft' culture and processes, as well as the 'hard' designs and structures. It is no use having a perfect reward plan sitting on the boardroom shelf. Our strategies need to involve and engage people, give them meaning and understanding, and address their personal needs. They need to allow time and provide the support for people to understand, accept and to cope with change. Reward strategies are not about 'big bang' revolutions or totally concerned with global strategic decisions. The pattern of successful reward changes, as we saw in Chapters 6, 7 and 8, is an evolutionary one, often of tinkering and improvement across a wide span of issues and practices, large and small. John Purcell's (2000) latest CIPD research on the links between HR strategies and business performance draws exactly the same conclusion.

Reward strategies can only have real meaning in the messy day-to-day realities of the lives of 'real' managers and staff, with all their idiosyncrasies and foibles and failings, in our organisations. Your strategy needs to provide the level of understanding and direction that ensures that these day-to-day issues – of how people are developed and involved, of how they are recognised, of how they are given feedback – are addressed in a common manner that is consistent with

Figure 21
A MORE BALANCED, PRACTICAL REWARD STRATEGY MODEL

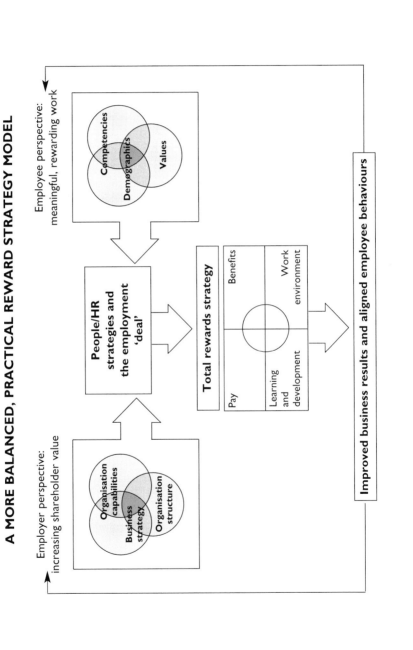

your reward goals and principles. And this is precisely why reward strategies are so critical, in that rewards are a tangible and very visible part of the environment and foundation for the employment relationship in our organisations. They can play a key role in creating and delivering the type of positive, high trust and business-aligned psychological contract that does so much to explain the prominence of the most successful organisations in today's highly competitive and challenging world.

Of course, these two 'sides' illustrated in Figure 21 – the business and the people, the hard and the soft – are not conflicting but complementary. We characterised the reward strategy process in Chapter 8 as circular, not in the sense of going back to the start every time, but in helping to create this self-reinforcing upward spiral, with incremental reward changes and improvements progressively adding to enhanced employee motivation and business performance. This is hardly a new concept, I accept, with Edward Cadbury observing before the First World War that 'employee welfare and business profitability are different sides of the same coin'. But it is a dual perspective that has sometimes been forgotten in our attempts to make our reward policies business-aligned and demonstrably adding value to the business.

I have largely eschewed the literature that attempts to 'prove' causal links between reward and HR practices and business performance, although I hope I have given plenty of examples of their positive associations. Frankly, I think that it is an impossible task. Rewards form part of the complex web of organisational, cultural and HR factors that together creates what Ghoshal and Bartlett (1999) call 'the internal environment that allows people to create far more value than they could if they were employed elsewhere ... the Fontainbleu woods in the spring-time', rather than 'downtown Calcutta in the summer'. Formal reward policies are only one way in which people are made to feel motivated to fully contribute to the success of the organisation, and as we have seen, the success of particular reward practices is heavily dependent on these complex interrelationships – the quality of performance management and leadership, the levels of communication and involvement and so on.

But, while not favouring Zingheim and Schuster's (2000) 'Top Gun' imagery, of reward specialists using their 'quiver of arrows' to aggressively shoot down malpractice and 'transform' their organisations, I think it would be safe to conclude that reward policies are playing an increasingly important role in helping to create and sustain this positive and productive environment.

In our era of competitive advantage through people, a declining welfare state, the increasing power of the knowledge worker and the 'me' generation, although executive 'fat-cattism' still grabs the odd headline, people now barely raise a well-lacquered eyelid at supermodel Naomi Campbell's earnings of £250,000 for a four-hour shoot, or raise a fist in protest at footballer Roy Keane's weekly wage of over £50,000. Daniel Goleman's (1998) research suggests that their employers are not crazy, but that high individual performers really can create such huge returns for their employers to justify these earnings levels, contributing over 1,200 per cent more than the average individual.

Reward strategy is ultimately a way of thinking that you can apply to any reward issue arising in your organisation, to see how you can create value from it. This was really brought home to me after witnessing a trial reward scheme in a major retailer with a stagnant share price, operating in one of the most cut-throat competitive sectors of the economy. They placed graduate specialists in a select number of stores to focus on marketing a high-margin product range. These specialists were comparatively expensive to hire and train, earning about twice the rates of a typical shop assistant. Yet all of them had paid for themselves within one year of trading, and some had added up to 10 per cent to total store profitability.

So given the success, why hadn't the company and store managers made this type of investment with such a high return before? Because people and their rewards were seen as a cost to be controlled and minimised, not an investment to be grown and multiplied.

> ‘The returns in taking a strategic approach to reward management are potentially greater than ever’

So the returns for you in taking a strategic approach to reward management, in addressing those difficult and sensitive issues and improving the situation, are potentially greater than ever. Hopefully this book has given you enough examples and ideas, and tools and techniques to help you start and progress your own journey in this direction. And it does have to be your own. That reward strategy does have to be sculpted to suit your own particular setting, and however attractive some of those reward strategy pathway diagrams from other companies look, you cannot import an effective strategy from outside.

My final and favourite analogy to help us define and understand a reward strategy is drawn from Canadian academic Henry Mintzberg (1990), the man who famously punctured the rhetoric of long-term strategic planning with a PhD that demonstrated that chief executives spent the vast bulk of their time flitting rapidly between issues and making short-term decisions. He contrasts the 'greenhouse' approach of forced, 'top-down' business strategies that inevitably cannot be implemented, with the 'seed-garden' approach in successful organisations, growing and nurturing the 'emergent' strategies that come 'bottom-up' from the skills, inputs and commitment of their staff.

This seed-garden approach (see the box below) is the way to make your reward strategy truly alive in your organisation and to give it real impact. This kind of broad, balanced and continuous approach is the means through which you really can deliver on the considerable potential of reward practices and processes to support this posi-

The new reward strategy approach

From	To
Tight 'greenhouse'	Looser 'seed garden'
Top-down, planned	Mix of broad plan and emergent components
Wholly business-driven	Balancing business, employee and market needs
Pay, maybe also benefits, focus	Total rewards
Systems-design focus	Goals and process focus
HR secret	Line and communication tool
Perfection	Incremental improvement
Big-bang change	Evolution

tive work environment and thereby contribute to business success, to arouse what one executive in a retailer referred to as 'the sleeping giants of organisational change' (Ashton, 1999).

So go out there and wake those giants, start that journey, make that investment, create that life and meaning, grow those seeds and make that music.

Bibliography

AMERICAN COMPENSATION ASSOCIATION. (1996) *Raising the Bar: Using competencies to enhance employee performance.* Scottsdale, Ariz., research report, May.

AMERICAN COMPENSATION ASSOCIATION. (1997) *Team Pay.* Field research project carried out with the University of Tennessee. Scottsdale, Ariz.

ARKIN A. (1999) 'Return to centre'. *People Management.* 6 May.

ARMSTRONG M. *and* BARON A. (1998) *Performance Management: The new realities.* London, IPD.

ARMSTRONG M. *and* BARON A. (2000) 'Out of the tick box'. *People Management.* 23 July.

ARMSTRONG M. *and* BROWN D. (2001) *New Dimensions in Pay Management.* London, CIPD.

ARMSTRONG M. *and* MURLIS H. (1997) *A Handbook of Reward Management.* 3rd edn. London, Kogan Page.

ASHTON C. (1999) *Strategic Compensation.* London, Business Intelligence.

BARON A. (2000) 'Advance beyond intuition'. *People Management.* 20 July.

BECKER B. E. *and* HUSELID M. A. (1996) *Managerial Compensation Systems and Firm Performance.* Paper presented at the National Academy of Management Annual Meeting, Cincinnati, Ohio.

BICHARD M. (2000) *Performance Management Report.* London, Cabinet Office.

BLOOM M. (1995) *The Bundle of Valued Returns: A psychological contract view of incentive pay.* Cornell University Centre for Advanced Human Studies, Working paper No. 95-1.

BLOOM M. *and* MILKOVICH G. (1995) 'Managerial compensation and social contracts'. *Trends in Organisational Behaviour.* No. 3.

BOWEY A. (1983) *The Effectiveness of Incentive Pay Systems.* London, Department of Employment Research Paper.

BRADDICK C. A. (1992) 'A look at broadbanding'. *Journal of Compensation and Benefits.* July/August.

BRONSON P. O. (1999) *The Nudist on the Late Shift and Other Tales of Silicon Valley.* London, Secker & Warburg.

BROWN D. (1996) 'Broadbanding: a study of company practices in the UK'. *Compensation and Benefits Review.* November/December.

BROWN D. *and* ARMSTRONG M. (1999) *Paying for Contribution.* London, Kogan Page.

BROWN J. (2000) *People Implications of Mergers and Acquisitions, Joint Ventures and Divestments.* London, CIPD survey report.

BROWN W. *and* HUDSON M. (1997) Referenced in Pickard J. 'Experts greet move back to collectivism'. *People Management.* 21 July.

BULLOCK R. *and* LAWLER E. E. (1984) 'Gainsharing: a few questions and answers'. *Human Resource Management.* Vol. 20, No. 1.

CARROLL S. J. (1987) 'Business strategies and compensation systems'. In Gomez-Mejia L. R. and Balkin D. B. *New Perspectives on Compensation.* New Jersey, Prentice Hall.

CARTER M. (2000) 'Cyber house rules'. *People Management.* 22 June.

CARTWRIGHT S. *and* COOPER C. (2000) *HR Know-how in Mergers and Acquisitions.* London, IPD.

CHANDLER A. (1962) *Strategies and Structures: Chapters in the history of industrial enterprise*. Cambridge, Mass., MIT Press.

COLLINS J. *and* PORRAS J. (1998) *Built to Last*. London, Century.

COX A. *and* PURCELL J. (1998) 'Searching for leverage: pay systems, trust, motivation and commitment'. In Perkins S. (ed.) *Trust, Motivation and Commitment: A reader*. Farringdon, SRRC.

CULLEY M. (1998) *The 1998 Workplace Employee Relations Survey: First findings*. London, ESRC/DTI.

DAVENPORT T. O. (1999) *Human Capital: What it is and why people invest in it*. San Francisco, Calif., Jossey Bass.

DEMATTEO J. S. (1997) 'Factors relating to the successful implementation of team-based rewards'. *ACA Journal*. Winter.

DOZ Y. *and* BOWER J. L. (1992) *Strategy Formulation: A social and political process*. New Jersey, Prentice Hall.

DUNCAN D. *and* GROSS S. E. (1998) 'Gainsharing plan spurs record productivity at Ameristeel'. *Compensation and Benefits Review*. November/December.

EGAN G. (1995) 'A clear path to peak performance'. *People Management*. 18 May.

ELLIG B. R. (1987) 'Strategic pay planning'. *Compensation and Benefits Review*. Vol. 19, July/August.

ELLIS *and* HAFTEL. (1992) 'Reward strategies for R. and D.' *Research and Technology Management*. March/April.

EMERSON S. M. (1991) 'Job evaluation: a barrier to excellence'. *Compensation and Benefits Review*. January/February.

FITZ-ENZ J. (1997) 'The truth about best practices'. In Ulrich D. (ed.) *Tomorrow's HR Management*. New York, John Wiley.

FLETCHER C. (1997) *Appraisal: Routes to improved performance*. London, IPD.

FRADETTE M. *and* MICHAUD S. (2000) *The Power of Corporate Kinetics*. London, Simon & Schuster.

GHOSHAL H. *and* BARTLETT C. A. (1999) *The Individualised Corporation*. New York, Harper Perennial.

GLUECK W. (1998) *Business Policy and Strategic Management*. Maidenhead, McGraw-Hill.

GOLEMAN D. P. (1998) *Working with Emotional Intelligence*. London, Bantam Books.

GOMEZ-MEJIA L. R. *and* BALKIN D. B. (1987) *The Effect of Organisation Strategy on Pay Policy*. Paper presented at the National Academy of Management.

GOMEZ-MEJIA L. R. *and* WELBOURNE T. M. (1987) *Compensation Strategy as an Emerging Research Area*. Paper presented to the Academy of Management National Conference, August.

GOOLD A. *and* CAMPBELL M. (1987) *Strategies and Styles*. Oxford, Basil Blackwell.

GRATTAN L. (1997) 'Perspectives on the future'. In Ulrich D. (ed.) *Tomorrow's HR Management*. New York, John Wiley.

GRATTAN L. (2000) 'A real step change'. *People Management*. 16 March.

GRATTAN L. (2000a) *Living Strategy*. London, Financial Times Prentice Hall.

GRINT K. (1993) 'What is wrong with performance appraisal'. *Human Resource Management Journal*. Spring.

GUEST D. (2000) 'Piece by piece'. *People Management*. 20 July.

GUEST D. *and* CONWAY N. (1998) *Fairness at Work and the Psychological Contract*. London, IPD.

HANSEN P. referenced in Brown D. (1998) 'The international reward balancing act'. *Benefits and Compensation International*. Vol. 28, No. 5. December.

HENDERSON R. I. *and* RISHER H. W. (1987) 'Influencing organisation strategy through organisation leadership'. In Gomez-Mejia L. R. and Balkin D. B. (eds) *New Perspectives on Compensation*. New Jersey, Prentice Hall.

HENDRY C., BRADLEY P. *and* PERKINS S. (2000) 'Performance and rewards: cleaning out the stables'. *Human Resource Management Journal*. Vol. 10, No. 3.

HUNT J. (1998) 'A salary can't buy happiness'. *The Financial Times*. 13 May.

HURWICH M. (1986) 'Strategic compensation: designs that link pay to performance'. *Journal of Business Strategy*. Vol. 17, No. 2. Fall.

INCOMES DATA SERVICES. (2000) *Pay and Conditions in Call Centres*. London, IDS Research Report.

INCOMES DATA SERVICES. (2000a) 'The EU economy, pay and labour costs'. *Employment Europe*. 464. August.

INSTITUTE OF PERSONNEL AND DEVELOPMENT. (1998) *Performance Pay Survey*. London, IPD. (Out of print.)

INVESTORS IN PEOPLE. (2000) referred to in 'Satisfaction is being paid lip service'. *Personnel Today*. 10 October.

KAPLAN R. *and* NORTON D. (1996) 'The balanced scorecard: measures that drive performance'. *Harvard Business Review*. January/February.

KATZELL M. E. (1993) 'Recognition, reward and resentment'. *Research and Technology Management*. July.

KERR S. (1975) 'The folly of rewarding for A while hoping for B'. *Academy of Management Journal*. Vol. 18, No. 4. December.

KESSLER I. *and* PURCELL J. (1992) 'Performance-related pay: objectives and application'. *Human Resource Management Journal*. Vol. 2, No. 3. Spring.

KIDDER T. (1995) *The Soul of a New Machine*. Boston, Mass., Back Bay Books.

KOHN A. (1993) *Punished by Reward*. Boston, Houghton Mifflin.

LANGLEY M. (1987) *Rewarding the Salesforce*. London, IPM.

LAWLER E. E. (1971) *Pay and Organisational Effectiveness: A psychological view*. New York, McGraw-Hill.

LAWLER E. E. (1994) 'Effective reward systems: strategy, diagnosis and design'. In Howard A. (ed.) *Diagnosis for Organisational Change: Methods and models*. New York, Guilford Press.

LAWLER E. E. (1996) 'Competencies: a poor foundation for the new pay'. *Compensation and Benefits Review*. November/December.

LAWLER E. E. (2000) 'Pay strategy: new thinking for the new Millennium'. *Compensation and Benefits Review*. January/February.

LAWLER E. E. (2000a) *Rewarding Excellence: Pay strategies for the new economy*. San Francisco, Jossey Bass.

LAWTON M. (1997) 'Death of a paradigm: looking at international reward'. *Benefits and Compensation International*. September.

LEWIS D. (2000) *The Soul of the New Consumer*. London, Nicholas Brealey.

LIKERT R. (1959) 'Performance review'. *Harvard Business Review*. Vol. 37, No. 4. July/August.

MACADAMS J. L. *and* HAWK E. J. (1994) *Organizational Performance and Rewards*. Scottsdale, Ariz., ACA.

MAKINSON J. (2000) *Incentives for Change: Rewarding performance in national government networks*. London, Public Services Productivity Panel, January. Available from the Public Enquiry Unit, HM Treasury.

MARGINSON P. (1993) *The Control of Industrial Relations in Large Companies*. Warwick University Paper on industrial relations, No. 45, December.

MCBEATH G. *Salary Administration*. Out of print.

MINTZBERG H. (1990) 'The design school: reconsidering the basic premises of strategic management'. *Strategic Management Journal*. Vol. 11.

MONTEMAYOR E. F. (1999) *Decisional and Interactional Fairness: Key sources of merit pay system satisfaction: cross-validation with American and Venezuelan samples*. Michigan University draft research paper, June.

OERTON S. (2000) referred to in 'E-business calls for rules to be rewritten'. *Personnel Today*. 10 October.

O'NEAL S. (1998) 'The phenomenon of total rewards'. *ACA Journal*. Autumn.

PEARCE J. A. *and* ROBINSON R. B. (1997) *Formulation, Implementation and Control of Competitive Strategy*. 6th edn. Richard Irwin.

PERKINS S. J. (1997) *Internationalisation: The people dimension*. London, Kogan Page.

PFEFFER J. (1998) 'Six dangerous myths about pay'. *Harvard Business Review*. May/June.

PFEFFER J. *and* O'REILLY C. (2000) *Hidden Value*. Boston, Harvard Business School Press.

PLACHY R. J. *and* PLACHY S. J. (1998) *Results-Oriented Job Descriptions*. New York, Amacom.

PORTER M. E. (1980) *Competitive Strategy*. New York, Macmillan.

PUCIK V. (1992) 'Globalisation and human resource management'. In Pucik V., Tichy N. M. and Barnett C. K. (eds) *Globalising Management*. New York, John Wiley.

PURCELL J. *and* AHLSTRAND B. (1994) *HRM in the Multi-Divisional Company*. Oxford, Oxford University Press.

PURCELL J., HUTCHISON S. *and* KINNIE N. (2000) 'Evolving high commitment management and the experience of the RAC call centre'. *Human Resource Management Journal*. Vol. 10, No. 1.

PURCELL J. *et al* (2000) 'Inside the box'. *People Management*. 26 October.

RHODES D. (1988) 'Employees: strategy makers or breakers?' *Journal of Business Strategy*. July/August.

SCHULER R. S. (1988) 'HRM choices and organisation strategy'. In Schuler R. S., Youngblood S. A. and Huber V. L. (eds) *Readings in Strategic HRM*. 3rd edn. St Paul, Minn., West Publishing.

SMITH I. (1982) *The Management of Remuneration*. London, IPM.

SPARROW P. R. (1996) 'Too good to be true'. *People Management*. 5 December.

THOMPSON M. (1992) *Pay and Performance: The employer's experience*. IMS Report No. 218.

THOMPSON M. (1998) 'HR and the bottom line'. *People Management*. 16 April.

THOMPSON M. (1998a) 'Trust and reward'. In Perkins S. (ed.) *Trust, Motivation and Commitment: A reader*. Farringdon, SRRC.

TOWERS PERRIN. (1994) *Improving Performance through People: HR issues in the utility industry*. London.

TOWERS PERRIN. (1997) *Learning from the Past, Changing for the Future*. London.

TOWERS PERRIN. (1997a) *The 1997 Workplace Index*. London.

TOWERS PERRIN. (1998) *The Role and Effectiveness of the Corporate Centre*. London.

TOWERS PERRIN. (1999) *Compensation Effectiveness Survey: Is pay delivering on its promise?* London/New York.

TOWERS PERRIN. (1999a) *Meeting the Global Rewards Challenge: A 15-country study of performance and reward management practices*. London.

TOWERS PERRIN. (1999b) *Revolutionary, Realistic or Reticent: A European study of total rewards into the 21st Century*. London.

TOWERS PERRIN. (2000) 'Pay attention: how to reward your top employees'. In *Perspectives on Reward Management*. New York.

ULRICH D. (1997) 'Judge me more by my future than by my past'. In Ulrich D. (ed.) *Tomorrow's HR Management*. New York, John Wiley.

UNIVERSITY OF CALIFORNIA. (1998) Referenced in 'More staff involvement the route to success'. *Personnel Today*. 10 August.

WALLACE BELL D. *and* HANSON C. (1989) *Profit Sharing and Profitability*. London, Kogan Page.

WINSTANLEY D. *and* STUART-SMITH K. (1996) 'Policing performance: the ethics of performance management'. *Personnel Review*. Vol. 25, No. 6.

ZINGHEIM P. K. *and* SCHUSTER J. R. (2000) *Pay People Right: Breakthrough reward strategies to create great companies*. San Francisco, Calif., Jossey Bass.

Index

With over 100,000 members, the **Chartered Institute of Personnel and Development** is the largest organisation in Europe dealing with the management and development of people. The CIPD operates its own publishing unit, producing books and research reports for human resource practitioners, students, and general managers charged with people management responsibilities.

Currently there are over 150 titles covering the full range of personnel and development issues. The books have been commissioned from leading experts in the field and are packed with the latest information and guidance to best practice.

For free copies of the CIPD Books Catalogue, please contact the publishing department:

Tel.: 020-8263 3387
Fax: 020-8263 3850
E-mail: publishing@cipd.co.uk
Web: www.cipd.co.uk/publications

Orders for books should be sent direct to:

Plymbridge Distributors
Estover
Plymouth
Devon
PL6 7PZ

Credit card orders:
Tel.: 01752 202 301
Fax: 01752 202 333

The E-Learning Revolution: From propositions to action
Martyn Sloman

This seminal work by a top training manager and leading UK authority on e-learning is a call to arms to his profession. For too long, he argues, the agenda has been driven by IT; it is time for all those concerned with organisational learning and development to discard the traditional models, ignore the hype of the vendors and become active players in the connected economy.

The book addresses:

- why barriers between knowledge management, performance management and training must fall to achieve competitive advantage through people
- how technology that offers learner-centred opportunities will redefine the way adults learn
- why expertise in 'soft' technology will give trainers new credibility
- what can be learnt from the different strategic responses to e-learning of blue-chip companies.

Price: £25.00
ISBN: 0 85292 873 4
216 pages
234 x 156mm
Pbk
March 2001

The Global HR Manager: Creating the seamless organisation
Pat Joynt and Bob Morton

At least one-third of all products sold anywhere in the world cross international boundaries on their way to market. Globalisation is no longer the future of business: globalisation is a fundamental part of the way business works today.

- How do human resource managers cope with the increasingly international aspects of their profession?
- How should they tackle the unique demands of international teamworking?
- How does international recruitment differ from domestic recruitment?

This book answers all these questions and more. Written by some of the world's leading HR authorities, including J. Stewart Black and Dave Ulrich, Linda Holbeche, Terence Brake, Gareth Jones and Rob Goffee, *The Global HR Manager* is your definitive guide to *the* HR issue of the new millennium.

The advent of the seamless organisation means that people-management policies and practices have to facilitate working across time, distance and culture not only in a practical, operational sense but also in creating a new mind-set in managers of thinking and operating internationally
Professor Pat Joynt, Henley Management College and Bob Morton, Ciba Speciality Chemicals PLC, Editors

There are individual chapters covering:

- The new frontier of global HR
- Organisational culture and international HRM
- The HR manager as global business partner
- International recruitment, selection and assessment
- International compensation
- International HR: career management
- Sustaining constructive relationships across cultural boundaries
- International teamworking
- Developing international management teams through diversity
- International HRM: an Asian perspective

Price: £25.00
ISBN: 0 85292 815 7
256 pages
Pbk
1999